THE LAWYER'S TALE

J. STEWART SCHNEIDER, J.D.

DEDICATION

Dedicated to the congregation of Community Presbyterian Church of Bellefonte, Kentucky, who gathered in a hurting politician and his family, and taught them how to be ministers.

Also dedicated to Charles Bowen and Kit Hathorn, my mentors, my disciplinarians, my conscience. And to my most esteemed son-in-law, Ryan Evans, hammer-wielder, armor-builder, maker of scrolls.

A special thanks to my wonderful editor, Pamela Bowen, of 2Bowens.com[1], who worked tirelessly on my tiresome errors.

And lastly, to my wonderful wife and daughter, Kathleen Schneider and Kat Evans. Never was a man more blessed than by these two wonderful women.

---

1   My suggestion of "When you messed it up so badly just one Bowen couldn't fix it" as a corporate logo has thus far fallen on deaf ears.

PREFACE

I don't think my childhood in the 1950s and 1960s, now half a century and more ago, was substantially different from that experienced by most of my schoolmates in the small town in which we all grew up. Sundays, for most of us, was church day, whether we wanted to or not. In my case, it was a choice between Dad's church, First Christian, or Mom's, First Presbyterian. In general, we went to Sunday School at First Presbyterian, where I learned useless things, such as how to color, and useful things, like the order of the books in the Bible. Following Sunday School, my brother and I would lobby for Dad's church, on the grounds that Brother Joe Faulkner would have us out by 11:30, whereas the Reverend Sam Curry at Mom's church could easily preach through a change of seasons.

I mention this, not to be critical of either pastor, who were both fine men, dedicated to their calling, but to emphasize the degree to which church was something inflicted upon us as an obligation by our parents. The activities we were engaged in were mostly designed by elderly women who had long ago forgotten what it was to be a child and whose goal was, primarily, to produce decent, inoffensive children. Their tool of choice in this enterprise was stories of heaven, depicting it as a place where everyone wore nightgowns and played the harp, and stories of hell, which was depicted as a place of fire to which no sane child would willingly repair. One moved closer to hell by committing sins. One moved closer to heaven by doing good deeds. One could also move closer to hell by entertaining bad thoughts, and that caused a great deal of consternation among the pubescent who had begun to find bad thoughts about the opposite gender to be very entertaining, indeed.

I objected to this teaching because it seemed to me, even then, to be self-centered. If one did good deeds, not out of compassion for those in need, but as a means to benefit one's self in an afterlife, how was this more than a business transaction? With the hubris of youth, I announced to my mother that I wanted to become a preacher. It was my unspoken goal to set people straight, although I didn't share that thought with my mother. She said that was a fine thing to be, but pointed out that I had not, up until that time, shown much enthusiasm for the activities at either church, and didn't I think I should become more familiar by voluntary attendance, rather than the usual tug and drag that accompanied me on the way to Sunday School?

And so, in desperation, I became a lawyer. Through diligent application of my resources to the job at hand, and attendance at countless Democratic Women's Club meetings, I became Commonwealth's Attorney for Kentucky's 32nd Judicial Circuit. But thirty-five years of the practice of law left me with an intense skepticism about judges and juries both. That's not a very popular thing to say, I suppose, but I became aware that as uncomfortable as it may be to leave your property or your liberty in the hands of a jury, it is unconscionable to entrust a human life to such a system, and so I became a failed politician.

I failed the people who elected me by telling them, when a death qualified case finally came before me, that I could not stand in front of a jury of my neighbors and argue to them that they were wise enough to order another's death. As a result, I was voted out of office. My colleagues in the Commonwealth Attorney's Association, with one exception, excoriated me. The one holdout was a Commonwealth's Attorney who was a dual vocation pastor of a Presbyterian church. The remainder of my colleagues vowed that as I was false to my oath to uphold the laws of Kentucky, I was unfit to serve further as a prosecutor. Five families similarly lost their livelihoods. Another prosecutor tried the defendants in my stead, and the jury declined to recommend death. Don't tell ME God doesn't have a sense of irony.

In the end, I filled in for pastors who were away from their churches and, completely out of the blue, was asked to pastor Community Presbyterian Church of Bellefonte, Kentucky. It took me quite by surprise, and I could only stutter, "I'd love to be your pastor, but you guys are Presbyterians. You can't do that." In the end, they did, anyway, and I went from a prosecutor who wouldn't follow the rules to a pastor who doesn't follow the rules. As I am not an ordained Presbyterian pastor, I cannot be recognized as pastor of my church. I am properly a pulpit supply speaker, and I have continued to speak for the past five years.

These little essays represent my thoughts on how we might relate to this thing we call "God" in ways that might be helpful to us and our neighbors, and pleasing to Him. More than that, they are my way of urging, begging, really, for the Gospel of Jesus Christ to become, in the heart of each of us, something more than what I fear it has become. From the first century on, the church of

THE LAWYER'S TALE

Christ speaks most authentically when it speaks in protest to culture. It is that voice of protest to the sinful systems in which we live that I hope to nurture.

Table of Contents

Introduction

In 1967, the state of Kentucky hired me as a University of Kentucky police-man. I was 21 years of age. My first task was to solemnly swear that I had not, since the adoption of the Constitution of Kentucky in 1792, engaged in a duel with deadly weapons. That oath is still required by Kentucky for commission-ing of law officers.

My next task was to procure a pistol, pistol belt and uniform. And handcuffs. Which I wound up locking myself into only to find that I did not have a key.

I worked that job for two years. My next job was as a dispatcher for the Lex-ington Police. I was moving in a trajectory toward a career in law enforce-ment, but I was also attending Law School. My idea was that a law degree would qualify me for a job with the FBI. I had no intention of practicing law.

Life intervenes, and I entered the practice of law in 1972. By 1976, I was the city prosecutor in Ashland. In 1977, I was hired as an assistant Common-wealth's Attorney, eventually becoming senior trial counsel. I entered poli-tics, ran for the office of Commonwealth's Attorney, and won, holding the of-fice for 13 years.

When people inquired how I was employed, I'd often tell them that I ruined people's lives for a living. They understood this as a joke, but it was only par-tially so. The actual task of a felony prosecutor is precisely that: to ruin peo-ple's lives by imposing upon those who have caused pain to others compen-sating pain sufficient to satisfy the injury done to the victim of the crime and to the society in which we live. It became an idée fixe for me — why are we so compelled to the notion that violence as an answer to violence will lessen vio-lence? It seems to me that violence done to us only frees the cogs which hold our own violence within, granting us permission to slip the dogs of war in re-taliation.

My judicial district was not a particularly deadly place. We suffered a homicide every two or three years, much below the national average, I should think. Certainly below the average for the nearby town of Huntington, West Virginia.

To understand how my life played out, you must understand that the popular imagination fails to grasp the legal subtleties of homicide prosecutions. In the popular imagination, any killing of a human being is likely to be referred to as murder. That's quite false. The killing of a human being is a homicide, but not all homicides are murders, nor even punishable as a crime. The killing of a home invader, for instance, is not a crime, generally speaking.

Neither are all illegal homicides murder. For a homicide to be characterized as murder, it must be done intentionally, or under circumstances so depraved that it is the moral equivalent of intentionally.

Finally, not all murders are death qualified. Only a jury may impose the death penalty, and only in those cases in which there are aggravating factors, which are statutorily defined, may a jury be urged to return a penalty of death. In my little part of the world, that did not happen, until, one night, it did.

On that night, two really nasty pieces of work named Nolan and Campbell went to the home of two drug dealers in Boyd County to buy marijuana. For reasons best left to those wiser than I, they decided to rob and kill them, shooting and knifing the man and his wife, then setting fire to the house to try and cover it up. Tragically, there were two children in the house when it was set ablaze. Thankfully, the children weren't physically hurt, but children are sympathetic victims, endangering others while committing a homicide in the course of a first-degree arson is one of those aggravating factors I spoke of, and suddenly, this was a death qualified murder case. It would be my job at trial to convince the jury that this would be a proper verdict for them to return.

When I say that this was a death qualified case I mean that the facts presented made a verdict of death a legally possible outcome. Not mandated, mind you, just possible. What penalty would be imposed is up to the jury. A death penalty case just means that a jury could, if they choose, return a death verdict.

So, here I was, the Commonwealth's Attorney of Kentucky's Thirty-second Judicial Circuit, sworn to uphold the law, and I had, after nearly a quarter century in law enforcement, a case in which I would have to urge a jury to return a verdict which would result in the death of two people.

At the same time, I'm a Christian, and a minister of the Gospel, under the care of the Christian Church (Disciples of Christ) of Kentucky.

So, I went to the Archabbey of St. Meinrad in Indiana to decide what to do about it, and I saw the heavens open, and a great staircase appear, and descending those stairs was the Archangel Gabriel, the message-bringer, and lo

... a choir of trumpets and seraphim, and Gabriel looked me straight in the eye saying, "You better NOT do that. Some of the people on that jury, we've been working on for years, and you're going to mess it up, and all I can say is you better NOT do any such thing."

OK ... I made up that part.

What I really did, before I left for St. Meinrad, was to visit the scene of the crime. I stood there in the ashes and imagined myself at the end of the case, urging a jury to return a decision that these two men, for whom I cannot, even now, dredge up any love, should die for their crimes. And I clearly heard a voice say, "The preacher said it would be all right to do that."

The preacher. Me.

What if someone heard those words, and took me to be speaking for the church as a whole? What if that person concluded that if the preacher said it, it must represent the teaching of the church?

What if there were someone on that jury with a poor opinion of Christians who heard me say that, and concluded, "Christians are hypocrites, just like I always thought. They talk about love, then turn around and try to get us to put these two fools in the electric chair."

Many times worse, what if someone on that jury, or someone in the public reading about the trial, was "on the bubble" about committing their lives to Jesus Christ, heard that and turned from the commitment? That happened, in another county. A Commonwealth's Attorney who was very active in her church argued for a death verdict. One of the members of the church heard that, and came to question her own faith.

What we DO, the positions we take and the things we act on define what Christianity IS for the time in which we live. If we are seen to take positions of hate and intolerance, then Christianity is perceived as the religion of hate and intolerance, in exactly the same way that Islamic extremists are defining Islam in the popular Western imagination as the religion of suicide bombers and generally homicidal crazies despite the long history of Islam to the contrary.

If we clothe ourselves, so that all can see, with compassion, kindness, humility, gentleness and patience, if we bear with each other and forgive whatever grievances we may have against one another, if we forgive as the Lord forgave us, as, indeed, we pray each and every Sunday, we will be perceived as the faith of compassion, the faith of kindness, humility, gentleness and forgiveness.

I could not tell those twelve jurors I hadn't even met yet that they had the power reserved to God alone to decide life or death, however carefully it was done. To do so might cause them to fall into the sin of believing they are wiser than God. I told the courts that I could not, and at the next election, I lost my job, my life's work; my twenty-four-year career. And the jobs of five other families who worked for me. I must now live with that decision.

There's one other thing. Many people in Boyd County think I threw away my career, and the jobs of my secretaries and my assistants for two criminals the world would do very well without. I could easily have kept the case, kept my mouth shut, plead it out for a life sentence, and maybe all those people would still have their jobs. All I had to do was to hide my faith under a basket. For better or worse, I chose not to do so. If we, as Christians, cannot stand up and give our Christianity as the very reason that we do the things we do, then there is no point in being a Christian. I did what I did, and I said why I did it as clearly as I could manage so that as many people as possible could know that Christianity is the religion of love.

My hope was that, at the least, a conversation in my community might begin about the death penalty. If it did, I have not seen evidence of it. We are so addicted to violence as our only response to violence that it seems impossible to even discuss the possibility of abandoning it.

The sermons in this book, I hope, will be a blessing to the readers, not because I'm trained in this art, but precisely because I am not. These are the thoughts that have come to me as I have journeyed into a ministry found from a career lost.

The Undertaking

"The undertaking is to recognize the presence of the ineffable within us and to act in accordance with it."

Luke 1:46-55

And Mary said,
'My soul magnifies the Lord,
  and my spirit rejoices in God my Saviour,
for he has looked with favor on the lowliness of his servant.
  Surely, from now on all generations will call me blessed;
for the Mighty One has done great things for me,
  and holy is his name.
His mercy is for those who fear him
  from generation to generation.
He has shown strength with his arm;
  he has scattered the proud in the thoughts of their hearts.
He has brought down the powerful from their thrones,
  and lifted up the lowly;
he has filled the hungry with good things,
  and sent the rich away empty.
He has helped his servant Israel,
  in remembrance of his mercy,
according to the promise he made to our ancestors,
  to Abraham and to his descendants for ever.'

A few years ago, in Lexington, Fred Craddock preached a sermon he titled "I Miss Mary." He noted that one of the casualties of the split between Protestants and the Roman church had to do with Mary. If you have time, and Internet access, go to the Catholic Encyclopedia and look up the article on "Mary, Blessed Virgin" for a sense of the attention to detail accorded Mary by the Roman church. Protestants, on the other hand, seem to relegate her to a place in the Nativity set on top of the TV. Kathleen Norris observes:

> Protestants have a limited attention span for Mary, the mother of Jesus. We unpack her from the box at Christmastime, and then pack her back up again, with our other decorations, after the holidays are over.[2]

Dr. Craddock's sermon focused on his sense of loss from the Protestant insistence on marginalizing Mary to so small a role in the Christmas story. I think I agree with him. I usually agree with him, come to that.

The Canticle we read from Luke is called "*The Magnificat.*" A Canticle is a song, so this passage is referred to as "The Song of Mary." In this Canticle, we can hear the clear voice of Mary, mother of Jesus, rising above the inevitable secular clutter of our Christmas season with some very important theology. We Protestants would do ourselves a big favor if we would listen to her witness, for in this exchange between Mary and Gabriel there are two concepts the importance of which, I feel, has escaped contemporary Christians. When Gabriel tells Mary, "The Lord is with you,," he reveals the mystery of the presence of the holy within God's Creation, including each of us. Notice that Gabriel didn't say, "The Lord is watching you," or, "The Lord has noticed you." He said, "The Lord is with you." It is this quality of God, that of immanence, that Gabriel is emphasizing. God is indwelling in all of his Creation, rather than being off in a heavenly realm keeping score.

When Mary speaks, we hear the voice of submission to the ineffable. In that voice of submission we learn much of our relationship with God, and our limitations.

I want you to tear down that mental picture of Mary you have in your mind. Church tradition tells us she was fourteen years old, tops. She's a child, to our eyes, not the mature woman depicted in your noggin. This is pretty heavy freight for a fourteen-year-old. It's pretty heavy freight for any of us to face the revelation that God is with us, here, right now. It is much easier to think of God as "up there" somewhere and to imagine that we can deal with God

---

2   Foreword to Blessed One: Protestant Perspectives on Mary, ed. by Beverly Roberts Gaventa and Cynthia L. Rigby Westminster John Knox Press; 1 edition (October 30, 2002)

when the time comes than to come face-to-face with God's immanence throughout His Creation, here and now. It is even heavier freight to examine the internal concept which we call "God" and to confess that we do not have the power to conceptualize God and thus may have been worshiping a creation of our own minds.

Over the past three and a half years, I have spoken a lot about the work and the responsibilities of being a Christian, but this is a real breath-taker. When I think of how often we fold up under the much less demanding responsibilities of being a Christian imposed upon us, I'm humbled by Mary's courage. Mary answers:

"I am the Lord's servant. May your word to me be fulfilled."

These simple dozen words are the first place where we sail right over an enormous expression of faith on our way to the cute little crèche on top of the TV set. It is God who empowers us, but it is we who must act and that is our task. The goal of this series of sermons is to ready us to carry out that task, for it cannot be undertaken without preparation. We are not puppets or passive observers of God's majesty. We are active participants. Fourteen-year-old Mary has just agreed to be *Theotokas*, the God-bearer. The church has understood Mary as the God-bearer for sixteen centuries, since the year 451 C.E.. Mary is going to bear God into the world. She is going to deliver the new covenant, God incarnate, into the world, and she has agreed to do so with the simple words, "I am the Lord's servant. May your word to me be fulfilled."

It is in this unique task — to be the bearer of God into the world — that Mary serves as the model for our relation to God. She shows us what it means to bear God into the world, to take that burden onto our shoulders by saying, in deepest humility, "I am the Lord's servant. May your word to me be fulfilled." In Paul's words:

I appeal to you therefore, sisters and brothers by the mercies of God, to present your bodies as a living sacrifice, holy and acceptable to God, which is your spiritual worship.[3]

If that is what we are to be about as Christians, and if Mary is the first to do so, have we not lost an important connection with the foundations of our faith by relegating Mary to a role as insignificant as that of a small blue statue

---

3   Romans 12:1

on top of the TV, a bit behind the ox, and to the right of the donkey?

✗ Since the time of that council in 451 C.E. which named Mary *Theotokas*, the church has understood and taught the nature of Jesus to be simultaneously fully human and fully divine. In the same way, the church is to be fully divine — empowered by the Holy Spirit, and fully human — acting through the agency of … well … us, individual Christians. Mary's task of bearing God into the world is our task of bearing God into the world.

The questions I would pose are this: Are Christians, as they are perceived among non-Christians, bearing God into the world? Among non-Christians, are Christians known as the people who act from love toward everybody, or is the working definition of Christians among non-Christians something harsher than this? More importantly, do Christians themselves perceive Mary's submission to God to be their undertaking, or do they envision their faith as an individual pursuit of heaven?

For many years, there was something called the Board of Heavy Metal Mining Appeals in the federal government. Their job was to hear appeals of denials of disability claims made by uranium miners. The law was poorly drafted and permitted the miners to bypass the Board of Heavy Metal Mining Appeals and go directly to court if their disability claims were denied. So who would take the extra step of appealing to the Board of Heavy Metal Mining Appeals if they didn't have to? Nobody. And nobody did. The Board had nothing to do, so they occupied their time by writing procedural rules to handle cases in the unlikely event they ever had one.

Forgive me, but I'm afraid that a lot of contemporary Christians think they are serving on the Board of Heavy Metal Mining Appeals. They don't see themselves as having any real job apart from seeking their own salvation, so they invent make-work. You see them getting into arguments with each other and the culture at large over irrelevant issues like evolution, or same sex marriages, or whether someone greets you with Merry Christmas or Happy Holidays, or whether Muslims worship the same God we worship. We like to quarrel. It makes us feel righteous and affirmed.

When you feel strongly about one of these divisive issues, try to measure it against the task Mary took on, then ask yourself, "Is this an issue that bears God into the world, or is this an issue that sets neighbor against neighbor, brother against brother?"

Undertaking to carry the name Christian into the world means that you have undertaken the work of a Christian, and the work of a Christian is not at all like sitting on the Board of Heavy Metal Mining Appeals. There is real work to do — hard work that will bring brother closer to brother, neighbor closer to neighbor. "The only work of a Christian," I hear Mary say, "is that of bearing God into the world." To represent yourself as a Christian is to offer your very self to the world as a life lived connected to the Holy Spirit.

How does that work? How do you do the work of Mary? One of the first steps is to seek out others who can hear what we say. It's important to realize that not everyone can hear what we say. Luke tells us that as soon as Gabriel departed,

> At that time Mary got ready and hurried to a town in the hill country of Judea, where she entered Zechariah's home and greeted Elizabeth.

She's excited. She needs to tell **somebody**, and the only somebody she can tell is someone who has experienced a similar miracle — her cousin Elizabeth, who finds herself expecting a child in her old age. Who else is going to believe her? God is ineffable. You cannot explain God. You don't have the language. The only way for your words about God to be received by another as anything is if God has prepared the way for you with that other person. The only person in the whole world to whom Mary could tell her tale is Elizabeth, and that's where she went.

Mary bursts through Elizabeth's door.

> When Elizabeth heard Mary's greeting, the baby leaped in her womb, and Elizabeth was filled with the Holy Spirit. In a loud voice she exclaimed: "Blessed are you among women, and blessed is the child you will bear!"

Mary then sings the Song of Mary, which begins

> My soul proclaims the greatness of the Lord,
> my spirit rejoices in God my Savior;
>   for he has looked with favor on his lowly servant.
> From this day all generations will call me blessed:
>   the Almighty has done great things for me, and holy is his Name.

This is the work of a Christian. God has prepared a way for Mary, and Mary has responded by bearing God to Elizabeth. She didn't bring arguments to Elizabeth about whose understanding of God is the better. She didn't involve herself in quarreling, and neither did she have to. Elizabeth was prepared and ready to receive what Mary bore. Not everyone to whom you speak will be prepared and ready to receive what you bear. Keep that in mind. Who can hear you and who cannot is not your business. Your business is to bear God into the world, not to measure the outcome.

We are called to present our bodies as a living sacrifice, holy and acceptable to God, which is our spiritual worship. We are part of something greater than ourselves. To prepare ourselves to bear God into the world, we embark upon preparation through Advent and journey the seasons of the liturgical year. The journey we embark upon is not only the story Christians have told for millennia in the passage of the seasons of the liturgical year. It is the story of the journey of every Christian through preparation, awakening and awareness of the entry of God into our lives. Once we have awakened to God's immanence and become aware that God is with us, not somewhere out there and far away, then we can view the sacrifice that will occur and see in the Resurrection proof that even at our worst we are not beyond God's grace.

This journey means a giving up of things we have treasured throughout our lives in order to successfully follow in Mary's steps, carrying Jesus into the world. But first, we must repent and accept that the God is with us so that we can join in the twelve words of Mary:

"I am the Lord's servant. May your word to me be fulfilled."

The Time of Preparation

The church year begins with Advent, a time of preparation and anticipation of the birth of the Christ Child. Of course, it's a little inconsistent to urge that we are "anticipating" the birth of a child when that event took place two-thousand years ago.

Instead, I'd like to suggest that what we are anticipating is a more personal journey which follows the trajectory of the story of Jesus, but which is, in reality, a journey each of us called to this story follow in our own lives. Advent is the beginning of God's entry into our lives as the driving force for what we do, say and live as His Creatures, even though we might not yet be aware of His influence. In Advent, we look about ourselves to find the first hints that we are not our own.

J. STEWART SCHNEIDER

The Need for Wonder

"God is our refuge and strength, a
very present help in trouble[4]. Not everyone can hear this,
and those who do are sometimes overcome with fear.
Those who cannot are given into the care of those who
do."

Matthew 24:36-44

*'But about that day and hour no one knows, neither the angels of heaven, nor
the Son, but only the Father. For as the days of Noah were, so will be the coming of the Son of Man. For as in those days before the flood they were eating
and drinking, marrying and giving in marriage, until the day Noah entered the
ark, and they knew nothing until the flood came and swept them all away, so
too will be the coming of the Son of Man. Then two will be in the field; one
will be taken and one will be left. Two women will be grinding meal together;
one will be taken and one will be left. Keep awake therefore, for you do not
know on what day your Lord is coming. But understand this: if the owner of
the house had known in what part of the night the thief was coming, he
would have stayed awake and would not have let his house be broken into.
Therefore you also must be ready, for the Son of Man is coming at an unexpected hour.*

There are more things in heaven and earth, Horatio,
Than are dreamt of in your philosophy.

Hamlet, Act 1, Scene 5

---

4   Psalm 46:1

I know. I know. It's lame to use Shakespeare to sound erudite, but it would be hard to find two better lines to express that which we now pursue than these two. The lines are spoken by Hamlet, Prince of Denmark, to his schoolmate, Horatio.

Horatio was a student at Wittenberg, and Wittenberg was a center of humanist thought. The humanists at Wittenberg were framing a world in which reality consisted of atoms, void and nothing more, the world in which we live today in fact. In the play, Horatio barges into a room in which Hamlet is speaking with the ghost of his father. There is no place for ghosts in Horatio's understanding, and as the ghost indisputably rattles around beneath the stage, Horatio can only sputter, "O day and night, but this is wondrous strange!"

Hamlet advises him:

> And therefore as a stranger give it welcome.
> There are more things in heaven and earth, Horatio,
> Than are dreamt of in your philosophy.

Hamlet and Horatio represent the two extremes of perspective in our world. Horatio's world, and that of Wittenberg, was one of objective, measurable, understandable things. There was no room at Wittenberg for things which could not be weighed, measured, tasted or observed, and still less for a confession that there are more things in heaven and earth, things beyond human capacity to grasp, than are dreamt of in the philosophy of Wittenberg.

Hamlet lived in a reality in which ghosts were not only possible, but a reality in which one could be motivated by conversations with ghosts. Hamlet perceived the unseen, the unspoken, the ineffable. For Horatio, that world was closed.

We live in a similar time, a time when there is a rejection of anything not subject to human understanding. If you can't net it in the coils of language, it is relegated to the rubbish heap as mere myth, fairy tale or worse.

It is an arrogance to assert that if the human mind cannot encompass a thing, it has no reality. As Hamlet insists, there are unseen things, things we will never net nor comprehend that affect us, that fill us with wonder, that challenge our assumptions like the ghost of Hamlet's father prowling beneath Horatio's very feet. It is with a new appreciation of such things that both wisdom and our Advent journey begins.

The church year begins with Advent for very good reason. Advent is a time of preparation. To follow the story we will embark upon over the next year, to adjust our perceptions from that of a student at Wittenberg to something more attuned to the wonder that is this world, certain preparations must be made. If we are to gain anything from the story of the Gospels beyond the comfort of dry repetition, we have to be able to discard those things we will not need for a successful journey. Jettisoning those things which will hold us back is the first part of our preparation. Among the things we shall have to leave behind is the preconception bred into us as children of our time, the certainty, indeed, that reality consists of atoms and void and nothing more. To gain from the Gospels we must discard Horatio, humanism and the University of Wittenberg and adopt Hamlet's wider perspective.

What would be the alternative? What if we just continue on in our accustomed way of viewing the world, a way in which we discount anything which we cannot weigh or measure? What if we continue to believe that the ineffable is unimportant, unreal or irrelevant?

I watched "Punkin Chunkin" on Thanksgiving. For those not familiar with the national sport of Delaware, Punkin Chunkin is a competition in which groups of men (and one group of women) devise enormous machines, the purpose of which is to launch a pumpkin as far as possible. One of the Punkin Chunkers, who rejoices in the name "Fat Jimmy," wore a shirt that said "Warning! I do dumb stuff." If we are not able to disconnect ourselves from our attachment to the arid world of Horatio and the University of Wittenberg to again embrace the larger world which once was our very DNA, I fear that the words from Fat Jimmy's T-shirt will be the verdict of history about us. I fear that future history books will say of us that we were too soon smart and too late wise, and that we were so busy being smart we never noticed that we were not wise.

There is an enormous difference, of course, between being smart and being wise. To be smart is to be born with an above-average gift of understanding. But to be wise requires much more than that. It requires the ability to step outside the assumptions of our very culture to gain an appreciation of the ineffable.

There are, it seems to me, two poles between which we oscillate in our relationship to the world in which we live. One pole is rooted in our understanding of our world and the way it functions. This pole of understanding has brought us television sets, iPhones and computers. It is no wonder that we grant this pole of understanding such great honor. These things are great fun.

The other pole is planted in our need for wonder, our sense of the ineffable. The pole of wonder brings us no gadgets nor theories, but stands in opposition to the idea that we can, in the words of Dr. Michio Kaku, come to read the mind of God.

It is to this pole, once so important to our being, that we have, I fear, turned our backs. We are the poorer for it, because the placement of ourselves in Creation, the mind of God if you like, is our essence, and however much Dr. Kaku would wish it, if God's mind could be read by such as we, He wouldn't be God. To re-embrace this vital pole of our being, we must be able to say, "I don't know," and that in the face of the astonishing discoveries the pole of knowledge brings us.

As our scientific pole produces ever greater understanding of the world, we become ever more enthralled with it, to the injury of our awareness of our existence as God's children, and this is the central problem. Instead of welcoming the pole of wonder into our world we oscillate between the two, and thus tragically fail to see the opportunity for synthesis. Even worse, we seem to have concluded that the pole of wonder and mystery that is the ineffable can be hauled to the pole of understanding and autopsied. This notion is quite false.

Abraham Heschel observed:

> As civilization advances, the sense of wonder declines. Such decline is an alarming symptom of our state of mind. Mankind will not perish for want of information; but only for want of appreciation.[5]

If we now understand the inside of an atom, the gravitational constant and what makes the fizz in bicarbonate of soda, then it can only be a matter of time before we understand God, so the thinking goes. This line of thought, which beggars our path to wisdom, represents our failure to appreciate that we are not going to puzzle out God, no matter how smart we get, for if God were a problem subject to our investigation, He wouldn't be God. The quicker we come to appreciate what a wonderful thing that is, the sooner we get

---

5   Abraham Heschel, *The Wisdom of Heschel*, Farrar, Straus and Giroux (September 1, 1986)

wise.

If you can accept that statement — that we are not going to puzzle out God because if God were a problem subject to our investigation, He wouldn't be God — then we have taken our first step together on our Advent preparation for the birth of Jesus.

That step is harder to take than you would think. Thanks to Horatio and the University of Wittenberg, the world we inhabit is one in which we perceive no question to be too large for us to undertake. To accept that God is not subject to our investigation, to confess, "I don't know," runs counter to everything we take as true. I told witnesses, when preparing them for cross-examination, that if you are asked something to which you don't know the answer, "I don't know" is the only truthful answer you can make, but this is enormously hard to do, since no one wishes to look uninformed. Nevertheless, if you don't know, the truthful answer is, "I don't know." My advice to them was not to guess. If you're asked what color socks the robber had on, as soon as you guess "white," that lawyer is going to open up his briefcase and pull out a pair of argyle socks.

The myth of our omnipotence is the first thing we must jettison on our journey to the manger, for trying to drag the foundational mystery of the world within the orbit of the pole of understanding always leads to calamity. Such efforts actually damage our understanding, by leading us to believe that we understand that which we do not, and by deadening the voice within us that yearns for connection with the ineffable. I am convinced that we need mystery and the awareness of the ineffable to survive. Without the confession that there are more things in heaven and earth than **can** be dreamt of in our philosophy, we will dream up alternative dreams, dreams with a faulty foundation that will lead us astray.

A proper appreciation for, and study of, Scripture is our best remedy to the sort of misery we inflict upon ourselves by our belief that we can understand God by bottling Him within the limited space of our minds. The wonder of Scripture is not that it will raise you to God's level so that you and He can examine His creation as equals, but that it will lead you to see your understanding for what it is, utterly inadequate to the task of raising you to equality with God. When your wisdom and understanding have spent their force against the ineffable, leaving you to breathe only, "Holy, Holy, Holy is the Lord," that is the beginning of wisdom. It is in that moment, when we are face-to-face with the limit of our understanding, that we finally admit, with Jesus, no less,

> But about that day and hour no one knows, neither the angels of heaven, nor the Son, but only the Father.

We want an explicable world, but we need a world of wonder. The tension between what we want and what we need leads us to believe that we know far more than we really do. Those who arise from time to time, claiming to know all these complicated details about the end times are asserting that they are smarter than Jesus. I don't think so.

But, admitting that we don't know something in Horatio's reality is admitting that we are less knowledgeable than others. It makes us look bad. To make our discomfort less, we imagine a tangible God, a God a lot like us, in other words, just bigger. And dressed in a white robe. With lightning bolts.

That isn't God. That's self-deception. Jesus, the Son of God, says "I don't know." Why should we be ashamed to confess as much?

Our arrogance in our own abilities has relegated wonder and the awareness of the ineffable to the status of fantasy. In such a world, one of our own creation, we have laid aside our appreciation for wonder in favor of electronic toys made by Chinese children working long hours for chump change. What is this need for wonder I keep going on about?

For most of my life I have gazed in wonder at the small copse of trees that would represent the extension of 39th Street past its intersection with Belmont, had 39th Street possessed the energy and determination to so extend itself. It seemed clear, from the lay of the land, that 39th Street once had every intention of doing so, forcing its way into the space occupied by that small forest, but had found its ambition somehow thwarted. Perhaps the trees were too ancient and powerful for a street as trivial as 39th Street to push its way through. Every time I traveled Belmont, I'd glance into the darkness below those trees and wonder what I might find if I were to one day park my car and travel along that unformed road. It was a mystery, and from that mystery, I always took comfort.

This year, for no reason that I can perceive, someone bulldozed all the trees, laying flat the little forest. Where once was wonder, there now is just fallen trees, and I can see that all that was ever there was just the rounded side of the hill below the cemetery. No secret roads. No secret, wondrous anything. Just a few logs and a hillside.

That, I think, is what Rabbi Heshel is speaking of. The march of civilization revealed to me my little fantasy for what it was — just a hillside — but the loss of wonder in that revelation has left me the poorer for it. I need wonder in my life. I need something wonderful that I don't understand if I am to retain my appreciation for my surroundings. I need to know that there is something beyond my wildest and greatest understanding, something which will always exceed my most thorough and far-reaching answers. I need a forest of trees which cannot be bulldozed, a purpose greater than my imagination, a loving hand whose compass I cannot trace nor net in the web of my language.

I need God.

That's what I am thankful for this season of Advent. I am thankful that God is beyond my wildest and greatest understanding. I am thankful that God will always be so. I am thankful that I am granted faith to trust in that which I cannot perceive nor encompass, but most of all, and greatest of all, I am thankful that this God who is greater than my fancy is so in love with me that he became man so that I could perceive Him.

J. STEWART SCHNEIDER

Satyagraha

"Cooperate enthusiastically with the inevitable for the in-effable is truth and hath force to make itself unavoidable."

Mark 1:1-8

The beginning of the good news of Jesus Christ, the Son of God.
As it is written in the prophet Isaiah,
"See, I am sending my messenger ahead of you,
who will prepare your way;
the voice of one crying out in the wilderness:
'Prepare the way of the Lord,
make his paths straight,'"

John the baptizer appeared in the wilderness, proclaiming a baptism of re-pentance for the forgiveness of sins. And people from the whole Judean coun-tryside and all the people of Jerusalem were going out to him and were bap-tized by him in the river Jordan, confessing their sins. Now John was clothed with camel's hair, with a leather belt around his waist and he ate locusts and wild honey. He proclaimed, "The one who is more powerful than I is coming after me; I am not worthy to stoop down and untie the thong of his sandals. I have baptized you with water; but he will baptize you with the Holy Spirit."

Advent. A coming into place, view, or being; arrival; onset, beginning, commencement, start. We start the liturgical year with the first Sunday in Advent. During Advent, we anticipate the arrival of Jesus Christ. An-other Gospel story comes into view as we try to get a handle on this enor-mously strange, enormously familiar, enormously over-laid event — the com-ing of Jesus Christ into the world as an infant. So Advent in year B, when we read from Mark, is always a little ironic. Mark says not a word about it. The Gospels of Mark and John contain no infancy narratives. No flight to Egypt.

No Wise Men. No Bethlehem, Drummer Boys, Santa Claus or mangers. Nothing. Just the simple statement:

The beginning of the good news of Jesus Christ, the Son of God.

Here is another irony. It is hard to see good news in Mark's telling of the story. In Mark's telling, those closest to Jesus constantly misunderstand Him, pressing on Him their own expectations then abandoning Him at the last. The only ones who recognize Jesus as the Son of God are His cousin John, the demons He casts out and, at the last, a lone Roman Centurion.

In the earliest manuscripts we have, there's not even a Resurrection. The text ends at Mark 16:8 on a note of inexpressible sorrow and loss as the women discovering the empty tomb flee.

Trembling and bewildered, the women went out and fled from the tomb. They said nothing to anyone, because they were afraid.

That was too heart-breaking. A later hand or hands added the longer endings of Mark[6] in which Jesus appears to Mary Magdalene and she reports to the others, who do not believe until Jesus appears to them. You'll see that as a footnote in your pew Bibles.

So, where's the good news in this bleak Gospel? Where is the happy anticipation of the arrival of the precious baby Jesus that we have come to expect as our due in this season? Where's the hope of Resurrection? Perhaps of more significance to the modern mind, why are there four different accounts of the life of Jesus? Which one is true?

It is upon the fulcrum of that last question that Hamlet and Horatio teeter. For Horatio and for most contemporary people, "true" means "historically correct." For Hamlet, truth can never be reduced to such a trifle. For Hamlet and for those who live in his reality, truth is incapable of being expressed or described in words. Truth is ineffable. It is only our human arrogance at our abilities which leads us to fancy that we can discover truth. For Horatio, truth is something we find. For Hamlet, truth is something that finds us. All the Horatios I have ever met will cry foul at this assertion and all the Hamlets will nod

---

6   Some manuscripts have the following ending between verses 8 and 9 and one manuscript has it after verse 8 (omitting verses 9-20): Then they quickly reported all these instructions to those around Peter. After this, Jesus himself also sent out through them from east to west the sacred and imperishable proclamation of eternal salvation. Amen.

assent.

Some years ago, I corresponded with a man who wished to learn to play the autoharp. His distinction was that he was profoundly deaf since birth. He had never heard a single sound. Concepts like a high note or a low note or a loud note versus a quiet note were completely beyond his grasp. He had no semblance of a context into which to fit them.

After some time and with the help of a number of people, he was able to push the right buttons at the right time and produce something like a melody. Eventually, the impossibility of the enterprise defeated him and he stopped.

The experience was very like that of discussing the immanent God with those in Horatio's camp who do not feel the call of the ineffable in their own lives. It is like arguing the existence of the color red with a color blind man or trying to describe the difference between a loud note and a soft one to one profoundly deaf.

Look at that riveting first line. Matthew and Luke, where all the good Christmas stuff is, make a big deal of proving to the reader that Jesus is who he is portrayed to be by demonstrating that nature itself announced his presence, through a star, through hosts of angels. Mark has none of that.

The beginning of the good news of Jesus Christ, the Son of God.

Mathew and Luke, speak to the identity of Jesus as something which can be contained within the categories of human understanding. "These are the signs of His coming," they proclaim. "Mortal, see and understand." Mark makes no effort to offer proof of Jesus' identity. That is not up for question in Mark's Gospel. There are no heavenly angels announcing the birth, no stars, no Magi because Mark starts from this simple statement: Jesus is the Son of God. Mark's Gospel is not about proving who Jesus is, nor explaining how that came to be. Mark's Gospel starts from that foundational statement, rather like the words attributed to Martin Luther fifteen hundred years later, "Hier stehe Ich. Kann Ich anders." — "Here I stand. I can do no other." In the manner of a Sixth Century BCE prophet, Mark speaks to us directly. "This is the way it is, the truth. It has force even if you cannot grasp it with your intellect," he tells us. As his story unfolds, Mark will also tell us, "This is the consequence of the way it is."

For many, many people Mark's approach is profoundly disquieting. It does not meet their need to understand who this Jesus is. When Kat was a little girl, we read to her at night and because I am a naughty daddy, sometimes I'd change one of her favorite stories, just to pull her chain. The result was always the same. "Nooo, daddy!" she'd wail. "That's not how it goes." That is the experience we have when we courageously read Mark's Gospel and face up to the places in it where it fails to follow our expectations of the story. "Noooo!" we cry. "That's not how it goes."

But it does. The Second Gospel, like a whooping big speed bump on our highway of happy thoughts proclaims, "The beginning of the good news of Jesus Christ, the Son of God" and there it has sat from the very beginnings of the early church. Eusebius of Caesarea quotes Papias about the Gospel and Papias was speaking about the year 120 or 130 C.E. For two thousand years, this odd little book has been treasured by the Church as the Inspired Word of God and yet it fails to deliver any sort of understandable explanation of the coming of the Christ child into the world beyond the single statement, "The beginning of the good news of Jesus Christ, the Son of God." If we want to read Mark's Gospel with integrity, we will have to take to heart the words of the Psalm today:

> I will listen to what the LORD God is saying,
> for he is speaking peace to his faithful people
> and to those who turn their hearts to him.

Reading Mark's Gospel with integrity means reading what is actually there, not pressing upon it our wishes and desires for things that aren't actually in it. Mark's Gospel isn't about confirming what you expected to hear. Mark's Gospel is about self-denying love, the lonely, unacknowledged servant path that Jesus walked alone. The way which cannot be understood through any lens but that of the cross. Keep that in mind this year. Mark's Gospel cannot be understood through any lens but that of the cross.

Mahatma Gandhi believed that the truth has force to make itself manifest and he coined the word "Satyagraha" loosely translated as "insistence on truth" or "truth force" to express this. It is precisely this that I hope to convey.

Many years ago, Kathy and I found our house, which we loved at first sight. My dad came and looked. Engineer that he was, he pointed out that the house is situated in a bowl. Water, he noted sagely, runs downhill.

We were so in love with the house, though, that we believed the sellers when they told us that the house never flooded. We tossed Satyagraha, insistence on the truth, under the bus in pursuit of our desire for the house. Guess what happens every spring? Satyagraha — the force of truth — enters the house and pools in my study to remind us that we live in a world with actual consequences, whether we choose to believe them or not. So it is with the way that Jesus showed us — the way God would have us treat each other and His Creation. There is force of truth in God's way. It will become manifest, though the forces of the world and the voices of practicality, greed, self-seeking and vengeance array themselves against it.

The force of truth which the Gospels convey tells us that the poor are given into our hands to care for, but the voices of the world tell us that the poor are so because they are lazy, or criminals, or addicted and so fail to meet our expectations for those to whom we extend our charity. Mark's story of Jesus is filled with friends who abandon Him, disciples who misunderstand Him, authorities who murder Him. Mark shows us clearly that none of these people meet our expectations of worthy people to whom to extend charity, but Jesus loves them, teaches them, blesses them. To read Mark with integrity is to jettison the distinction between the deserving and the undeserving poor.

We are told to love our neighbor as ourselves, but the voices of the world lock us into works of force, violence and passion. We are told to love even our enemies, but the voices of the world demonize our enemies and whisper that they must be killed, to a man. Mark's telling of the story of Jesus shows us that even death will not halt the way, the truth and the light, for the truth will manifest itself.

The way Jesus taught tells us to love the Lord with all the force of our being, but the voices of the world whisper to us that such is impractical and unworkable and must be moderated, as if there were realistic alternatives to the Word of God. Jesus walked with his eyes open to the cross in self-denying obedience to the sovereignty of God and shows us that the way of God is not an alternative or an opinion.

Mark shows us that the life Jesus experienced was not like the life we experience. Our families and friends comfort us and tell us we do not go alone. Jesus' path is that of one walking that lonesome valley by Himself. I watch Kathy "playing with her house" as the years spin by, changing the decorations to match the season, now snowmen and Christmas trees, later spring flowers and bunny rabbits, then summer and fall. I watch her preparing for Thanksgiving, waving a wooden spoon and shouting at those who put up Christmas decorations before the turkey's done. In her beautiful, warm, smiling face I see the comfort the whole family experiences from the regularity of the seasons and her maintenance of the traditions we pass on to Kat and Ryan and I am content.

Jesus had none of that. The Son of Man has nowhere to lay his head, Matthew and Luke tell us. When we open Mark, we enter the world Jesus inhabited, one with no comfort and we are called upon to leave our expectations behind if we are to understand the beginning of the good news of Jesus Christ, the Son of God.

Maybe that is, in the end, the reason Mark is so comfortless, for we are given hope by Jesus' acceptance of a comfortless life. Mark lets us see the world from Jesus' eyes so that we can know the price of the hope we hold.

The hope Jesus gave us sustains us even though the world we find ourselves in offers little room for the values Jesus taught.

Like the disciples, pressing on to Jesus their expectations of who and what the Messiah would be, we press upon Mark our expectations of how the story must be. When we read from Mark, we cry, "Nooo! That's not how it goes." But, yes, it does. In Mark we take up kingdom eyes and see that the voices of the world, to which we give such heed, do not speak the truth. The expectations of the world are not those of God. The coming of the Christ into the world is not something to debate — for it comes with Satyagraha, the force of truth that surpasseth all understanding.

Only those who can disconnect themselves from the voices of the world sufficiently to perceive the call of the ineffable will be able to respond. The rest of humanity are then in the care of those who heed.

Everything To Do With Break-fast

"A Christian is one who follows Christ. Such a one is called to respond to suffering. Commitment to the Way of Christ erases the distinction between deserved and unde-served suffering."

James 5:7-10

Be patient, therefore, beloved, until the coming of the Lord. The farmer waits for the precious crop from the earth, being patient with it until it receives the early and the late rains. You also must be patient. Strengthen your hearts, for the coming of the Lord is near. Beloved, do not grumble against one another, so that you may not be judged. See, the Judge is standing at the doors! As an example of suffering and patience, beloved, take the prophets who spoke in the name of the Lord.

This news just in. Four Jewish subway riders were attacked and injured Friday in New York by ten attackers because they answered, "Happy Hanukkah" to them when they yelled, "Merry Christmas." Even more serious injury was prevented by a Muslim college student who came to the aid of the Jews and fought off the Christians. I don't think I'm the only one who feels that Christmas has gotten a little out of hand. What with the shopping, and the decorating and the assaulting people of other faiths ... it's no wonder everybody's exhausted!

I left church Monday after telling Linda, the church secretary, that I did not know <u>what</u> I was going to preach this Sunday. The Lectionary Texts just didn't speak to me. As I was leaving, Linda reminded me of a bit of shopping I had to do, so off to the mall I went, through a cold rain and into the warmth of the 21st Century's answer to the Romans' gladiatorial arena. There were reindeer up to here, and Santas everywhere and wrapped display packages and people with determined expressions, and, ever so gently, the thought began to form that this might be the time for the "real meaning of Christmas" sermon.

I had hardly formed that thought, though, when I ran into two friends from First Christian. They were particularly exercised because they had seen a television on-street interview of passers-by in New York. The interviewer had asked random people why we celebrate Christmas and had gotten the expectedly random answers about buying presents and showing loved ones that we care about them, but nothing about Jesus. "What do we do," they asked, "to get the young people to know that the babe in the manger is our God?"

That's a very good question. A very good question, indeed, and appropriately asked in New York — considering what's going on in the subways. How did Christmas come to be all about gifts and nothing about Jesus? Why can there so easily be Christmas without Christ, but Christmas without gifts is unthinkable? Growing up, even my Jewish neighbors had a Hanukkah bush!

The other thing that happened that Monday, which now seems a lot fuller than I first thought, was that Linda and I had a conversation venting some frustration she felt over a family which had asked the church for help, but who had gotten a little testy with her because we couldn't bring the food to them and who was equally upset to learn that the church couldn't buy whatever her children wanted for Christmas.

Quite a lot for a Monday, now that I look back on it, and two very different views of the "Christmas problem." My friends at the mall see Christmas as a time to educate the world about our faith. The woman who called the church sees Christmas as a time in which she is entitled to have food and presents delivered to her and her family. Without my being aware of it, my Monday had presented me with two examples of what we might call the "Christmas problem."

On the one hand, Christmas seems overwhelmed by its secular dimensions. Christians feel marginalized by a perceived preempting of the celebration of the birth of Jesus by commercial and non-Christian interests. Their natural inclination is to jump to the defense of "their" holiday.

On the other hand, a woman with real need but few social skills had approached the church with that need, and the church was unable to respond to it in a way she expected it to have done at least partially because Christmas is such a rushed time for churches.

I have to be honest with you here — I don't think Christmas has much to do with Christ, and, historically, it never has. The winter festival we celebrate as Christmas has much earlier origins in the Roman festival of *Dies Natalis Solis Invicti*, the *Saturnalia*, the Assyrian celebration of the goddess Ishtar and the Persian celebration of Mithras, among others. The early church grabbed on to the the date and, since the existing celebrations were too popular to prohibit, declared it the Mass of Christ. Protestants didn't like that because it was too papist and prohibited Christmas celebrations. "Keeping Christmas" would have gotten you a spell in the stocks in Puritan communities. Until sometime in the 19th Century, that was the position of the Presbyterian Church, and most other Protestant churches. As late as the time of my great grandparents, Christmas as a religious observance would have seemed a novel, and a bit of a daring, undertaking.

Looked at in that light, our problem isn't so much "putting Christ back in Christmas" as it is "Finding Christ in a historically secular celebration." Now, how might we do that?

One Christmas, when I was a child, Dad decided that Christmas had become too much about gifts, and that we needed to refresh our memory of the real meaning of Christmas. He announced that before we could open our presents, there would be a reading of the Christmas story, by which he meant the account of the birth of our Lord from Luke's Gospel.

I'm a minister of the Gospel of Jesus Christ. I really <u>believe</u> in Bible study. But telling an eight-year-old and a ten-year-old that they can't open their Christmas presents until they have heard a Bible passage read in Elizabethan English from an elderly King James translation is not an ideal way to focus their attention on the meaning of Christmas.

I have a confession to make: Dad couldn't immediately find the Christmas story in the Bible that Christmas. Mom was a determined Presbyterian and Dad a devoted DOC, but we were obligatory Christians — Christians who attended church and said grace before meals because that was the way decent people behaved and because it was good for us. We were not informed Christians. The Bible was something you put on a table, not something you read. Dad undertook the reading of the Christmas story in the same way — it was something that would do us good, in some poorly understood way. Reading a pas-

29

sage of Scripture because it will do you good, or in times of stress, won't put Christ in Christmas. Putting Christ in Christmas is going to take a lot more effort than that.

Sometimes, I'm that close to giving up on Christmas. The societal forces are so overwhelming, the force of tradition is so great, I just become too tired to fight it. "Oh, let the reindeer have Christmas," I think. "Maybe we can save Easter. The Easter Bunny just doesn't have the same marketing muscle. He's a little guy. I think I can take him."

Then, on Tuesday, just as I had myself all Grinched up, out of nowhere comes a news story about a man going through Starbuck's in Greensburg, Pennsylvania, who paid for the coffee for the car behind him, for no reason at all. That person, pretty surprised that a stranger should do something nice for her, paid for the coffee of the car behind her. It went on like that for two hours, an unbroken chain of 100 cars. A gift bestowed. A gift received. I left the house, went to McDonald's and bought breakfast for the car behind me, then ran like crazy in case she thought I was some kind of masher.

What do my Monday experiences teach me about Christmas? Is "keeping Christ in Christmas" honored more by leaping to the defense of our faith at this special time of the year against the heathenish attacks of the "happy Hanukkah" or "happy holidays" people, claiming the 25th of December as ours and only ours, or is it honored more by responding to the need of the woman who called? Who acted in a Christ-like way, the thugs in the subway, or the man in line at Starbuck's?

But, why did the first man do that at just this time of the year? Isn't it because he, in turn, was responding to the gift of Jesus? Didn't he pony up for a venti cinnamon dulce latte, sugar free, soy, no whip because he realized that long ago and far away God gave us His Son, just as I bought breakfast for a stranger in Kentucky because somebody in Pennsylvania bought coffee for a stranger? That's a pretty good Gospel message there. Why am I being such a Grinch about gift-giving? Honestly, I'm not against giving loved ones gifts. I just wish we weren't under so much pressure to do it at this time of the year. I think it confuses the Christmas message. It's not the sort of gift that God gave us when He sent His Son.

To my mind, the gift of Jesus to the world is entirely different from the Christmas gift-giving to which we've become accustomed. If I buy Uncle Fred the fishing pole he hinted he wanted, I'm showing him that I value him. It's a nice thing to do, and he might keep me in the will.

It's an entirely different thing to offer to buy something for the stranger behind you. You don't know what the stranger's needs are. You might have come in for a two dollar cup of coffee (assuming there still is such a thing as a cup of coffee that costs only two dollars anymore). The car behind you might have ordered ten or twelve dollars' worth of coffee drinks. You have no way of knowing, yet you are opening yourself to that stranger's needs freely, making yourself vulnerable to the needs of someone you don't know.

Sort of like the life of Jesus, in miniature, don't you think? No shopping. No running around. No pressure. Just "I'd like to satisfy a need of the stranger behind me. I know it's a tiny need. I know it will cost me money. I know that the person won't thank me because I'll be gone before he or she can do so."

It's exactly the sort of giving this church has practiced for the past 52 years, when we distribute toys and food at Christmas time. Some of the people to whom we give are embarrassed. Some are driven by a sense of entitlement, perhaps like the woman who gave Linda grief that Monday. Some are grateful. It doesn't matter. We aren't after a response. We're responding to a need.

The stranger behind me might take the breakfast I bought and grumble about where was I when she needed groceries last week. She might be very wealthy and be insulted that I might have thought she needed charity. I don't really care what the stranger's reaction might be. I just want that person to know that for a second or two, for a small amount of money, I valued them, just as I value Uncle Fred.

No, that's not true. I do care what the stranger's reaction might be. I'm just not interested in what the stranger's reaction toward me is. I hope that she will think about passing on the favor to another stranger. Jesus' message was not so much, "Do as I do and be holy" as it was, "Be holy and you will do as I do." Move as Jesus did, in obedience to the Communion of the Holy Spirit, and you will find yourself doing the most amazing things. If my small gift of breakfast awakened in her an awareness of the Spirit of God speaking to her, she will buy breakfast for others and more than that, as well.

This is the place that my chance meeting with my friends really lit my fuse. It is not a baby in that manger. It is God. God, who saw that we could not raise ourselves up to Him, so He came to us. God, who saw our need and answered it. <u>THAT</u> is the gift we are to emulate in our giving — a selfless, unconcerned, unstressed totally vulnerable giving that has nothing really to do with reindeer.

But everything to do with breakfast.

The Cosmological Constant

"The very complexity of Creation cries loudly for the presence of a Creator in the same way footprints testify to the presence of a foot."

Isaiah 61:1-4, 8-11

The spirit of the Lord GOD is upon me,
because the LORD has anointed me;
he has sent me to bring good news to the oppressed,
to bind up the brokenhearted,
to proclaim liberty to the captives,
and release to the prisoners;
to proclaim the year of the LORD's favor,
and the day of vengeance of our God;
to comfort all who mourn;
to provide for those who mourn in Zion—
to give them a garland instead of ashes,
the oil of gladness instead of mourning,
the mantle of praise instead of a faint spirit.
They will be called oaks of righteousness,
the planting of the LORD, to display his glory.
They shall build up the ancient ruins,
they shall raise up the former devastations;
they shall repair the ruined cities,
the devastations of many generations.
For I the LORD love justice,
I hate robbery and wrongdoing;
I will faithfully give them their recompense,
and I will make an everlasting covenant with them.

Their descendants shall be known among the nations,
and their offspring among the peoples;
all who see them shall acknowledge
that they are a people whom the LORD has blessed.
I will greatly rejoice in the LORD,
my whole being shall exult in my God;
for he has clothed me with the garments of salvation,
he has covered me with the robe of righteousness,
as a bridegroom decks himself with a garland,
and as a bride adorns herself with her jewels.
For as the earth brings forth its shoots,
and as a garden causes what is sown in it to spring up,
so the Lord GOD will cause righteousness and praise
to spring up before all the nations.

John 1:6-8,19-28

There was a man sent from God, whose name was John. He came as a witness to testify to the light, so that all might believe through him. He himself was not the light, but he came to testify to the light.

This is the testimony given by John when the Jews sent priests and Levites from Jerusalem to ask him, "Who are you?" He confessed and did not deny it, but confessed, "I am not the Messiah." And they asked him, "What then? Are you Elijah?" He said, "I am not." "Are you the prophet?" He answered, "No." Then they said to him, "Who are you? Let us have an answer for those who sent us. What do you say about yourself?" He said, "I am the voice of one crying out in the wilderness, 'Make straight the way of the Lord,'" as the prophet Isaiah said. Now they had been sent from the Pharisees. They asked him, "Why then are you baptizing if you are neither the Messiah, nor Elijah, nor the prophet?" John answered them, "I baptize with water. Among you stands one whom you do not know, the one who is coming after me; I am not worthy to untie the thong of his sandal." This took place in Bethany across the Jordan where John was baptizing.

THE LAWYER'S TALE

I think everyone has a know-it-all in their lives. You know the guy — the one that can hold forth on any topic, no matter how exotic, and who never, ever admits to being wrong. I remember a school trip to a farm to watch a farrier make horseshoes. Our class know-it-all was holding forth for the whole class about the different types of horseshoe. He idly reached over and picked one up to demonstrate some point, failing to notice that it had just come out of the forge.

Everybody laughed at him as he jumped back and dropped the horseshoe, and somebody said, "Don't know as much as you thought you did, huh?"

With great dignity, hiding his burned fingers in his pocket, and biting his lip, he replied, "Nawww. It just doesn't take me very long to look at a horseshoe."

If we're going to function in this world, we have to have a baseline amount of confidence in our abilities and in our understanding of how the world works, but it must be balanced by the humble admission that we DON'T actually understand everything. A little humility is essential to a successful life as a human being. Unfortunately, like my classmate, we're much happier hiding our limitations, even from ourselves, than we are facing up to them.

Of course, the truth is that our lives, our very existence, is as a result of things we aren't aware of — things that we take purely on faith, if we think of them at all. There really are things we don't understand or aren't aware of that actually have a very big effect on our lives, even though we don't understand them. Here's an example: There is a number called the "cosmological constant" which describes the way in which space itself expands. Einstein proposed it as an addition to his General Theory of Relativity, then abandoned it. Lately, it has been resurrected. Chances are, you've never heard of it. Doesn't matter. The thing you need to know about it is that it appears that if it were even one millionth of one percent different than it seems to be, the universe either would have blown itself to pieces, or crushed itself into a black hole shortly after the Big Bang. If this number were even infinitesimally different, we wouldn't be here. Your very existence is by virtue of a mathematical function that you've never heard of and so never think about.

Here's something else. The protein in our blood that carries oxygen to our cells does so because of its shape. Oxygen molecules fit into it like a hand in a glove. Unfortunately, it binds even tighter to another molecule — carbon monoxide. This is why it is such a very bad idea to sit in a garage with the motor running. The finesse of the thing is that normal processes in our bodies produce small amounts of guess what? Carbon monoxide. How come we don't poison ourselves?

Turns out the protein in the blood that we're speaking of has the power to change its shape slightly in the presence of low concentrations of carbon monoxide so that the carbon monoxide doesn't fit the protein anymore. Think of that! A protein that has the smarts to change its shape to tolerate low concentrations of carbon monoxide. I bet you never heard of that, either, but if it were otherwise, you wouldn't be here. You pay it no mind, but it absolutely determines your continued existence.

Even so mundane a thing as switching on the light when you enter a room places you at the apex of an monstrously complex chain of events leading from a swamp in the Carboniferous period a third of a billion years ago to a coal mine in West Virginia through some baroque machinations involving copper and magnets to your home.

We're pretty resourceful thinkers. We can imagine that these things we are not aware of, and thousands of others I haven't mentioned, came to be this way by random processes. That seems a stretch for me. For me, it is as if the universe itself, from the moment of the Big Bang, has been arraying itself to graciously welcome life. Though we never think about how unlikely a thing it is that we can be here at all, let alone be able to switch on a light and read Scriptures that have been transmitted to us over three and a half millennia, the writer of Psalm 100 remind us:

Rejoice in the miracle of every day.
Shout for joy to the Lord, all the earth.

Each day IS a miracle. That we are able to be here and experience it is so improbable a thing that you would be a fool to bet your hard-earned money on it, yet, against all odds, here we are. So, why DON'T we pay attention to these critical factors that permit us to live? Now that I've told you about them, why don't we demand that WSAZ include a report during the 5 o'clock weather on the state of the cosmological constant?

Of course, the world does contain people who do just that. They are called cosmologists and they spend their days thinking about the cosmological constant. You might say they are Einstein intoxicated. They are the elect, called to beat their brains out over these questions. It is their bliss and their pleasure to think about such things. If we want to be courageous Christians, I think we have to face up to the realization that for many people in this country, thinking about God is on a par with thinking about the cosmological constant. Some do, most don't.

It's as if we are all sailing on a beautiful cruise ship, but we all have internal cabins. We can't see the great sea that supports us, and we are unaware that we are traveling. In general, the passengers are unconcerned about either possibility. Their interest is in enjoying the comfortable surroundings. For some, it is given to them to glimpse the sea and sense the motion. If these few try to tell the others, the most common reaction will be a shrug, and the statement, "Oh, all that stuff doesn't matter to me. Personally, I'm more interested in the buffet. Try the shrimp."

Does this old world contain nice, considerate, moral people who are plain baffled by any talk of God or Jesus? Yes, church, it does. Does this old world contain nice, considerate, moral people who marry and raise children, and care for their aged parents and give as much thought to God's love and grace as they do to the state of the cosmological constant? Yes, church, it does. It is not so that everyone on the planet, or even everyone in our own community, hears the call of God. For some people, the entire topic is just closed to them.

So, what do we make of this? Is an interest in religion just one more obsession some people develop? Some people like to collect butterflies, other people like to sit in pews and sing old songs?

I think not. I'm compelled by my own experience to assert that there is, behind the stained glass and familiar hymns, a reality, a cosmological constant, an inexpressible mystery, access to which some are granted, and some are not. Some in the church hear Isaiah proclaim

> The spirit of the Lord GOD is upon me,
> because the LORD has anointed me;
> He has sent me to bring good news to the oppressed,

and know what he means, because they have experienced it. Those both inside and outside the church who have not experienced it hear it as mumbo-jumbo or self-delusional thinking. Like my classmate with the horseshoe, they will hold forth at length about the delusional way church people think about their experience. It's closed to them. Naturally they don't understand us.

Left to our own devices, this is just exactly the hole in the road we'd get stuck in. Left to our own devices, those touched by God would carry on about hearing the voice of the Spirit and being Spirit guided, and those outside the church would be tolerant of the delusions of church people at best, or actively hostile to those in the church for being self-righteous bigots at worst. It would be a big mess.

Fortunately, we're not left to our own devices. Once upon a time, God handed us a hot horseshoe. As my know-it-all classmate found out, you just can't ignore a hot horseshoe. You can pretend that it's not hot. You can pretend you didn't experience it, but you can't credibly ignore it. In our passage today, the horseshoe's name is Jesus. You can't ignore Jesus. You can hold forth against the church's understanding of Jesus and his message, you can agree with the church's understanding, but you can't ignore Him.

The people confronting John are described as "priests and Levites." The priests would claim descent from Aaron, Moses' brother, and the Levites from the tribe of Levy. These would be the religious professionals of the time, the ones whose business it would be to know who was who and what was what. The thing they weren't able to know, the thing that John DID know was the reality behind the events which were playing out before them. Failing to understand that a world-changing event had happened, they wanted to bang events into the shapes they knew. They asked John if he was the Messiah. They asked him if he was Elijah. (Elijah, Scripture says, was taken up to heaven while still alive, and was believed to come again to announce the Messiah. Jews to this day set an extra cup at Seder for Elijah, should he arrive at their door.) They asked him if he was the prophet whose coming Moses had promised in Deuteronomy:

> The Lord your God will raise up for you a prophet like me from among your own people; you shall heed such a prophet.

"No," John told them. "I'm none of these. But there's a game changer standing among you that you do not know, and I am not worthy to untie his shoelace."

In First Century Judea, something happened. "Jesus something from somewhere up north," unconnected with the religious center at Jerusalem, appeared and changed everything. The people who witnessed reacted with shock and awe, and "Jesus something from somewhere up north" became the man known throughout the globe. Even the Qur'an honors him.

"Jesus something from somewhere up north" is the most famous man to ever walk the face of the earth, but he could be overlooked in a crowd. The church teaches that Jesus was God incarnate, the Word made flesh, but Rome could kill him with no difficulty whatsoever. The church and the experience of millions of people through time teaches that on the third day He arose from the grave. Those outside the church can assert that it just doesn't take them very long to look at a horseshoe, but to assert that it's all wishful thinking is to discount both the record of history, which documents that "Jesus something from somewhere up north" existed, and the experience of millions of people worldwide who testify, just as John did, to the reality and accuracy of the accounts of Jesus.

Our very existence may depend on the nature of something called the cosmological constant. Our proteins may be wise enough to change their shape without our being aware of it. The fact that we don't understand or acknowledge generally the realities behind our existence does not change them — it simply reflects our limited understanding. If we're going to function in this world, we have to have a baseline amount of confidence in our abilities and understanding of how the world works, but it must be balanced by the humble admission that we <u>don't</u> actually understand everything. One of the ways God teaches us humility is by handing us a hot horseshoe, just when we are holding forth as a know-it-all, when we are at our most self-assured and confident in our own abilities.

In this "Jesus something from somewhere up north," there was what Celtic Christianity calls a "thin place," a place through which we can look to see the limits of our understanding, and from which we can experience the reality behind the stained glass. This "Jesus something from somewhere up north" is a porthole in our cruise ship through which we can see the great ocean speeding by. Not everyone will look, but for those who do, such a glimpse shocks and awes those who have been given that opportunity and grants to them true humility.

Here is that reality, as I glimpse it: if the cosmological constant were even one millionth of a percent greater or lesser, the universe we live in wouldn't have formed and we wouldn't be here. If the sun's energy output were a tiny bit different, we would have broiled or frozen before we could have evolved the ability to think about it. If the ratio of matter to anti-matter in the universe was only slightly different, the whole shebang would have blown up eons ago. From the very instant of the big bang, the universe was preparing itself for the presence of life on a tiny planet around an insignificant star. You can believe that happened by chance if you want. I can't. It's just too improbable. I believe it happened because some force, call it, oh ... God ... willed it so.

But that's not enough! Being convinced that the universe was called forth by an ineffable God so great that He is beyond our ability to describe isn't enough. The other piece we need is to be convinced that this God cares about us, right down to the least of us. This is the piece that's lost on so many today. We live in an objectified, secular world. By virtue of our decision to be respectful of all beliefs we teeter on seeing religious understanding to be a personal opinion. Jesus is the hot horseshoe that forces each of us to take a position. You can be a professing Christian and assert your belief in Jesus. You can say it's all a load of dingo's kidneys and wishful thinking, but you have to take some position on Jesus.

The complexity of Creation cries loudly for the presence of a Creator. This is what I urge you to think about this Advent. Jesus is coming into the world. What does that mean for you?

The Wheelhouse

"The life of a Christian begins with
the awareness of a relationship
with an immanent, transcendent God."

Luke 1:26-38

*In the sixth month the angel Gabriel was sent by God to a town in Galilee
called Nazareth, to a virgin engaged to a man whose name was Joseph, of the
house of David. The virgin's name was Mary. And he came to her and said,
"Greetings, favored one! The Lord is with you." But she was much perplexed
by his words and pondered what sort of greeting this might be. The angel said
to her, "Do not be afraid, Mary, for you have found favor with God. And now,
you will conceive in your womb and bear a son, and you will name him Jesus.
He will be great, and will be called the Son of the Most High, and the Lord
God will give to him the throne of his ancestor David. He will reign over the
house of Jacob forever, and of his kingdom there will be no end." Mary said
to the angel, "How can this be, since I am a virgin?" The angel said to her,
"The Holy Spirit will come upon you, and the power of the Most High will
overshadow you; therefore the child to be born will be holy; he will be called
Son of God. And now, your relative Elizabeth in her old age has also con-
ceived a son; and this is the sixth month for her who was said to be barren.
For nothing will be impossible with God." Then Mary said, "Here am I, the
servant of the Lord; let it be with me according to your word." Then the angel
departed from her.*

J. STEWART SCHNEIDER

O ur passage from Luke depicting the angel Gabriel bringing a surprising announcement to a young woman named Mary is called "The Annunciation.." When I say "young" I mean very young. It's so excep-
tionally hard not to read back into the First Century our expectations and assumptions about what life was like for these folks, but we really need to resist
that temptation. The life Mary knew was nothing like you might expect. A boy
child became "son of the Law" at 13. A female child was marriageable at that
age and perhaps as young as twelve for the betrothal. We think of Mary as a
poised, mature woman. We'd do better to think of her as a little girl.

She's not just any little girl, either. She is a little Jewish girl of Nazareth, and
given that the people of her time couldn't **get** to the far side of the moon,
Nazareth is about as far away from the center of things as they could manage.
Recent excavations indicate that Nazareth in Jesus' time was a tiny village of
perhaps 480 persons[7], about half the size of Bellefonte. That's a pretty small
speck in the world.

Mary's dominant status was that she had none. She was not a great leader like
Deborah, who judged Israel. She was a little girl from a town so tiny it left virtually no archaeological record to excavate. She would have had no education
apart from those things her mother might have taught her that a woman
would need to know to run a household. It's almost unthinkable that she
would have been able to read or write. Books as we know them had not been
invented and it's unlikely she ever saw written material of any sort in any
event.

Luke seeks to give her royal blood by telling us that her child will inherit the
throne of his ancestor David, but if you recall, David's son, Solomon, had 700
wives and 300 concubines[8]. Setting aside the question of why the wisest man
in history would put himself in a position in which a thousand women are all
mad at him at the same time, I think the mathematics of the situation would
indicate that if he had children with only some of his wives and concubines,
there would be no one in Judah a thousand years later who couldn't claim descent from David. I think, whatever Luke has to say about it, that Mary was
just as I've described — a little Jewish girl from the sticks of no particular status at all.

7   E. Meyers & J. Strange, Archaeology, the Rabbis, & Early Christianity Nashville: Abingdon,
      1981; Article "Nazareth" in the Anchor Bible Dictionary. New York: Doubleday, 1992.
8   First Kings 11:1-3

THE LAWYER'S TALE

It is Mary's status, or, rather, her lack of it, that draws me back to the image I used last Sunday of a cruise ship. If you recall, I asked you to imagine that we are on a cruise ship equipped with the finest of luxuries. Fifty-two-inch plasmas in each stateroom, with ESPN, an Xbox and a Wii. In the dining hall, the Grand Buffet is stocked with the finest of food and drink 24/7. There are concerts and Broadway shows, a great gym, a huge library. There are walking paths and swimming pools and casinos galore. No expense has been spared. Our accommodations are the finest, BUT ... we all have interior cabins, with no portholes.

It's no surprise, then, with so many distractions, that most people settle into the Grand Buffet, stake out a good seat at the game, and think nothing at all about how they came to be here. There are on board, however, some few who have been granted a peep outside. They have seen that we are on a ship, supported by a vast, blue sea. By the wake in the water, these elect can see that we are on a journey — a journey guided by an unseen hand in the wheelhouse. It's a life-changing revelation. We are all on the same journey! We're all in the same boat!

If these few try to share their revelation, they will find that it frightens their fellow passengers. It's scary to trust an unseen hand in the wheelhouse. What if the unseen hand in the wheelhouse isn't paying attention? What if he doesn't know what he's doing? What if he is malicious, and is deliberately taking us to doom? I think these questions are scary enough that most of the people on the boat would rather not think about them. I think they would bury themselves in the entertainment possibilities and drive thoughts about this out of their heads. They might even take the position that there is no one in the wheelhouse because there is no wheelhouse, and we're not going anywhere in any event. That's certainly more comfortable than putting our trust in something we can't see or even, by definition, prove scientifically.

Thinking about Mary and her lack of status brought this image to mind for me because there are other passengers on our ship. For these, there is no Grand Buffet, no gym, no fifty-yard seats. These live beyond a locked door, in the bowels of the ship. For those in steerage, there are very few distractions. And among these passengers, in the poorest accommodations, is Mary. Very soon, there will be another passenger in steerage, Mary's son, Jesus.

Why would Gabriel go to a little Jewish girl from the sticks to bring his message? Why wouldn't he go to the virtuous wife of the banker, or to the caring physician, or to someone else on the upper decks who would be in a position to spread this good news ship-wide? If the idea is to spread good news that there IS a hand on the wheel, and that he wishes only good for his charges, why go below decks to do it? If the idea is to assure us of our safety in his hands by sending his only Son to share our journey, why start at the bottom? Isn't it because the news Gabriel brings isn't good news at all to those on the upper decks? Isn't it that the same good news that offers hope to those in need demands sacrifice from those who live in plenty?

"But," I hear you say. "Can't you be wealthy and influential **and** virtuous?" Well ... yes, you can. It's just infinitely harder. I would draw your attention to one Nikolaos of Myra. He was born about the year 270 in Patara, a port in present-day Turkey, and lived in Myra, eventually becoming its Bishop. He was known for his generosity. It is said that he would secretly go about the town, leaving coins in shoes that were left out for him. Through a series of translit-erations of his name, he was known in Holland as Sinterklaas. As anyone who has watched "Miracle on 34th Street" with Natalie Wood knows, we call him Santa Claus.

So, yes, you can be wealthy and virtuous, but how common is it? There are philanthropists, of course, but they give from their plenty, not from their essence. He gives nothing who does not give of himself. Look at what is being required of Mary:

> And now, you will conceive in your womb and bear a son, and you will name him Jesus.

We're not talking about a tax deduction here! Mariam, the little Jewish girl from the sticks is going to go through a pregnancy, labor and delivery because some random guy told her she would. And her reply?

> "Here am I, the servant of the Lord; let it be with me according to your word."

That, church, is self-denying faith. Above decks, the party roars on. Only in those below decks, where there are no distractions, can you find such a re-sponse. Only those who live in darkness and are forced, by their circum-stances, to confront it are equipped to see the light.

Above decks, the coming of a child to a little girl in a rural community wouldn't make a human interest spot on the five o'clock news. Above decks, only those few who have been granted a glimpse outside realize that all within are supported by the sea. All of us, rich and wretched, virtuous and villain, are on a journey directed by an unseen hand in the wheelhouse. When these prophets bring their words to their fellows, at best they are asked to move aside and stop blocking the TV because the game is coming on. At worst, they may be attacked.

Below decks, a little Jewish girl of no background replies with the *Magnificat*:

> My soul proclaims the greatness of the Lord,
> my spirit rejoices in God my Savior;
>   for he has looked with favor on his lowly servant.
> From this day all generations will call me blessed:
>   the Almighty has done great things for me, and holy is his Name.

Can you be privileged and virtuous? Can you live above decks and show compassion to your brothers and sisters? Yes, but it is much more difficult. Those below decks, who share suffering, can relate to it better than those above deck who live lives of privilege. This is why we so often hear stories of someone's mother who, though struggling for her family during the Great Depression, would still provide a hot meal to a hobo. She knows what it is to be hungry and because she has suffered hunger, she can relate to the hunger of others with compassion. That's much, much more difficult if you have a reserved seat at the Grand Buffet. It is also the most pressing challenge for those of us who sail on the upper decks. The life of a Christian begins with the awareness of a relationship with an immanent, transcendent God. Through that relationship, it becomes possible to approach God's Creation with compassion.

The 14th Dali Lama observes:

> The first beneficiary of compassion is always oneself. When compassion, or warmheartedness, arises in us and our focus shifts away from our own narrow self-interest, it is as if we open an inner door. It reduces fear, boosts confidence and brings us inner strength. By reducing distrust, it opens us to others and brings us a sense of connection to others, and sense of purpose and meaning in life.

The distractions of a privileged life make compassion for the suffering of others much more difficult to experience. This is why, when I discuss the lot of those below decks with my fellow "A" deck passengers, I don't often hear words of compassion. Instead, I hear statements like, "Get a job," or "Take a bath." I hear words like "lazy" and "criminals," hurtful words directed at the dehumanized masses of suffering children of God, as if all who suffer do so through their own fault, even those who were working until their companies laid them off. Even older workers who can't find a job anymore but still must pay dearly for their medications. Even children. It was recently reported that more than 29,000 Kentucky children have no place to call home[9].

Are there villains below decks? Yes. Are they all villains because they are below decks? No. Remember, there are villains above decks as well, some of them committing offenses that far exceed those committed by those below decks. People are people, above decks or below.

And so, Mary will bring forth her child, who shall be called holy, in poor accommodations, in a manger. In his adulthood, he will speak words of condemnation to those distracted by the Grand Buffet and words of comfort to those who confront the darkness of hunger and hopelessness. He will teach "Blessed are the poor" for the poor, having supped at want's table, are truly blessed to feel the suffering of others. As the Dali Lama notes, "The first beneficiary of compassion is always oneself."

Beyond all that, He will teach that there is a wheelhouse. There is a hand on the wheelhouse who is so competent that He would send His only son to share the journey with us. The lessons Jesus will flesh out begin before he is born because the lesson of Mary at the Annunciation is also one of self-denying faith. Mary's lesson is bound up in her words,

> "Here am I, the servant of the Lord; let it be with me according to your word."

I want to close with a thought from Cantor Mark Perman:

> If everyone were to recognize the common ethical and spiritual thread that binds all of humanity, wouldn't that help us to move beyond the superficial differences that seem to endlessly divide?

Those above decks who have seen a peek at the ocean realize that we are all

---

9   http://www.homelesschildrenamerica.org/documents/PublicNewsService_KentuckyHomelessNumbers.pdf

in the same boat together. Those below decks, who share the suffering of the poor, know it as well. Our challenge on the "A" deck is to recognize the common ethical and spiritual thread that binds all of humanity. We must take to heart Mary's lesson of self-denying faith. We must also take to heart the Dali Lama's words that "When compassion, or warmheartedness, arises in us and our focus shifts away from our own narrow self-interest, it is as if we open an inner door."

Can you do it, church?

J. STEWART SCHNEIDER

From Awakening to Awareness

Although Christmas and Epiphany, for largely commercial reasons, have been run together in our culture, they represent two distinctly different way stations on our journey to connection with God. Just as the Christ Child entered the world on Christmas, unnoticed by hardly anyone outside His family, so the indwelling Spirit promised by Jesus enters our lives, often unnoticed. In the telling of the story, it was only much later, perhaps two years or so, before the world, in the person of Herod the Horrible, client king of Judea, became aware of His presence. When Herod did become aware of it, he recognized such a one as Jesus as disruptive and dangerous and acted promptly to attempt to remove the Christ Child.

Many of us react the same way to an awareness of God's presence in our lives. We see the Holy Spirit as dangerous to our comfortable way of life and disruptive to our plans for our future.

J. STEWART SCHNEIDER

The Commonplace

"The world in which we live is the common place where we encounter God."

Luke 2:22-40

When the time came for their purification according to the law of Moses, they brought him up to Jerusalem to present him to the Lord (as it is written in the law of the Lord, "Every firstborn male shall be designated as holy to the Lord"), and they offered a sacrifice according to what is stated in the law of the Lord, "a pair of turtledoves or two young pigeons."

Now there was a man in Jerusalem whose name was Simeon; this man was righteous and devout, looking forward to the consolation of Israel, and the Holy Spirit rested on him. It had been revealed to him by the Holy Spirit that he would not see death before he had seen the Lord's Messiah. Guided by the Spirit, Simeon came into the temple; and when the parents brought in the child Jesus, to do for him what was customary under the law, Simeon took him in his arms and praised God, saying,

"Master, now you are dismissing your servant in peace,
according to your word;
for my eyes have seen your salvation,
which you have prepared in the presence of all peoples,
a light for revelation to the Gentiles
and for glory to your people Israel."

And the child's father and mother were amazed at what was being said about him. Then Simeon blessed them and said to his mother Mary, "This child is destined for the falling and the rising of many in Israel, and to be a sign that will be opposed so that the inner thoughts of many will be revealed — and a sword will pierce your own soul too."

There was also a prophet, Anna the daughter of Phanuel, of the tribe of Asher. She was of a great age, having lived with her husband seven years after her marriage, then as a widow to the age of eighty-four. She never left the temple but worshiped there with fasting and prayer night and day. At that moment she came, and began to praise God and to speak about the child to all who were looking for the redemption of Jerusalem.

When they had finished everything required by the law of the Lord, they returned to Galilee, to their own town of Nazareth. The child grew and became strong, filled with wisdom; and the favor of God was upon him.

Just before Christmas, I saw a display of carolers cut from plywood and painted in Edwardian dress. They were in good voice, each face up-tilted, each mouth caught mid-syllable. For some reason I thought of these plywood figures spending most of the year in the back of the garage, their faces still uplifted in hope, their mouths still open in praise, heard by none, ignored by all until the Christmas season again rolled around. Then they would be retrieved from behind the bicycles and the lawn mower, given a quick scrub with soap and water to remove the accumulated detritus of the year, and posted again in their accustomed place.

Little Mary had no such luxury. For her, Christmas was not a season to be repeated each year. It was a responsibility every day of the year. Her son had to be fed, and clothed, and he must have a place to rest his head where he would be safe. For Mary, Christmas ushered in her life as a mother, a role she fulfilled with some enthusiasm, for Mark tells us, recounting a later event in Jesus' life:

> Is not this the carpenter, the son of Mary and brother of James and Joses and Judas and Simon, and are not his sisters here with us?'

The Roman Catholic Church teaches as a foundational understanding of the faith the perpetual virginity of Mary. These children, the church reasons, must therefore be children of Joseph's first marriage to some other, unnamed, Mrs. Joseph. This is why Joseph is always pictured as an older man. It really makes no difference if these children were of her body or not. She is the mama, and it's her responsibility to care for them, not just at Christmas time, but all year long.

Here, in a nutshell, is the balancing act that we must accomplish in our faith. We must treat Christmas and the coming of our Lord with the celebration that it deserves without losing sight of what a commonplace event it really was — the birth of a child under less than ideal circumstances, to a little girl, far from home in Luke's telling.

Luke and Matthew, the two Gospels which contain infancy narratives, are at great pains to convince us, and their first century readers, of the magnitude of this event. Stars move. Wise and important men from hundreds of miles to the east journey to tiny Bethlehem. Angels appear to shepherds. Even Herod the Horrible is aware that the foundations of common life have been shaken by an event so powerful that the heavens are moved, but the actual physical phenomenon — the initiating event — is a thing of such commonality as to be all but unnoticeable. It was the birth of a child under less than ideal circumstances, to a little girl, far from home.

I think we could be forgiven for taking from the Gospel stories only the magnificence of the event, and overlooking the ordinariness of it, but there is a danger there. We might be mislead into believing that God must always act with pomp and ceremony. This is the wrong lesson to take from the the story of the Nativity of our Lord. God works in inconsequential events. God acts in the commonplace.

Kentucky nurtured a real, gosh-for-shooting holy man in the person of Thomas Merton. For a man of the stature of Merton, you would expect a stars-moving, heaven-shaking sort of a beginning of his awareness of God. Merton's epiphany was nothing like that. He wrote of it in "Conjectures of A Guilty Bystander". I cannot possibly explain it with more clarity than did Merton:

> In Louisville, at the corner of Fourth and Walnut, in the center of the shopping district, I was suddenly overwhelmed with the realization that I loved all those people, that they were mine and I theirs, that we could not be alien to one another even though we were total strangers.
> . . .
> Then it was as if I suddenly saw the secret beauty of their hearts, the depths of their hearts where neither sin nor desire nor self-knowledge can reach, the core of their reality, the person that each one is in God's eyes. If only they could all see themselves as they really are. If only we could see each other that way all the time. There would be no more

war, no more hatred, no more cruelty, no more greed...I suppose the big problem would be that we would fall down and worship each other. But this cannot be seen, only believed and "understood" by a peculiar gift[10].

I have always thought that Merton's choice of the word "overwhelmed" was a happy one. He wasn't "suddenly aware", he didn't "notice", it wasn't a conclusion reached while preparing something for a talk. He was overwhelmed. We're so confident of how thoroughly competent we feel that we forget what it means to be overwhelmed, to be stopped in our tracks, to have the divine roll or surge over us with such force and clarity that it is impossible to ignore. Such was Thomas Merton's experience in Louisville, at the corner of Fourth and Walnut, in the center of the shopping district. Such was also the experience of little Mary.

A picture is worth a thousand words. We take as our internal representation of the Nativity story the Nativity set on top of the TV. As lovely as the Nativity is, it's a Hallmark Cards version. It's much too tidy, and it scribbles over all the human parts. Mary is as overwhelmed as Merton was, and she didn't even have to go to Louisville.

Two weeks ago, we read of the visit of Gabriel to Mary predicting the birth of Jesus.

And he came to her and said, "Greetings, favored one! The Lord is with you." But she was much perplexed by his words and pondered what sort of greeting this might be.

Perplexed or not, Mary signed on to carry the child, saying, "Here am I, the servant of the Lord; let it be with me according to your word."

Last week, Luke told us of the visit of the shepherds and again, Mary had perplexing things to ponder.

When they saw this, they made known what had been told them about this child; and all who heard it were amazed at what the shepherds told them. But Mary treasured all these words and pondered them in her heart.

This week, forty days after the birth of Jesus, Joseph and Mary, she only a

---

10 Thomas Merton, *Conjectures of A Guilty Bystander* (Image, January 9, 1968)

month post-natal, go from Nazareth to Jerusalem, a distance about the same as from here to Morehead, on foot. With a baby.

Mary and Joseph took upon themselves the burden and responsibility to do for Jesus what we celebrate only once a year and they did it in the real world, with real journeys and real sacrifices. That which we celebrate during Advent and the Twelve Days of Christmas, they undertook for the childhood of this most strange and holy child. For that time, they, and the child, were as invisible to the world as the plywood carolers behind the lawn mower in the back of the garage, heard by none, ignored by all until Epiphany, when the world came to know of Him.

We live in a commonplace world, filled with commonplace events. We are called to act where we are, to keep in our vision the holiness of this commonplace world and to share that vision with our fellows, for God Himself became a member of the human race.

Again, Thomas Merton says it better than I can:

> It is a glorious destiny to be a member of the human race, though it is a race dedicated to many absurdities and one which makes many terrible mistakes: yet, with all that, God Himself gloried in becoming a member of the human race. A member of the human race! To think that such a commonplace realization should suddenly seem like news that one holds the winning ticket in a cosmic sweepstake.

> I have the immense joy of being man, a member of a race in which God Himself became incarnate. As if the sorrows and stupidities of the human condition could overwhelm me, now that I realize what we all are. And if only everybody could realize this! But it cannot be explained. There is no way of telling people that they are all walking around shining like the sun[11].

It is a reality that each of us must face that not everyone is conscious that they belong to God. To many, that is a closed book. Some few get to peek outside and become conscious that we all, each of us, belong to God. This does not make us better or superior beings or anything of the sort. It means that in addition to doing that which everyone else does, we have the additional duty to carry the child, the Son of God, into the world.

---

11 Ibid.

55

At Jerusalem, when the parents brought in the child Jesus to do for him what was customary under the law, they were met by two people: Simeon and Anna. From these two seers, Mary and Joseph again were reminded of the divine within the commonplace and they were amazed at what was being said about him. I'm not surprised. It is a shock when the divine meets us here, where we are. It's disorienting, just as Merton said.

Disorienting or not, the commonplace of life is where we meet God and realize that He was here, with us, all along. God's creation is the common place where both the secular and the holy commune. Here is where we live, and here is where God came to meet us in the form of a baby. Here, in the common place God has chosen for us, we meet Him and receive from Him His teaching which we are to spread to all we meet. That is your job, church. It is your job to see to it that the good news of Christmas isn't hidden behind the lawn mower, heard by none, ignored by all. You are to bring the certainty that within the commonplace events of human lives is the holy. Bring LIFE church, LIFE into God's creation. Be for all a reminder that God acts within the commonplace.

"The ineffable God cannot be contained within the categorizing mind. To attempt to do so is to worship your own self."

Galatians 3:23-25; 4:4-7

Now before faith came, we were imprisoned and guarded under the law until faith would be revealed. Therefore the law was our disciplinarian until Christ came, so that we might be justified by faith. But now that faith has come, we are no longer subject to a disciplinarian.

But when the fullness of time had come, God sent his Son, born of a woman, born under the law, in order to redeem those who were under the law, so that we might receive adoption as children. And because you are children, God has sent the Spirit of his Son into our hearts, crying, "Abba! Father!" So you are no longer a slave but a child, and if a child then also an heir, through God.

John 1:1-18

In the beginning was the Word, and the Word was with God, and the Word was God. He was in the beginning with God. All things came into being through Him, and without Him not one thing came into being. What has come into being in Him was life, and the life was the light of all people. The light shines in the darkness, and the darkness did not overcome it.

There was a man sent from God, whose name was John. He came as a witness to testify to the light, so that all might believe through him. He himself was not the light, but he came to testify to the light. The true light, which enlightens everyone, was coming into the world.

He was in the world, and the world came into being through Him; yet the world did not know Him. He came to what was his own, and his own people did not accept Him. But to all who received Him, who believed in his name, he gave power to become children of God, who were born, not of blood or of the will of the flesh or of the will of man, but of God.

And the Word became flesh and lived among us, and we have seen his glory, the glory as of a father's only son, full of grace and truth. (John testified to Him and cried out, "This was He of whom I said, 'He who comes after me ranks ahead of me because He was before me.") From his fullness we have all received, grace upon grace. The law indeed was given through Moses; grace and truth came through Jesus Christ. No one has ever seen God. It is God the only Son, who is close to the Father's heart, who has made Him known.

A s I looked over the passages for today's sermon, I was really struck by the focus on Words. I have spent forty years earning my daily bread with words. I have lined them up in sentences and sold them to book publishers and to National Public Radio. I have spoken them into microphones connected to radio transmitters and wondered time and again if there were other people on the other end of the vibrations listening to my words. I have spoken countless thousands of words, many of them embarrassingly meaningless, in courts all over the Commonwealth of Kentucky, and I've spent three and one-half years now jabbering to you eighteen minutes at a time, fifty-two times a year. The sheer weight of the words that have passed my lips over four decades weigh me down. As I and the other old men leave the Chapel of St. Starbuck after Vigils and Lauds, in my imagination I see the Sexton with his broom brushing all the words we have spoken into great piles to be hauled off to the trash.

Words. Piles of words. Important words. Trivial words. Sometimes hurtful words. Words of judgment. Words of forgiveness. I have a belly full of words. One of my friends was celebrating her 41st anniversary, and as she was telling her husband how much she loved him, she said, "Words are not enough." She's right. They are not.

Nevertheless, a word popped into my attention from the radio this week — Diane Rehm's show, in particular. She was talking to the author of a new book on the birth of Jesus or some such, and she remarked that what happened to the family of Jesus after the birth, but before we take up the tale again 30 or so years later was a "mystery." That's the word that caught my ear — "mystery"

— and that's what I want us to think about this week — words and mystery, and how the two interplay with each other.

"Word," as John uses the term, means something other than the noise that comes out of our mouths virtually every waking moment of our lives and "mystery," as we speak of it here, doesn't mean a puzzle that can be examined and explained in words. That's a strange thing for me to say, since that is exactly what we DO mean when we use the terms "Word" and "Mystery" today. To us in the 21st Century, words are utterances. Mysteries are puzzles to be solved. It was not always so. The one who seeks wisdom would do well to recover the older meaning of these words. In the older meaning of these words, the Word of God is the creating and sustaining force behind everything in Creation. "Mystery" is the reality which remains when we have expended the full force of our reason and found it inadequate to reach the ineffable reality within which we live.

The one who would connect with this older meaning will find it immeasurably challenging. Our cultural understanding of these words binds us to our assumptions about words and mystery. To reconnect with these words is to jettison the cultural expectations of these words. For us, mysteries are problems to be solved and words are a kind of a fishing net we use to catch reality. Wisdom cannot be gained from these definitions. They will lead you astray, for more times than we realize, it is the fisherman, not the fish, who is netted. When we try to capture big concepts like "mystery" in our net of words it is our own thoughts which are netted, and we fool ourselves into thinking we understand things which we do not understand at all. It is the difference between someone describing to you a wonderful meal at a restaurant, and biting into the burger for yourself. You might decide that the description you heard really was accurate, or you might disagree, but no one would confuse the description with the burger. Except us, when the burger is the mystery of the Incarnation. Then we get all confused between the words and the reality.

When we attach words to big things, like "mystery," we attach everything we understand about the word to the concept, so that the concept comes to be bent out of shape by the weight of the baggage our words carry. N.T. Wright points out that if you hear the phrase, "I'm mad about my flat," from an Englishman, it means that he is crazy about his apartment. If you hear it from an American, it means he is angry about a flat tire. Without knowing the nationality of the speaker, the sentence is really meaningless. Without knowing the nationality of the speaker, you will attach your own nationality to it, and make of it what you will.

Not only national differences make words unreliable. Words change over time, too. If we would understand another's words, we have to know the time in which they were spoken. In the 13th century "girl" meant any young person, female or male. To distinguish between the two, a female was sometimes known as a "gay girl" and a male as a "knave girl." "Idiot" was once used to describe an ordinary person. Idiot gradually came to mean a layman, as contrasted with a clergyman. Since few people outside the church were educated, the term became associated with an uneducated person, hence an ignorant or foolish one, and ultimately with a person who was mentally deficient.

Even allowing for nationality and chronology, there is a world of difference between asking "What's this thing called 'love'?" and "What's this thing called, Love?" The latter might be explained. The former, I am convinced, cannot be netted in words. Love is a mystery that exceeds our capacity to explain.

When we approach the mystery of the stable and the birth of Jesus words are not enough. How do we get behind the words and the images that have been burned into our brain since we were babies ourselves to approach the mystery in the manger?

This is the time of the year in which we are to dedicate ourselves to this very task. The time between Christmas Eve and Epiphany is called "Christmastide" or the Twelve Days of Christmas. That means you should have gotten a partridge in a pear tree yesterday, and two turtle doves today. Do those words help us understand mystery better? The lyrics DO have a hidden meaning, once well-known, but it's so obscure that no one knows it today apart from theologians and scholars. The rest of us just wonder when the ten lords are going to stop their endless leaping and do something to earn their keep. Words are not enough to understand, to really enter into, the mystery of Christmastide.

"Well, what's the big mystery?" you might well ask. "We celebrate the birth of Jesus. That's not too mysterious."

I beg to differ. The birth of any baby is a sufficiently mysterious event that we should be in awe of it, but the birth of THIS baby ... ah ... that's something entirely different. THIS baby the church understands to be the second person of the Godhead. This baby the church understands to be fully human and fully divine. THIS baby represents God's own Self in the world in the most vulnerable way imaginable. When we try to approach THIS baby, words are not enough. Any words you apply to it will trivialize the birth and rob it of its power. Understanding the birth of Jesus, like understanding the meaning of love, can only be done emotionally, with the heart.

Because of the focus of the celebration, we are focused on the baby, and babies, like words, have the power to snare us in our own nets. We see the baby. We miss seeing the Word, capital W. I don't know if any of you got to see "The Best Christmas Pageant Ever" at the Paramount, or have read the book, but there's a line in it announcing that the part of the baby Jesus is played by a 40-watt light bulb. That's the part we tend to miss. In the manger is not just a baby. It is the Word of God.

How are we to understand this mystery? Words are not enough. We cannot net this mystery in the net of our words, for it is larger than we, and deeper. It is for this reason that I spoke of mystery as the reality remaining after we have expended the full force of our reason upon it. Such is the child in the manger. The Second Person of the Godhead in the manger is the reality which remains after you have expended the full force of your reason upon it and found your words and concepts to be inadequate.

But even that which we cannot understand we can form our lives around. At the end of the first century, the writer of the Gospel of John struggled with the same limitations of language that frustrate me today. How do you put into words that which is too large for words? His take on it was:

> In the beginning was the Word, and the Word was with God, and the Word was God. He was in the beginning with God. All things came into being through Him, and without Him not one thing came into being. What has come into being in Him was life, and the life was the light of all people. The light shines in the darkness, and the darkness did not overcome it.

The book of Genesis tells us, at its inception, the first chapter:

> In the beginning God created the heaven and the earth.
> And the earth was without form, and void; and darkness was upon the face of the deep. And the Spirit of God moved upon the face of the waters.
> And God said, Let there be light: and there was light.

This was the instant of creation, and that which God spoke — the Word — was with God, and the Word was God. All things came into being through Him, and without Him not one thing came into being. How would we approach such a thing in a manger, in a stable so long ago?

I would suggest we would be wrong to try, because we would try by applying words to it, and words are not enough. The moment of creation, when the Word of God brought all things into being, is too large for our nets. To pull in such a catch of mystery would tear our nets and capsize our boats.

The history of words is the history of the Law, by which the people of Israel tried to find their way to God. Fifty years or so before the Gospel of John, Paul wrote his letter to the Galatians, a portion of which we heard today. It is sometimes called the Christian Magna Carta, for when Paul tells his church at Galatia

> Now before faith came, we were imprisoned and guarded under the law until faith would be revealed. Therefore the law was our disciplinarian until Christ came, so that we might be justified by faith. But now that faith has come, we are no longer subject to a disciplinarian.

he is telling them that they cannot find their way to God through the words of the Law. Rather, it is God who has found us.

It seems to me that the coming of our Lord in so mysterious a fashion — the creative and creating Word of God through whom all things came into being, and without whom not one thing came into being, appearing as a baby in a manger — challenges us to take one of two paths: we may have faith in our words, our nets of reason, or we may have faith in the story, the power, the wisdom of God who seeks us out in such a passionate way.

This is no trivial challenge, church. We are so accustomed to trusting our thoughts, our words, our understanding of the world that it is disorienting and frightening to acknowledge that our vision is faulty, our mental processes inadequate to the task. At first it is like being a blind man, dependent on others to lead us. It is only later that we understand that once we were indeed blind, and now we see. It's not surprising that the process brings on a little vertigo. That's normal.

In "The Allegory of the Cave," Plato offered a description of people living chained in constant darkness in a cave looking only at a blank wall. They could perceive things only by the shadows they cast on the walls of the cave. One day, one of them escaped the cave into the light and saw things for what they were. When he brought the good news to his companions, they thought him a fool, as the evidence of their own eyes contradicted what he said.

That is us before the mystery of the manger. When we stand before the manger in which the Word of God lies, we are faced with a choice. We can try to net the story in our inadequate words, or we can react as the carol teaches us:

> A thrill of hope the weary world rejoices,
> For yonder breaks a new and glorious morn.
> Fall on your knees! Oh, hear the angel voices!
> O night divine, the night when Christ was born;

We can either see a baby or we can see our own sins and shortcomings revealed in the Light of the World and go therefrom with new eyes, new humility, and new gladness.

Clearing the Way

"To live in relation to God, we must stop forming God in our minds and allow Him to form us instead."

Matthew 2:1-12

In the time of King Herod, after Jesus was born in Bethlehem of Judea, wise men from the East came to Jerusalem, asking, "Where is the child who has been born king of the Jews? For we observed his star at its rising, and have come to pay him homage." When King Herod heard this, he was frightened, and all Jerusalem with him; and calling together all the chief priests and scribes of the people, he inquired of them where the Messiah was to be born. They told him, "In Bethlehem of Judea; for so it has been written by the prophet:

`And you, Bethlehem, in the land of Judah,

are by no means least among the rulers of Judah;

for from you shall come a ruler

who is to shepherd my people Israel.'"

Then Herod secretly called for the wise men and learned from them the exact time when the star had appeared. Then he sent them to Bethlehem, saying, "Go and search diligently for the child; and when you have found him, bring me word so that I may also go and pay him homage." When they had heard the king, they set out; and there, ahead of them, went the star that they had seen at its rising, until it stopped over the place where the child was. When they saw that the star had stopped, they were overwhelmed with joy. On entering the house, they saw the child with Mary his mother; and they knelt down and paid him homage. Then, opening their treasure chests, they offered him gifts of gold, frankincense, and myrrh. And having been warned in a dream not to return to Herod, they left for their own country by another road.

New Years are like the first day of school. You go to school with a bunch of shiny new pencils, crisp notebooks and empty heads. The goal is to leave at the end of the year, heads stuffed with new knowledge, and pencils and notebooks utterly consumed. The torn and soiled notebooks and chewed up pencils are the fuel that powers our search for education.

Our torn-up and soiled lives are like the pencils and notebooks, the fuel that powers our search for a more perfect relationship with God. And every year, we would do well to take stock of what went well, and what didn't, then clear away the detritus.

Usually, though, what we do is make a New Year's resolution to go to the gym and lose some weight. This resolution does not normally make it past Epiphany. I want us to talk about some more sweeping resolutions. We've already determined that you're not going to lose weight. I'm not, anyway. I want to see if we can clear the way to making some more important changes in our relationship with God.

Surprisingly, the first thing I'd like to see us clear away is our perception of God and I bet you didn't see that one coming! The problem of our perception of God, as I see it, is that we think we **can** perceive God. What we end up doing is imagining somebody like us, only bigger. Or someone like us, only more powerful in some way. If your idea of God is an old guy with a long white beard sitting on a throne, you may be worshiping Galdalf the Magician instead of God.

It was in preparation for this sermon that I recently bored you with an astronomy lecture. I wanted you to get some emotional feel for the scope of God's creation. Trust me on this, church. We are not going to make an intellectual connection with God. We need to make an emotional one, and that's not so easy for 21st Century Americans.

Here's what I mean: I can't imagine traveling at the speed of light, and I can't imagine how far ten billion light years is, even if I wrote it out with a gazillion zeros on a piece of yellow paper. I really cannot imagine the difference in scale between the star Betelgeuse and our sun. I'm just sure an old guy with a long white beard sitting on a throne can't either. Our God, the one we worship, the one who took on flesh and became one of us, spoke that whole creation into existence. Knowing that I can't perceive God's creation helps me to understand that I can't perceive God in His Wholeness. Any attempt to do so inevitably winds up by putting God in a box — a box made of my own limitations — and that's where we get into trouble. We stop worshiping God and start worshiping our **understanding** of God. The idea that we can contain God in such a box is something that needs to be cleared away so that we can reach a more perfect relationship with God.

After you've spent a lifetime living with, praying to, and feeling uplifted by the old guy with the long white beard, it's not an easy thing to clear away. Let's try some lateral thinking. Sometimes, it's easier to look at the mote in our brother's eye to get a sense of the beam in our own. Let's look at radical Islamists.

Why do they wish to kill Christians? We've been led to believe that it is because Christians don't worship Allah, and that makes us infidels. Who is Allah? It is the Arabic word for God. To whom do Arabic Christians devote their prayers? To Allah. Because Allah is the Arabic god? No, because "Allah" is the Arabic **word** for God. Does the Qur'an direct followers of Islam to murder Christians and Jews? No, the Qur'an actually refers to Christians and Jews as "People of the Book" and treats them favorably. The Qur'an states:

> ... You will find the people most affectionate to those who believe are those who say, "We are Christians." That is because some of them are priests and monks and because they are not arrogant.[12]

Why, then, do radical Islamists believe that they are to kill Christians and Jews? Because they have substituted their own understanding of God's teaching for God. Would they agree with that estimate? Not for a minute, just as you are having an uncomfortable time hearing me tell you that the old guy on the throne isn't God, but only your perception of some part of God's glory.

For the new year, the first thing I'd like to clear away is the notion that I can perceive God in His Glory.

The second thing I'd like to clear out of the way is the idea that we can't truly connect to God, except through a specially trained intermediary. Actually, that's a pretty reasonable thing to think about a God who could speak such

---

12 Surat al-Ma'ida, 82

imaginable grandeur into existence with a mere word. I can't connect to the planet Jupiter and Jupiter, large as it is, is an infinitesimal part of God's creation. How in the world can I reach out to God? It's gonna take some powerful magic to do that.

Paul encouraged his church at Ephesus by saying:

> I pray that the God of our Lord Jesus Christ, the Father of glory, may give you a spirit of wisdom and revelation as you come to know him, so that, with the eyes of your heart enlightened, you may know what is the hope to which he has called you, what are the riches of his glorious inheritance among the saints, and what is the immeasurable greatness of his power for us who believe.

The portion of this text that really caught my eye was the phrase "I pray that God ... may give you a spirit of wisdom and revelation." This is at the core of a declaration to become a Christian — God grants to us a spirit of wisdom and revelation. While we lack the power to perceive God's wholeness, God, who loves us individually, grants to us individually the spirit we need to enter into a relationship with Him. It does not flow from a preacher or a priest with especially good mojo. It is a free and undeserved gift of faith to each of us from God, Himself.

The Presbyterian Church believes strongly in an educated clergy. It is easy to drift from that worthy goal to a perversion of it whereby we come to think that the whole business of religion is so complicated that we have to hand it over to a professional, educated class. If we do that, we are refusing to acknowledge God's gift of individual grace to each of us. I wouldn't be happy if I gave Mrs. Schneider a Christmas gift and she referred it to an expert. There's no reason to think God would be happy about our handling of His gift of grace in such a way.

The third thing I'd like to clear away is the idea that a Christian is someone who does good deeds, or is a "nice" person. Boy Scouts and Girl Scouts do good deeds. The 14th Dali Lama is, by universal acclaim, a nice person. Neither the doing of good deeds nor a pleasant personality define a Christian. Christians are different because they insist on measuring everything they do against their relationship with God. If everything you do is weighed in the scale of how it affects your relationship with God and your brothers and sisters, you will, inevitably wind up doing good for God and to His Creation and children, but non-Christians do a lot of good things, too.

The idea that Christians are "nice" people, or that Christians are the people who do good things is dangerous because it leads to the notion that people who are **not** Christians are neither nice people nor do good things. When you take a minute to think about it in that way, it's clear that this is not true. It's just hard to look at it critically because the idea that Christians are the good guys is flattering to us, and hence hard to evaluate objectively.

Thinking of Christians as "nice" people also tempts us to gloss over our own sins. I was reading "Hagar the Horrible" in the funnies. The monk told Hagar that he should repent his sinful ways. Hagar thought to himself, "I'd like to co-operate, but I don't know which of my ways are sinful." We aren't very good at evaluating our own sins. Thinking of ourselves as "nice" people makes it all the more difficult.

This is not to say that Christians aren't nice people. Mohamed advised his followers to seek out Christians because they were "friendly." Emperor Julian the Apostate (361C.E. — 363C.E.) complained that Christians "not only feed their own poor, but ours also. See their love feasts and their tables spread for the indigent. Such practice is common among them and causes a contempt for our gods."

We are not kind, sharing and friendly people because we are the good guys. We are kind, sharing and friendly people because we have accepted with gratitude the free offer of grace from God and committed ourselves to following the indwelling spirit which leads us to a kind, sharing and friendly lifestyle.

Three things to clear out of the way:

1. the misconception that the mental image of God we form **is** God in his wholeness;

2. the misconception that connection with the Spirit is so difficult that we can only learn about it through the intervention of religion specialists, and never experience it for ourselves;

3. the misconception that Christians are the good guys who do good deeds and the rest of the world is "the enemy."

I think you could make your own list of things to clear away for the new year. This is just my list. Whatever you come up with, though, it is my wish that you do so with intentionality, with a commitment to and determination to find your own route to the relationship God is offering. May you be blessed in the coming year, you and all your loved ones.

Mr. Dumpty's Dilemma

"The awakening we seek is the discovery that we are part of something greater than our own needs, and that we are called upon to submit to something outside of our own desires and needs."

Jeremiah 31:7-14

Thus says the LORD:
Sing aloud with gladness for Jacob,
  and raise shouts for the chief of the nations;
proclaim, give praise, and say,
  "Save, O LORD, your people,
  the remnant of Israel."
See, I am going to bring them from the land of the north,
  and gather them from the farthest parts of the earth,
among them the blind and the lame, those with child and
  those in labor, together;
  a great company, they shall return here.
With weeping they shall come,
  and with consolations I will lead them back,
I will let them walk by brooks of water,
  in a straight path in which they shall not stumble;
for I have become a father to Israel,
  and Ephraim is my firstborn.
Hear the word of the LORD, O nations,
  and declare it in the coastlands far away;
say, "He who scattered Israel will gather him,
  and will keep him as a shepherd a flock."
For the LORD has ransomed Jacob,
  and has redeemed him from hands too strong for him.
They shall come and sing aloud on the height of Zion,
  and they shall be radiant over the goodness of the LORD,

over the grain, the wine, and the oil,
  and over the young of the flock and the herd;
their life shall become like a watered garden,
  and they shall never languish again.
Then shall the young women rejoice in the dance,
  and the young men and the old shall be merry.
I will turn their mourning into joy,
  I will comfort them, and give them gladness for sorrow.
I will give the priests their fill of fatness,
  and my people shall be satisfied with my bounty, says the LORD.

John 1:1-18

[1]In the beginning was the Word, and the Word was with God, and the Word was God. [2]He was in the beginning with God. [3]All things came into being through him, and without him not one thing came into being. What has come into being [4]in him was life, and the life was the light of all people. [5]The light shines in the darkness, and the darkness did not overcome it.

[6]There was a man sent from God, whose name was John. [7]He came as a witness to testify to the light, so that all might believe through him. [8]He himself was not the light, but he came to testify to the light. [9]The true light, which enlightens everyone, was coming into the world.

[10]He was in the world, and the world came into being through him; yet the world did not know him. [11]He came to what was his own, and his own people did not accept him. [12]But to all who received him, who believed in his name, he gave power to become children of God, [13]who were born, not of blood or of the will of the flesh or of the will of man, but of God.

[14]And the Word became flesh and lived among us, and we have seen his glory, the glory as of a father's only son, full of grace and truth. [15](John testified to him and cried out, "This was he of whom I said, 'He who comes after me ranks ahead of me because he was before me.'") [16]From his fullness we have all received, grace upon grace. [17]The law indeed was given through Moses; grace and truth came through Jesus Christ. [18]No one has ever seen God. It is God the only Son, who is close to the Father's heart, who has made him known.

Humpty Dumpty sat on a wall.
Humpty Dumpty had a great fall.
All the king's horses and all the king's men
Couldn't put Humpty together again.

Why do you think that would be? Wouldn't you think that the king would pick horses and men who were capable of looking out for the odd emergencies that you could foresee happening around the old kingdom? If you're going to let someone as fragile as Humpty Dumpty entertain himself by sitting on walls, shouldn't you have in place the right horses and men to take care of what, I would humbly suggest, is an easily foreseeable eventuality?

Perhaps, before we become too critical of the king and his senior appointees, though, we should pause to consider the magnitude of the problem. Humpty Dumpty was clearly an egg. All historical research has tended in that direction, and I think it is established to such a degree that to continue the debate would simply be perverse. Humpty Dumpty was an egg, and dropping an egg produces such a mess that no reasonable person could conceive of a way to reassemble the estimable Mr. Dumpty. Perhaps the ineffectiveness of the king's horses and the king's men is not so much a reflection of incompetency by the administration as it is an acknowledgement of a problem which is, in the last analysis, impossible to solve. It is regrettable, but one of the dilemmas of life is that some problems life presents aren't resolvable. As much as we would like them to be one way, sometimes, we have to face the fact that they are quite another way. That is Mr. Dumpty's dilemma.

If you think long and hard on the problems presented by the unfortunate Mr. Dumpty's accident, and the difficulty in ameliorating **his** injuries, you might get an idea of how the people of Jerusalem viewed their future at the time Jeremiah uttered this prophesy of hope. They were truly up the creek and had neglected to bring a paddle. The particular creek they were up was the river of Babylon, for when Jeremiah spoke of hope in Jerusalem, anybody of any importance had already been taken off into captivity in Babylon where they sang:

> By the rivers of Babylon —
> there we sat down and there we wept
> when we remembered Zion.
> On the willows there
> we hung up our harps.
> For there our captors
> asked us for songs,
> and our tormentors asked for mirth, saying,
> "Sing us one of the songs of Zion!"
>
> How could we sing the Lord's song
> in a foreign land?
> If I forget you, O Jerusalem,
> let my right hand wither!
> Let my tongue cling to the roof of my mouth,
> if I do not remember you,
> if I do not set Jerusalem
> above my highest joy.

Jeremiah was left behind in Jerusalem with the small, the poor, the ineffective remnants of David and Solomon's great kingdom because he had earlier prophesied that the attack by Babylon was a punishment from God, and had counseled the people to surrender. The Babylonians thus did not force him into captivity, and he chose to stay in Jerusalem.

You think sticking an egg back together would be tough? One hundred fifty years earlier the Assyrians had done the same thing to the northern tribes of Israel, and they disappeared. The only reasonable expectation is that Judah, the southern tribes, would disappear, as well, into captivity in Babylon and that this is the end of the story of God's chosen people.

Of course, **we** know that it was not the end of the story of God's people, but the poor, the terrified, the dispirited people who were left in Jerusalem with Jeremiah didn't know that. What sort of song were they singing, with their city and their Temple, the very House of God, laying in ashes around them? They were hopeless, and for good reason.

THE LAWYER'S TALE

My in-law's house burned once. It was a smoky fire. I remember picking our way through the house. What wasn't burned had been soaked by the hoses of the firefighters. What wasn't burnt or wet had been suffused by smoke. We'd pick up some treasured item, saying "Look! This wasn't hurt!" only to have it crumble in our hands. I still remember the expressions on the faces of the family as we tried to find some small thing that might have survived the destruction — something which could bridge us from the devastation we saw to the happier times of the past, some connection from which we could find a glimmer of hope.

There was nothing. I think the people left behind with Jeremiah must have felt that way, as they went from street to street, looking to find a familiar house or a familiar face, only to find them all gone, even the Temple! How could they stand it? How could they seek hope, find only desolation and bear to listen to Jeremiah's words of singing aloud in gladness?

Church, you can't reach the age most of us here have reached without sharing the experience of the remnant of Judah. This one has buried parents. That one has lost a home, a job, a spouse. This one has buried a son. All of us at one time or another have looked out on desolation and known hopelessness and powerlessness and the feeling of being abandoned. Inevitably, someone, with the best intentions in the world, will try "to make you feel better."

"It's not as bad as it could be," they'll tell you. But you know, down to your bones, that it is exactly as bad as it could be, and if it were any worse, you would die from the weight of it.

"Time will heal the wounds," they'll tell you. But you aren't ready to begin healing, because you have to process the grief you are feeling before you can begin healing. You have to walk through the valley of the shadow of death from end to end and there are no shortcuts.

All of us have shared this experience with the remnant of Judah. We all know that the wounds do not heal, but they become less insistent, less intrusive, only aching at anniversaries or when special thoughts are brought to mind, and then, we experience them less as active grief and more as sadness. Time doesn't heal, but it renders pain more bearable.

This is where we live, church! We live in a world in which the Babylonians can come, burn our town and take us into exile. We live in a world that offers up sadness. And we, poor children, can imagine a world without sadness, and that makes it worse. If that were the end of it, I don't think we could live with the sadness.

That isn't the end of it, though, for the people did return from Babylon, and the line of David continued, and Jesus was born among us, and because of that, we have hope.

There are very few passages of Scripture that induce in me a greater sense of awe than the great beginning of the Gospel of John.

> [1]In the beginning was the Word, and the Word was with God, and the Word was God. [2]He was in the beginning with God. [3]All things came into being through him, and without him not one thing came into being. What has come into being [4]in him was life, and the life was the light of all people. [5]The light shines in the darkness, and the darkness did not overcome it.

> [14]And the Word became flesh and lived among us, and we have seen his glory, the glory as of a father's only son, full of grace and truth.

The call of the Gospel is to view ourselves not as an end to be protected and glorified, but as a part of something bigger. We are called to be a part of a larger Body, the Body of Christ. Here, in the opening of John's great, misty, spiritual Gospel is that call. John's Gospel opens with a great trumpet blast announcing that we are part of something greater than our own needs, and that we are called upon to submit to something outside of our own desires and needs. Our place in God's Creation isn't a platform from which we defend our own existence. It is a pulpit from which we proclaim the eternal implications not only for our own selves, but the implications for others, for all of creation.

I suppose I could say something about Humpty Dumpty's fall resulting in good after all. Maybe they made a great omelet and fed the hungry. We all want to find the silver lining in every cloud, no matter how dark. It makes us feel better when we have suffered. I think that's the wrong approach, though. Jeremiah's prophesy that the northern tribes would return and be united once again with Judah is unfulfilled even now, 2,600 years later. Sometimes, a smashed egg is just a smashed egg.

Instead of trying to honey coat the suffering we experience by trying to find an ultimate good behind it, we should instead, use the suffering we inevitably experience in this world as the opportunity to focus our hearts and minds on that which escapes us — the transcendent Word of God, which took on flesh and shared with us our time on earth. "For God so loved the world," John tells us, "that He sent His only begotten Son." The birth of Jesus was motivated by love. The God who was motivated to become flesh did so because smashed eggs are sometimes smashed eggs, and He loves us, and wishes us to know that, though we may not see it, we are part of something greater than ourselves.

J. STEWART SCHNEIDER

Epiphany

An epiphany is that category of experience in which we understand, beyond cavil, that life has changed for us in irreversible ways. The Christ Child has made His entrance with no disturbance. He has become known to the world and stirred up only hostility in the court of Herod, and the death of many innocent children.

For us, as individuals growing into our calling as Christians, epiphany is the acceptance and certainty that the time line of the world, once so neatly planned out, is now impossible.

J. STEWART SCHNEIDER

JC's Coming

"Submission to God means abandonment of your own goals and self-interest. This comes as a shock to all."

Matthew 2:1-12

In the time of King Herod, after Jesus was born in Bethlehem of Judea, wise men from the East came to Jerusalem, asking, "Where is the child who has been born king of the Jews? For we observed his star at its rising, and have come to pay him homage." When King Herod heard this, he was frightened, and all Jerusalem with him; and calling together all the chief priests and scribes of the people, he inquired of them where the Messiah was to be born. They told him, "In Bethlehem of Judea; for so it has been written by the prophet:

'And you, Bethlehem, in the land of Judah,

are by no means least among the rulers of Judah;

for from you shall come a ruler

who is to shepherd my people Israel.'"

Then Herod secretly called for the wise men and learned from them the exact time when the star had appeared. Then he sent them to Bethlehem, saying, "Go and search diligently for the child; and when you have found him, bring me word so that I may also go and pay him homage." When they had heard the king, they set out; and there, ahead of them, went the star that they had seen at its rising, until it stopped over the place where the child was. When they saw that the star had stopped, they were overwhelmed with joy. On entering the house, they saw the child with Mary his mother; and they knelt down and paid him homage. Then, opening their treasure chests, they offered him gifts of gold, frankincense, and myrrh. And having been warned in a dream not to return to Herod, they left for their own country by another road.

81

When growing up in First Presbyterian at Ashland, I don't recall ever hearing the word "epiphany." That was a long time ago, and I guess the church didn't feel that following the festivals of the year was important. If you ask me, that's a darn shame. The church year offers us such a richness of opportunities to walk with Jesus. The church, half a century ago, seemed to turn its back on all of it. What a loss! I'm much happier with the church today, choosing to get involved with the liturgical year. And today is Epiphany Sunday. Today we'll talk a little about this strange word and the celebration of the arrival of the Three Kings.

The Nativity scene, complete with a donkey, a lamb, an ox, three camels, an equal number of wise men and the little drummer boy is on top of everybody's television set for Christmas, so it's often a shock to learn that Epiphany, or the arrival of the Three Kings, didn't happen on Christmas Eve, according to the Gospels, but two years after the birth of Jesus. Properly, Epiphany is celebrated on January 6, the day the old people often called "Old Christmas." For some reason, here in Appalachia, the old people believed the animals could speak at midnight on Old Christmas. Why? I don't know.

An Epiphany is more than an opportunity for farm animals to address us directly, so we have to dig a little deeper to understand why the church has, for so many years, celebrated the arrival of the Three Kings as a separate celebration from Christmas. What is different about Epiphany? What exactly are we celebrating? What does the word even mean?

An "epiphany" is a sudden, intuitive perception of or insight into the reality or essential meaning of something, usually initiated by some simple, homely, or commonplace occurrence or experience. Well, that's not very helpful, is it? I think, if we're going to work with a word like "epiphany" we are going to have to have a more concrete example. I dug around in my trunk of memories, and this is what I came up with:

When I'm not putting nice Presbyterian congregations to sleep, I sometimes play old-time music. One night, I was coming back from playing in Carter County. I was on old U.S. 60, behind a car just full of people. The car was going about 40 miles an hour and was all over the road. It was clear that the driver was impaired.

In my earlier career in law enforcement, I lost any tolerance I might have once had for DUI drivers. I had my phone with me, and dialed up KSP, identified myself, and reported that I was behind an impaired driver.

The dispatcher responded in the clipped fashion of dispatchers everywhere, "10-4, Mr. Schneider. JC is in route." JC is one of the troopers. I stayed behind the car so that I could help recover bodies if the worst happened.

We got to 180 and 60, near the Dairy Queen, and we still hadn't seen the trooper. I called again.

"I'm still behind that impaired driver. We're on 60, turning inbound," I told the dispatcher.

"Don't worry," she replied. "JC's coming."

"OK," I said, "but we're heading toward Ashland now, and there's more traffic."

"10-4," the dispatcher answered. I fell in behind the car. When he got to the red light at the mall, he turned left, against the light.

"Dispatch? He just disregarded a red light and turned into the mall. He's in the mall parking lot. This would be a really great place to make a stop."

"10-4," Dispatch replied. "JC is in route. He'll be there. Trust me."

Well, I did trust her, and I knew JC, a quiet, very tall and very reliable man who had worked for many years on the road. I trusted JC, but we had a bad situation brewing here. Even if you trust JC, it's hard to wait when a lot is on the line. Drunks do unpredictable things. Drunks behind the wheel kill people. I was getting a little bit antsy. I stayed on the approach road and watched as the car disappeared behind Burger King. At least in the drive-through of Burger King, he wasn't likely to kill anybody.

After about two minutes, he came out and pulled past me on the access road, heading for U.S. 60. I could see that there were five people in the car. The driver was laughing and driving with one hand, the other hand holding a burger.

"Great," I thought. "A drunk, trying to drive one-handed and eat at the same time. This should end well ... "

I tried to call Dispatch again to report that he was turning outbound, toward the Interstate, but before they could answer, there was an enormous noise, as of the beating of hundreds of angel's wings. I knew that sound. That was the sound of a Crown Vic police interceptor engine getting down to business. With a flash of gray, literally out of nowhere, JC swooped down on the impaired driver like an eagle on an salmon.

THAT, church, is an epiphany, just as the definition specified,

1. It was sudden. I don't to this day know where JC came from.
2. Intuitively the people in the car and I both immediately understood that life had just changed radically for them.
3. That intuitive understanding gave both of us an insight into the reality of something, in this case where the driver and some of the passengers were going to pass the remainder of the night AND
4. It was initiated by a far too commonplace occurrence or experience.

Epiphanies, by their nature, interrupt us. They stop us in our tracks as we suddenly come to an intuitive perception or insight into the reality or essential meaning of something. Our lives go along, day after day, about as they always have, then BAM! something happens, something commonplace and otherwise unremarkable, and we suddenly see that which we hadn't seen before. Epiphanies are what drag us out of the rut we've been walking in, and lift us up so that we can see around us. It is my hope that the driver of that car that JC pounced on has come to see that drinking and driving don't mix.

The Epiphany we celebrate today, the one involving the discovery of another JC by the world beyond His family, was like that. The world was going on about as it always had, day after day, but after the birth of this JC, nothing would ever be the same again.

The people of the time understood their relationship with God in one way based on the Covenant at Sinai. That had been their understanding for a thousand years. The Greeks around them understood themselves to be in relationship with many gods. That had been their understanding for a thousand years. No one had suggested a new, unifying relationship with the one God. That was about to change. Clearly, no one is happy about sudden changes. Epiphanies put our teeth on edge.

One church I served once had an attendance of nearly 200. It had a large sanctuary, but the congregation was reduced to 13 by the time I arrived to fill their pulpit one Sunday. Nevertheless, they each sat in the same pew they had sat in when the church was full. It was comforting. It was non-threatening to be in your "own" pew. They wanted no changes, and as the building crumbled around them, each went to their accustomed place, sang the same hymns and dozed through a brief sermon.

The people on the cusp of the Epiphany we celebrate today wanted no changes, either. Their relationship with the Divine, however they imagined it, wasn't broken, as far as they could see, and did not require fixing. They were wrong about that. It DID need fixing. It had ceased to involve them at a heart level. If you do something the same way for long enough, that's what happens: it becomes automatic and ceases to involve you at a heart level. How many of you have ever tried to recite the Lord's Prayer, while thinking about every word? I bet if you do that, you'll stumble. Reciting the Lord's Prayer is something we've done forever and it often just pours out of us without engaging our conscious attention in the slightest. I recall an Elder called upon to lead the Lord's prayer, who started out, "I pledge allegiance ... "

When worship becomes automatic in that way, it ceases to be worship. It becomes ritual. It no longer involves us at a heart level, and it thus ceases to be of any benefit to us at all. When that happens, we stand in need of an epiphany — something to take us out of the ritual, and into the relationship with God that worship is supposed to nurture. Worship isn't supposed to be comfortable. It is supposed to be challenging and empowering. Worship should challenge us by reminding us of our failures to live into God's Grace, and it should empower us to do better. It certainly shouldn't put us to sleep. It should wake us up! That's why we need epiphanies.

Jesus arrived in a stable in Bethlehem something like 76 years before the Romans would destroy the Temple. God's people at the time of the birth of Jesus couldn't know that soon the accustomed, traditional, automatic worship forms they had followed for centuries would become impossible. It was time for a new Covenant, a new way of understanding the relationship between God and His people. That's what we need now, church. In place of empty pews, and struggling churches, we need a new Covenant, a new way of under-standing our relationship with God that is something more than the automatic recitation of ritual as we have always known it. We need JC to swoop down on us with the mighty sound of angel wings!

An epiphany is what I wish for you for the coming year. I wish for you a sud-den, intuitive perception into the essential meaning of the birth of Christ. The Creator of everything seen and unseen, the God that misdirected followers of both Jesus and Mohammad try to characterize as a God of fearsome ven-geance, took upon Himself the flesh of a helpless infant, grew in the love of a human family, suffered and died in pursuit of us, to bring us the epiphany we need.

The realization of that miracle should be for you like JC's blue lights were to the impaired driver. We do Epiphany and ourselves a disservice by mushing Epiphany in with Christmas. It is entitled to its dignity as a separate Celebra-tion, for on Epiphany, the world came to be aware that everything was about to change, and that nothing would ever be the same again. On Epiphany we each, individually, look to the commonplace event of the birth of a baby and experience a sudden, intuitive insight into the essential meaning of that birth with all the immediacy of flashing Kentucky State Police blue lights in your rear-view mirror.

I wish for you to go from this place, church, into God's Creation, and carry with you the Epiphany that has been entrusted to you. I wish you to speak the Gospel wherever you go, in love, in respect of the sometimes baffling beliefs of others, and from confidence in your own relationship with God.

I wish for you one other thing, and I give you the gift of a phrase long hon-ored in Jewish tradition: mip'nei tikkun ha-olam ("for the sake of perfection of the world"). For the sake of perfection of the world, take up the example of the life of Jesus and make it your own. For the sake of perfection of the world, use your life thus transformed to make of your society a more compassionate society. For the sake of perfection of the world, guide that society in ways to make of your country a more loving country. Perfect the earth with the power of the Gospel you have been given, for it is the garden of the Lord. Do so be-cause JC is in route. He'll be there. Trust me.

Response

The unnoticed entry of the Holy Spirit into our lives, the beginnings of awareness and the certainty of epiphany as we realize that something unexpected
has altered us for all times demands a response. The nature of that response
is complicated and, I suspect, unique for all of us as we find ourselves led into
the new paths and new roles prepared for us.

J. STEWART SCHNEIDER

The Baptism of our Lord

"Finding the proper response to the calling of the Holy Spirit is an individual undertaking, but it begins with baptism."

Mark 1:4-11

John the baptizer appeared in the wilderness, proclaiming a baptism of repentance for the forgiveness of sins. And people from the whole Judean countryside and all the people of Jerusalem were going out to him, and were baptized by him in the river Jordan, confessing their sins. Now John was clothed with camel's hair, with a leather belt around his waist, and he ate locusts and wild honey. He proclaimed, "The one who is more powerful than I is coming after me; I am not worthy to stoop down and untie the thong of his sandals. I have baptized you with water; but he will baptize you with the Holy Spirit."

In those days Jesus came from Nazareth of Galilee and was baptized by John in the Jordan. And just as he was coming up out of the water, he saw the heavens torn apart and the Spirit descending like a dove on him. And a voice came from heaven, "You are my Son, the Beloved; with you I am well pleased."

Mark's telling of the baptism of our Lord by John is unnerving. It's too abrupt. There are no angels, no heavenly choirs, no wise men. There's really nothing that we can romanticize in this account — nothing we could put with the Nativity set on top of the TV — but there is some deep water in this beginning of Mark's Gospel. Let's see if we can find our way.

The first thing that strikes me is WHAT sins? John the baptizer proclaimed a baptism of repentance for forgiveness of sins. I thought Jesus was without sin. What would Jesus have to repent of? This is the problem we must face when we try to capture God in a net of words. God is eternal. The meanings we attach to words aren't. Words change their meaning over time.

Here's an example I bet you didn't know. To the ancient Greeks living in Athens, an "idiot" was someone characterized by self-centeredness and concerned almost exclusively with private — as opposed to public — affairs. Mature, educated Athenians put the good of their community ahead of their own good. Idiocy was the natural state of ignorance into which all persons were born and its opposite, citizenship, was effected through formalized education. Idiots were born and citizens were made, you might say.

So, as far as the ancient Greeks of Athens were concerned, an idiot was one who put his own good above the good of others. You may make of that what you will, politically. I bring it up only to note that that's not what we mean by the word today. The meaning that we ascribe to words isn't absolute. Words, and their meanings, change with time, and you'd have to be a serious idiot to contest that.

Even in our lifetimes, we have watched words morph into other meanings. As recently as the Second World War, a "computer" was a woman who did arithmetic with pencil and paper, and a "typewriter" was one who operated a "typing machine." To older people, a "mouse" is a rodent. To younger people, it is a device attached to a computer. To older people, an "album" is a black vinyl disk with recorded music on it. To younger people, the word has no meaning at all, and they'd have to Google it to know what you're talking about. That's what makes reading the King James version sometimes hazardous. The compilers of that translation spoke the same language as Shakespeare, and we all remember what a treat that was to puzzle out in high school.

Apart from allowing me to observe that a good education is what a country uses to turn a bunch of idiots into good citizens, the changing meaning of words makes it imperative that we make very, very sure that the meaning we are attaching to the words of Scripture is the same meaning that the writer had in mind, keeping in mind that we are reading a translation from an entirely different language. Two of those words we must be careful about are "sin" and "repentance." To 21st Century ears, sin is a bad thing that you do, and repent is synonymous with regret or remorse. We have to ask if that is the meaning that Mark intends.

Regret and repent are two very different things. Regret is the emotion we feel in response to something we have done wrong. Repentance is a conscious decision to change our way of life so as not to repeat the mistake. Regret is the emotion I felt when they wheeled me into the ER with a heart attack and my cigarettes fell out of my pocket onto the floor. Repentance is the decision I made to stop smoking right after the nurse picked up the cigarettes and said, "I see you USED to be a smoker." Regret is us slapping ourselves in the forehead. Repentance is us courageously setting forth on a new trajectory. Regret permits sorrow over the past to invade our present. Repentance leads our present into a more positive future.

As all of us know, repentance is terrifically difficult to do. To repent is a moral and spiritual revolution to the core of our being. Regret is just being caught in our own self-centeredness — being an idiot as the ancient Greeks would say. I remember a line by Bart Simpson from the Simpsons about regret. Bart had been caught doing something stupid, self-defeating and indefensible and an explanation was demanded. He replied, "I don't know! I don't know why I did it. I don't know why I liked it, and I don't know why I'm going to do it again!" Regret, even sincere regret, doesn't carry with it any obligation to change our behavior, whereas repentance means a complete re-ordering of our lives.

When we read the account of the baptism of our Lord and read "repentance" as synonymous with "regret" we get all confused and ask, "What had Jesus done that He regretted?" I don't think Mark means that at all. I think Mark is speaking of the new direction Jesus' life is taking. I think he has in mind the full meaning of the Greek word "metanoia" which he used to describe John's baptism. Metanoia means "a change of mind, as it appears to one who repents, of a purpose he has formed or of something he has done.[13]"

Certainly, "metanoia" can mean regret for something one has done, but it has the additional meaning of "a change of mind." I think this is the sense that Mark has in mind — a change of course, a change of life. The baptism which Jesus experienced with John was the point at which his life took a change of direction from what it was, to what it would be, precisely as we should understand the word "repent." When we perceive the call of God in our lives, we

---

13 Strong's G3341.

are to abandon our earlier way of living, however much we enjoy it, and take a new path. The new path is the path God has laid out for us.

The other word we must be careful with is "sin." To 21st Century ears, "sin" means bad things you do. Stealing is a sin. Lying is a sin. Murder is a sin. Viewed in that way, it doesn't take much imagination to fancy that just by not lying, stealing or murdering people, we aren't engaged with God's creation in a sinful way. That's a great way to lead yourself astray by pridefully thinking more of yourself than you ought.

I think we'd do much better if we thought of "sin" as the things we do, the attitudes we hold, the way we interact with God's creation and God's children that obscures the internal voice of the Holy Spirit. Seen in this way, the baptism of Jesus can be viewed as a symbolic passing from the ordinary earthly life of a rural laborer that Jesus had followed up until that time, to a life filled and directed by God's purpose into which Jesus would now enter. Jesus turned from His original idea of His purpose to embody God's purpose for His life.

That may sound a bit strange to your ears. We're more comfortable with the stories from Matthew and Luke in which Jesus is proclaimed from birth. If you do that, though, your mind will inevitably start to ask what Jesus did from birth to about the age of thirty. That's a very human question to get yourself involved in. Ancient writers imagined Jesus as a lad doing all manner of fanciful things like striking a playmate dead who displeased him, then raising him from the dead. Those sorts of imaginings don't move the story. They're distractions. We have to walk right by the distractions to get at the meat of what Mark is telling us. Mark tells us that Jesus changed his life and the Holy Spirit came upon Him.

The thing that intrigues me about Mark's telling is the parallel between what happened to Jesus, and what happens to each of us who encounter the Holy Spirit. Jesus was living an ordinary life for the time when he came into contact with John. Perhaps Jesus saw his life laid out before him, the inoffensive life of a country laborer. He would work at the trade he had learned from Joseph. Perhaps he would marry, have children.

Then, he met John. He was captured by the words John spoke. They made sense to him. A switch was thrown — a decision made. Jesus saw that his life up to that point was not the life for which he was destined. Something caused him to reassess all of that, and to change His mind about the direction of His life. He "metanoiaed," if you will. He turned from that which was to the life for which he was born, just as we are called to do. In that baptism, Jesus turned from the well-worn and familiar cultural expectations of his life to a whole-hearted cooperation with the inevitable. He turned from a life of relative comfort to a life of sorrow. In that instant of decision and repentance

> ... he saw the heavens torn apart and the Spirit descending like a dove on him. And a voice came from heaven, "You are my Son, the Beloved; with you I am well pleased."

This is the sort of repentance God seeks from us. Smacking yourself in the forehead in remorse and regret does no good for anyone unless you are motivated by the discomfort you feel to turn from your self-seeking life to an other-directed life, the life of a servant shown us by the example of Jesus. Just as the ancient citizens of Athens believed that everyone is born an idiot but can mature to be public-minded citizens, we are born with a childish "Me! Me! Me!" perspective, then we are called by the Holy Spirit to repent of our self-centered lives to take our place as citizens of the Kingdom.

Repenting of a life centered on the wellbeing of self and family just seems awkward in the mouth to say. Changing the trajectory of your life to that of a servant, putting aside private concerns in favor of the good of others seems scary. This is what Jesus did. This is the course that lead Him directly to the cross. Jesus embraced the new life he saw, even though it was one of horrible suffering, in the same way a soldier will sometimes throw himself on a grenade to save his fellows, showing by his action that His concern for others is greater even than His concern for His own well-being. Jesus saw the Holy Spirit directing the trajectory of his life in the only way it could go — the inevitable consequence of perceiving rightly the Holy Spirit. This is our call, as well — whole-hearted cooperation with the inevitable.

I don't want to stir up pride in this congregation, but I clearly see the working of the Holy Spirit here. When a need is expressed, there is an instant response. This is so contrary to the self-centered life of a Greek idiot, that I am convinced that it could not occur if the Holy Spirit were not active right here, in Bellefonte, Kentucky. This is not something to boast of. This is something to give humble thanks for. For you, this congregation, this church, this place of spirit-working, I humbly give thanks.

J. STEWART SCHNEIDER

Come and See

"Life is this simple. We are living in a world that is absolutely transparent, and God is shining through it all the time. This is not just a fable or a nice story. It is true. If we abandon ourselves to God and forget ourselves, we see it sometimes, and we see it maybe frequently."

John 1:29-42

John saw Jesus coming toward him and declared, "Here is the Lamb of God who takes away the sin of the world! This is he of whom I said, 'After me comes a man who ranks ahead of me because he was before me.' I myself did not know him; but I came baptizing with water for this reason, that he might be revealed to Israel." And John testified, "I saw the Spirit descending from heaven like a dove, and it remained on him. I myself did not know him, but the one who sent me to baptize with water said to me, 'He on whom you see the Spirit descend and remain is the one who baptizes with the Holy Spirit.' And I myself have seen and have testified that this is the Son of God."

The next day John again was standing with two of his disciples, and as he watched Jesus walk by, he exclaimed, "Look, here is the Lamb of God!" The two disciples heard him say this, and they followed Jesus. When Jesus turned and saw them following, he said to them, "What are you looking for?" They said to him, "Rabbi" (which translated means Teacher), "where are you staying?" He said to them, "Come and see." They came and saw where he was staying, and they remained with him that day. It was about four o'clock in the afternoon. One of the two who heard John speak and followed him was Andrew, Simon Peter's brother. He first found his brother Simon and said to him, "We have found the Messiah" (which is translated Anointed). He brought Simon to Jesus, who looked at him and said, "You are Simon son of John. You are to be called Cephas" (which is translated Peter).

I've aways been intrigued by these words of Jesus, "Come and see." That's such a simple thing to say, but when you try to put it into terms of our lives today, would you go? Come where? See what? I think modern people would be inclined to make an appointment and get back to Jesus on that. John's two disciples heard the words of their teacher, John, and on the strength of his words, they approached Jesus and asked, "Rabbi, where are you staying?" The text tells us that they stayed the rest of the day, and whatever they saw was sufficiently noteworthy that Andrew sought out his brother Simon and brought him, too.

That must have been some afternoon! What did Andrew see?

Celtic Christianity offers us the concept of the "thin place." Let me remind you of the quote from Thomas Merton that I shared with you earlier:

> Life is this simple. We are living in a world that is absolutely transparent, and God is shining through it all the time. This is not just a fable or a nice story. It is true. If we abandon ourselves to God and forget ourselves, we see it sometimes, and we see it maybe frequently. God shows Himself everywhere, in everything —in people and in things and in nature and in events. It becomes very obvious that God is everywhere and in everything and we cannot be without Him. It's impossible. The only thing is that we don't see it[14].

A "thin place" is an actual space, or a well-loved prayer, or a mantra said during meditation, or even the life of an actual person through which we can see God shining. Finding thin places is why we worship. I think that is what Andrew saw in his afternoon with Jesus — I think that Jesus was for Andrew a thin place, and that got him energized.

As you have probably guessed by now, the question I'm really posing is this: if Andrew came here, what would he see?

I don't think Andrew would find the same things here that he found there. I'm not talking about just at this church, but any contemporary church. I think he

---

14 Quoted by Marcus Borg, from an audiotape of Merton made in 1965. Prof. Borg thanks Rev. David McConnell, a United Methodist pastor in Montana for the quotation. Quoted in *The Heart of Christianity* (Harper-Collins, 2003)

could find some exciting music at the churches that offer "contemporary" services, and that might well excite him. I think he could find some nice people, but I just can't think that what he would see would excite him in the way John reports him to have been energized.

Come and see. Come where? See what?

Later in the Gospel of John, Jesus describes Himself as "The Way, the Truth and the Life" and, indeed, the earlier followers of Jesus were called "Followers of the Way." I'd like to suggest to you that this is exactly what Andrew found — the truth of a way of **life** — a way of life in which God's presence is felt in everything. I'd also like to suggest that we have somehow converted that great teaching into a way of death — suck it up while you're here, pie in the sky when you die. Jesus was teaching how to live. We have converted that teaching into instruction on how to die. Who can blame the unchurched if they come to us with all the enthusiasm of someone going to the lawyer's office to draw a will?

Put aside any notions that I'm arguing that the church should be more attractive as a marketing strategy. I'm not. The church is the church. What I'm talking about is turning our emphasis away from death and returning to the teachings of a truthful way of **life**. The model for that is the life of Jesus Christ. What I'm talking about is that we must start taking the words of Jesus seriously and incorporating them into our lives. And that means we must stop short-circuiting His teachings into something trivial.

A friend of mine was explaining to me why sermons are too long. He said,

> You don't need to know all of that stuff. All you need to know to get into heaven is to do the best you can, and God will forgive the rest. That's what it's all about, isn't it? Getting into heaven?

Well … no…I don't think that's what it's all about at all. I'm afraid that we've whittled the way of life taught by Jesus into something as trivial as my friend sees it. It's no wonder the world at large has trouble relating to it.

Our emphasis on heaven when you die has a real capacity to distract us from living the true way of life Jesus taught. If everything we do is all about winning heaven points, if we view life on this earth as just a sort of test of worthiness for heaven, then we're going to have an awful time loving our neighbors as ourselves, because everything we do is focused on ourselves. It would be like saying that I married Mrs. Schneider to get my shirts done and my supper cooked.

God is the God of the living. What Andrew saw in that afternoon so long ago was not a way to die, but a way to live, and it consumed his mind and his heart and his attention. Can we regain The Way?

You bet! But it means we have to change our focus from "What's the least I can do and still get to heaven?" to "What have I left undone for my neighbor and my God this day?" It means that we have to change our focus from "up there" to "right here," and from measuring belief to dedication of action.

As I survey the history of our faith, it seems to me, and to a number of scholars whose works I read, that there has been a change in our understanding of certain words and what it means to be a Christian. The most important one of these words is the word "believe."

As you know, I come from a tradition that is suspicious of creeds when they are used as a test of brotherhood. The notion that you MUST believe such and such in order to belong to a church is anathema to the understanding of the Christian Church (Disciples of Christ). In the Presbyterian Church, though, we affirm our faith from just such a creed every Sunday, and I lead it. Am I being hypocritical? No, I do not feel I am being hypocritical. Here's why.

We understand the word "believe" to mean something on the order of "agreement." When we say we believe something, we mean that we agree that the something is true. I believe that the sky is blue. The more tedious pedants of my acquaintance will explain to me that there's no object up there called "the sky" which I could touch, and that it's not blue in any event. They would explain that the atmosphere absorbs or reflects the other colors of sunlight making the air above my head appear blue, but there is no sky and it isn't blue. I believe that the sky is blue anyway. I love to look at it. The scientific explanation does nothing to reduce the joy I experience in a clear blue sky. The effect on my mood is a real effect. The changes a blue sky can bring about in my life are real. The scientific explanation makes me sleepy.

The word "believe" is derived from the same root as the German "liebe," meaning to love. When we say we believe something, we really should understand it to mean "we give our love to something." This is the part of the original meaning of "believe" which we have lost. When we say we believe in God the Father Almighty, maker of heaven and earth, we shouldn't understand ourselves to be saying that we assent to God being the Father Almighty. We should be saying we **belove** acknowledging God's place in our lives. We should be saying that we **belove** contemplating that we are created by God, that we are loved by God, that we are so desired by God that He pursues us even into taking on human form in His courting of us. This is something we give our love to, and it should inform our practice of life as a Christian.

I used the words "practice of life as a Christian" purposely because I think that our pursuit of "believe" as agreement has blinded us to the requirements of practicing a Christian life. We've moved from doing Christian things to believing Christian things. That does no one any good. I think this is exactly the thing we have lost and the underlying reason that Andrew would not see, in a visit with us, the exciting thing he saw in his afternoon with Jesus. In our pursuit of heaven, we've moved our faith from being something we practice here to being something we believe up there. I think we need to restore the idea of practice.

One of the five pillars of Islam is to pray five times a day. Do Christians practice that? One of the practices of Judaism is to remind oneself upon rising up and upon lying down, "Hear, Oh Israel. The Lord your God. The Lord is One." Do Christians practice that? How did we come to the understanding that all Christianity is about is giving assent to the right group of statements which will then guarantee a cheap ticket to heaven? Whatever happened to "thy kingdom come, thy will be done, on EARTH as it is in heaven?"

Our text doesn't tell us what was discussed on that afternoon with Jesus. My guess would be no better and no worse than yours, but I think what Andrew saw was a man, Jesus, who was practicing the true way of a Christian, the way that leads to a truthful life, and seeing this, Andrew saw the glory of God peeping through the thin place that was Jesus' life.

The thin places, places like the life of Jesus, or the recitation of the creeds and prayers to which we have become accustomed, help us to see the inevitability of God. That's good. That's how we are spiritually nurtured.

But what of the unchurched who haven't yet learned to peek through the thin places that worship offers? They need a hand up. That's your job.

For them to find the thin places in worship, you have to be the thin place for them. That's what I want to get across to you in the idea of the practice of being Christian. Jesus taught that the greatest command is to love the Lord your God with all your heart and with all your soul and with all your strength and with all your mind and to love your neighbor as yourself. The practice of being a Christian is to direct your life always with compassion for others and in connection with God. Your every thought, word and deed should reflect the model presented to you by the life of Jesus. If your every thought, word and deed is not motivated by compassion for others and awareness that you cannot be without God, the unchurched who look to you will see that, and your words will be to them tinkling brass and crashing cymbals.

Let God worry about Heaven. Heaven is God's responsibility anyway and God is well able to handle it without your help. Instead, begin today the task that has been given you — the practice of being a Christian, following the commands you have been given. Be for the world a thin place so that you, too, can say, "Come and see."

Disruption in the Cheap Seats

"A relationship with God can be, indeed MUST be, enormously disruptive to us in our ordinary lives back here in the cheap seats, theologically speaking, where most of us live."

Matthew 4:12-23

When Jesus heard that John had been arrested, he withdrew to Galilee. He left Nazareth and made his home in Capernaum by the sea, in the territory of Zebulun and Naphtali, so that what had been spoken through the prophet Isaiah might be fulfilled:

"Land of Zebulun, land of Naphtali,
on the road by the sea, across the Jordan, Galilee of the Gentiles –
the people who sat in darkness have seen a great light,
and for those who sat in the region and shadow of death light has dawned."

From that time Jesus began to proclaim, "Repent, for the kingdom of heaven has come near."

As he walked by the Sea of Galilee, he saw two brothers, Simon, who is called Peter, and Andrew his brother, casting a net into the sea – for they were fishermen. And he said to them, "Follow me, and I will make you fish for people." Immediately they left their nets and followed him. As he went from there, he saw two other brothers, James son of Zebedee and his brother John, in the boat with their father Zebedee, mending their nets, and he called them. Immediately they left the boat and their father, and followed him.

Jesus went throughout Galilee, teaching in their synagogues and proclaiming the good news of the kingdom and curing every disease and every sickness among the people.

We had an interesting discussion Tuesday in the ladies' Bible study group. One of the ladies believes very strongly that the Apostle John wrote the Book of Revelation. I was asked to come in and put my head on the block so people could line up to take a swing at me.

As best I could, I lined out the understanding of the scholars who study these things that John the Apostle probably did not write the Book of Revelation. At the end of my explanation, the lady responded, "I still believe John the Apostle wrote it."

That's the thing about beliefs. Sometimes, it's very hard to tell the difference between beliefs and preferences. This lady is obviously comforted by her preference of John the Apostle as the author of the Book of Revelation, so, as she says, she prefers to believe that. There's a word for reading our needs into the text. When we read into Scripture things we need to be there, we say we are reading *eisogetically*. We all do it. We feel comforted by such and such a position, so we search Scriptures for something that can be made to sound like support for whatever we believe in, then take our comfort from the knowledge that "it's in the Bible."

Don't get me wrong! Our relationship with God should comfort us. Not for nothing did Isaiah tell his people, "Comfort, comfort my people, says your God." We turn to God for comfort in times of grief and sorrow and anxiety. It is a great blessing. This lady apparently derives comfort from her understanding that John the Apostle wrote the Book of Revelation. Or maybe she was just being stubborn. We all do that, too.

The question that the conversation posed to me, though, was this: Is our relationship with God always one of being comforted? After spending some considerable time with this text this week, I think not. I think a relationship with God can be, indeed MUST be, enormously disruptive to us in our ordinary lives back here in the cheap seats, theologically speaking, where most of us live. Not surprisingly, for many of us a disruptive relationship with Jesus is not something earnestly to be sought after, and so we run and hide from it. There's an irony there, too. As the old Spiritual has it, "Oh sinner man, where you gonna run to?" Where would you go to escape the disruption of your plans that a relationship with God entails?

What sort of plans? The sort of plans that involve living comfortable lives uncomplicated by the demands of God that we do disquieting things. That sort of plans. Woody Allen said, "If you want to make God laugh, tell Him your plans."

If we're going to understand this passage of Scripture, we're going to have to get disruptive right away, because it's important to realize that this is not the only account we have of the call of Andrew and Peter. Recently, we read the account of the first meeting between Andrew, Peter and Jesus as recounted in the Gospel we call John. Today we read the account of the first meeting between Andrew, Peter and Jesus as recounted in the Synoptic Gospels, the one we call Matthew, in this case. We refer to Matthew, Mark and Luke as the "Synoptic Gospels" because they see the story of Jesus with "one eye" — in very similar terms. The Gospel of John almost never agrees with them in its narrative. Although four views of the life of Jesus grant us much better understanding, as we'll see by comparing the two accounts, it can be disruptive for those Christians who are Biblical literalists. For such of our brethren, it is central to their faith that the Bible is infallible and literally true, word for word. They derive great comfort from this understanding of Scripture.

It's not my place to be critical of the understanding of my brothers and sisters. Rather, I would like to suggest something we hit upon in the ladies' Bible study this week — believe what you like, but first ask what does the story **mean**? It is only by searching out the meaning of the accounts we have of the life of Jesus that we can come to a relationship with Him as close as we have been talking about the past two weeks — as close as the air in your lungs and the water in your cells.

This is exactly what I mean when I speak of disruption in your life. Understanding Scripture sometimes means that we have to abandon old ways of understanding in favor of new. Coming to a new relationship with God means abandoning old ways of relationship in favor of new. That can be terrifically upsetting and disruptive.

If we want to see just HOW disruptive things can get, we need look only so far as our account today. Jesus had received word that his cousin, John the Baptist, had been arrested by Herod Antipas, tetrarch of Galilee. When learning of this, Jesus relocated to Capernaum, and began to preach, "Repent, for the kingdom of heaven has come near."

Metanoia, the Greek word translated here as "repent" carries the meaning of turning from past courses to a new way of life. When Jesus tells his listeners to repent, he isn't asking them to feel remorse for their past mistakes as we often understand the word. He is asking them to turn from their past course of life, and accept a new way of relating to the world and to God's children within it. If we understand "repentance" as we usually do — feeling sorrow for past misdeeds — we can't understand this story at all. If we want to understand what the story **means**, we have to acknowledge that this isn't a story about feeling bad.

From what we've learned, then, we might better express the message Jesus began to preach as, "Abandon your previous understanding of your relationship with my Creation, accept this new way, and live within it for the kingdom of heaven has come near." That announcement is much more than a teaching. It is a command, and one spoken with authority. Jesus' preaching in Capernaum doesn't begin with teaching. It begins with a disruptive command to abandon an old way of life, and begin a new sort of life. How do we understand this?

When we delve into this story, what elements do we find? The first element I notice is the order of who approaches whom. In John's account, Andrew and the other disciple are disciples of John the Baptist — they have already embarked on a religious life. Their meeting with Jesus was only a change of teacher. The students, seeking a new teaching, approached Jesus, which was the ordinary course of things in 1st Century Israel. In Matthew's account, there is a reversal of roles — the teacher calls the students with a command, not an offer of teaching. "Follow me, and I will make you fishers of men." That's not the way 1st Century teachers worked. Students sought out teachers. Teachers did not seek out students.

Jesus sought out Andrew and Peter, rather than the other way round which underlines something we have been talking about for many weeks now. God pursues us and meets us where we are. It's not a question of our having to be special, or having to jump through hoops, or any of the things that we usually think of when we think about becoming "better people." Jesus didn't ask for the fishermen to admire His teaching, or approve of His ethics or even to accept Him as their Savior. He commanded them to follow Him, for the betterment of all the world.

I shared with you a bit of dialog from "My Name is Earl" once before.

> "Earl, Jesus loves you just the way you are. And He loves you too much to leave you like that."

I would be hard put to express it any better than that. You don't have to be good enough or smart enough or special enough. Jesus loves you just the way you are and He loves you too much to leave you self-centered and asleep. When He enters your life He will disrupt it mightily, and your brothers and your sisters and the entire world will profit from your new direction!

The second element I notice is that of ordinariness. We're not talking miracles or magic here. Everything about this story is ordinary. Jesus is not portrayed with a big honking halo walking on the water. Jesus is walking on the shore. The people Jesus called were the most ordinary of people — fishermen. I'm pretty sure that Andrew and Peter didn't spend their time thinking deep thoughts theologically. They were in the business of murdering fish. I would be astonished to learn they could even read and write, let alone be sufficiently educated as to be students of a great teacher. Matthew is hammering home the point that God meets us where we are — back here in the cheap seats where most of us live, rather than in magical encounters among specialists.

The next thing I notice is that when Jesus enters the ordinary, extra-ordinary things happen. A random guy shows up on the beach and says, "Follow me, and I will make you fish for people," it's a little hard to imagine them dropping their nets and doing so. Nevertheless, that's exactly what Matthew tells us that they did, without a single question or protest.

Suppose that last Tuesday, you got up, had a bite of breakfast, and got your day started. You had errands to run or a job to do. You were totally involved in the responsibilities of the day when some guy wandered up and said to follow him. Without a word to your boss or your family you dropped what you were doing. You left the cart in the aisle, walked out of the grocery, left the sentence unfinished on your computer, the hole by the broken water main undug, and followed him. That's what Matthew is telling us happened in his story of this call of the first disciples.

Frankly, given the time in which they lived, and their position on the food-chain, sociologically speaking, I can't think of a single reason to explain why Andrew and Peter, James and John obeyed the command of Jesus to follow him. On this hand, they have some guy on the shore saying "Follow me" and on the other hand they have the sure and definite knowledge that if they don't look after themselves, no one else will, and they'll starve.

Believe what you like about whether Andrew and Peter had met Jesus before then or not. What does this story **mean**? You can spend your time deciding whether John's account or Matthew's account represents what really happened, or constructing ways for both of them to be historical, but what does the story **mean**? Unless you delve into that question, you haven't engaged the story at all.

What does this story mean? Can we not take from this that the new way, disruptive as it is, is sufficient for our needs, even if we can't immediately see how? Can we not understand God saying to us, "Trust me. I know more about this than you do. You won't starve, and My Creation will benefit for through your actions, My Glory will shine?"

That's the last element I see in the story of the call of Andrew and Peter — a demand that we turn from a focus on "what's good for me?" to a focus on "what's good for my brothers and sisters, and good for God's creation?"

That's really disruptive! I'd much rather hear from God, "Well done, good and faithful servant. As you were. Don't change anything." This is a story about totally disrupting your life. It's breath-taking, and scary as all get-out! The command of Jesus is to disrupt your life, turn from concerns about yourself, and adopt a new motivating concern for the welfare of all of God's children, and God's creation.

This is Matthew's message to us. God pursues us from love. God meets us in the ordinary and calls us to be more than ordinary. God has a real and present ability to look after us. God's call is to change our focus from what is good for us to what is good for His children. The more we mentally move our relationship with God into the rarefied realm of magical thinking, the less disruptive that relationship becomes, and, thus, the less intense and real. The more we accept our relationship with God as one of love, ordinariness and service, back here in the cheap seats where we live, the closer and more intimate that relationship becomes. Jesus in the clouds is very easy to ignore. Jesus on the shore, beside us in the grocery, sitting beside us at work, much harder.

God's Eyeglasses

"We are much more capable of seeing life as a seeking after what we want than a seeking after what is good for
our brothers and sisters, and the result is that we suffer.
Life is suffering, you might say, and the root of suffering
is desire. The best we can do is to enter into the suffering
of the world, and bring it comfort."

Micah 6:1-8

Hear what the LORD says:
Rise, plead your case before the mountains,
and let the hills hear your voice.
Hear, you mountains, the controversy of the LORD,
and you enduring foundations of the earth;
for the LORD has a controversy with his people,
and he will contend with Israel.
"O my people, what have I done to you?
In what have I wearied you? Answer me!
For I brought you up from the land of Egypt,
and redeemed you from the house of slavery;
and I sent before you Moses,
Aaron, and Miriam.
O my people, remember now what King Balak of Moab devised,
what Balaam son of Beor answered him,
and what happened from Shittim to Gilgal,
that you may know the saving acts of the LORD."
"With what shall I come before the LORD,
and bow myself before God on high?
Shall I come before him with burnt offerings,
with calves a year old?
Will the LORD be pleased with thousands of rams,
with ten thousands of rivers of oil?
Shall I give my firstborn for my transgression,
the fruit of my body for the sin of my soul?"

He has told you, O mortal, what is good;
and what does the LORD require of you
but to do justice, and to love kindness,
and to walk humbly with your God?

Matthew 5:1-12

When Jesus saw the crowds, he went up the mountain; and after he sat down, his disciples came to him. Then he began to speak, and taught them, saying:

"Blessed are the poor in spirit, for theirs is the kingdom of heaven.

"Blessed are those who mourn, for they will be comforted.

"Blessed are the meek, for they will inherit the earth.

"Blessed are those who hunger and thirst for righteousness, for they will be filled.

"Blessed are the merciful, for they will receive mercy.

"Blessed are the pure in heart, for they will see God.

"Blessed are the peacemakers, for they will be called children of God.

"Blessed are those who are persecuted for righteousness' sake, for theirs is the kingdom of heaven.

"Blessed are you when people revile you and persecute you and utter all kinds of evil against you falsely on my account. Rejoice and be glad, for your reward is great in heaven, for in the same way they persecuted the prophets who were before you.

You might think we live in north-east Kentucky, but do you know where we <u>really</u> live? We live in our assumptions. We could move from here to the moon, but we'd take our assumptions along with us and continue to live in them, no matter where we pitched our tent.

What are our assumptions, you ask? Our assumptions are the foundational suppositions that we take for granted so that we can get through the day without having to rethink every last thing we put our hand to. Men get up in the morning, put on a shirt, and assume that the buttons are on the right hand side and the buttonholes on the left. Ladies put on a blouse and somehow effortlessly button it up, even thought the buttons and buttonholes are clearly backwards. We know how high a stair step should be, and where the doorknob is likely to be on a door. Our assumptions are sort of like our eyeglasses. We don't think about them, we're generally not even aware we are looking through them, but they affect everything we see and do. In a real sense, they are the foundations for everything else we do. They are the things we don't think about because they are just the way things are.

There is a technical word for our assumptions that unfortunately has a different meaning in day-to-day usage, making it confusing to talk about. The word is "myth." The collection of assumptions we make about the way things are is called our "myth."

When I flush the toilet, the water in the bowl goes down a pipe into the sewer. I never give that a second thought because part of my myth, the framework of my thoughts within which I think about other things, contains some rough idea of how plumbing works.

My cat, on the other hand, has no such myth to guide him so every time I flush the toilet, he runs around back to see where the water went. Our myth is our assumed way of thinking about other things.

Unfortunately, to us in the 21st Century, a myth is a made-up story — a fiction or a fairy tale, so to avoid that meaning, I'd like to use the word "viewpoint" instead. Our viewpoint is our combined assumptions about the way things work — where the buttons on a shirt are; where the doorknob is located; which way to turn a ketchup bottle lid to take it off — that allows us to function without having to re-think everything all the time. They are the things we don't think about because they are just the way things are.

Anyone who has tried to negotiate a set of stairs after being fitted for their first pair of bifocal glasses can tell you that if your eyeglasses aren't right, you can be led pretty badly astray. Our myth or viewpoint, like our eyeglasses, has the power to lead us pretty badly astray if it is is defective as well, simply because we don't ever take it out and dust it off.

Everyone knows the ham story. A newlywed wife cuts the end of the ham off before she cooks it. Her husband asks why and she says, "I don't know. My mother always did that."

Husband asks the mother, who similarly replies that she doesn't know. Her mother always did that. When new husband asks grandma why she cut the end off the ham, she replied, "The pan was too short."

Unexamined viewpoints, the things we always thought or were always taught, can lead us rather badly astray if we don't understand their limits. That's why I'm going to pose a really tough question today about a part of everyone's viewpoint that we never talk about, and it is this: "Why should God care what we do?"

I know … I know. You have been taught all your life that God will get you if you don't act right. That's part of your viewpoint — God is the ultimate trip to the principal's office if you don't do right. I want you to examine that teaching for a minute. I'm not saying it isn't correct. I'm just asking you to pose the question to yourself, "Why should God care what we do?" God is God, after all. You would think He would be above such concerns. Yet, the Scriptures, from beginning to end, just don't read that way. Again and again God is portrayed as INVOLVED with His creation and His creatures. We understand this as God caring what we do, but I'd like to suggest a slightly different lens through which to view this. I want to suggest that God cares most of all about our viewpoint — our assumed way of thinking about other things. I'd like to suggest the possibility that God is less interested in grading our behavior than He is in changing our viewpoint to better accord with His viewpoint. If we change our assumed way of thinking about other things, we will see God's children differently, and we'll see our relationship with Him differently, too.

The reason I'm proposing that you ask yourself such an outlandish question relates to the conclusion we reached last week with the ladies' Bible class: "Believe what you like, but first ask what does it MEAN." An unexamined faith is not worth following, you might say. Unless you push yourself to understand what the words we speak here mean, you will be following only sound bites.

So, "Why should God care what we do?" Are we even sure that He does? Why is the fat preacher taking something simple, like the faith I've held all my life, and trying to make something complicated out of it? Can't I just think what I've always thought?

Well, yes, of course you can. But we've been talking about God in <u>relational</u> terms, and in doing so, we've talked about just how close a relationship with us that God pursues. We've said a couple of times that we are already IN a close relationship with Jesus whether we acknowledge it or not. This is part of what we mean when we speak of God's Immanence. God is within the universe and within each of us in that God is our sustaining cause. No God, no us. What we are about is becoming more aware of it.

Let me say that again, just in case you were thinking about where to have lunch after church and not paying attention. We are already IN a close relationship with God whether we acknowledge it or not, and what we are about, as intentional Christians, is becoming more aware of it. Our calling and vocation as Christians is to become ever more aware of that relationship, and what it entails. Sometimes, that means adjusting the prescription for our eyeglasses to more closely approximate God's glasses.

If we look at the closing verses of our passage from Micah, we read:

> "With what shall I come before the LORD,
> and bow myself before God on high?
> Shall I come before him with burnt offerings,
> with calves a year old?
> Will the LORD be pleased with thousands of rams,
> with ten thousands of rivers of oil?
> Shall I give my firstborn for my transgression,
> the fruit of my body for the sin of my soul?"
> He has told you, O mortal, what is good;
> and what does the LORD require of you
> but to do justice, and to love kindness,
> and to walk humbly with your God?

Micah is rhetorically asking if we really believe that God needs rivers of oil or thousands of rams. The obvious answer is "No," so Micah then tells us what God <u>does</u> require of us. God pursues us to teach us to adopt His point of view, which is one of doing justice and loving kindness. We are to walk humbly with our God, and view things through the lens of compassion that He insists on. We are to look at God and His creation through God's own eye glasses. If we view things through God's glasses, our behavior will take care of itself, because God's viewpoint, as improbable as it seems, is one of loving us.

If our underlying viewpoint is similarly one of love, it is simply unthinkable that we should behave in an unloving manner.

Puppies, for instance. Who doesn't love puppies? Well ... most people love puppies. The viewpoint of almost everyone is one of adoration when faced with a cute little puppy. From that viewpoint, how likely are you to drop kick a puppy? Not so much. Your foundational assumptions about puppies are that they are to be cuddled, and those assumptions lead you to treat puppies well.

Why do we have such overwhelming difficulty viewing God's children, all of them, as a basket full of puppies? God seems to do so. If we adopt God's viewpoint, we will as well. And if we do, our behavior toward others and toward God's creation will change.

You see, church, if we cling to the idea of God looking over our shoulder, constantly grading our every action, two bad things happen. We move God to the principal's office way up there, far, far away from us, and we start to imagine that "sin" is a laundry list of bad things we can avoid just by not doing them. I'd love to think that I could wash myself clean of sin AND get on God's good side just by not drinking a beer or cleaning up my language, or whatever particular sin you think God hates worst, but I just don't get that from Scriptures at all. What I get from Scripture is a crying, intimate, agonized plea for me to change my viewpoint, and view God's creation and God's children with compassion.

If we think of God as offering us His own personal eyeglasses, His viewpoint, and if we then look at ourselves and our brothers and sisters through God's glasses, we become aware of just how near the kingdom of God has come — as near as our very breath. Through God's eyeglasses, we see God's Immanence — His presence within us and within our brothers and sisters. It is for this reason that Buddhists, when they meet, make a nemaste, acknowledging and bowing to the presence of God within their brother. Any conversation between two people that begins with an acknowledgment of the indwelling Spirit of God within the other is much more likely to go well than will a conversation that begins in conflict and judgment. How does the world look through this changed viewpoint?

When we use God's glasses to read the Beatitudes, look at what a difference we find! They aren't filled with "thou shalts" and "thou shalt nots." They are filled with perspective! You are blessed if you are poor in spirit — that is, lacking in pride, ego and arrogance. You are blessed if you feel the brokenness of the world and those around you, indeed, the brokenness of your own self so acutely that you mourn, for God will comfort you. Blessed are you if you seek righteousness with an urgency that is as commanding as hunger or thirst, if you view the suffering around you with mercy, if the goal and intention of your life is to bring peace into creation.

This is how Scripture tells us God sees the world. The Beatitudes are the world as seen through God's glasses — glasses that show us the suffering of life, and permit us to enter into that suffering that it might be comforted. If we look at the world through God's glasses, how could we respond otherwise?

I would be less than an honest preacher if I tried to tell you that God's eyeglasses are rose-colored, and that all is a basket full of puppies when viewed through them, for Matthew tells us

Blessed are those who are persecuted for righteousness' sake, for theirs is the kingdom of heaven.

Blessed are you when people revile you and persecute you and utter all kinds of evil against you falsely on my account. Rejoice and be glad, for your reward is great in heaven, for in the same way they persecuted the prophets who were before you.

When we confess the reality of sin in common life each Sunday, we acknowledge that the world does not always see itself through God's eyeglasses. However hard we try, we end up seeing ourselves through self-seeking, self-justifying, imperfect lenses. We are much more capable of seeing life as a seeking after what we want than a seeking after what is good for our brothers and sisters, and the result is that we suffer. Life is suffering, you might say, and the root of suffering is desire. The best we can do is to enter into the suffering of the world, and bring it comfort.

For this reason, did Jesus turn his steps toward Jerusalem.

J. STEWART SCHNEIDER

Birds on a Wire

"For most of our lives, we are like birds on a wire, contentedly settled in, while power hums beneath our feet, unnoticed and unacknowledged. Connection with what flows beneath our feet takes us unawares."

Isaiah 40:21-31

Have you not known? Have you not heard?
Has it not been told you from the beginning?
Have you not understood from the foundations of the earth?
It is he who sits above the circle of the earth,
and its inhabitants are like grasshoppers;
who stretches out the heavens like a curtain,
and spreads them like a tent to live in;
who brings princes to naught,
and makes the rulers of the earth as nothing.
Scarcely are they planted, scarcely sown,
scarcely has their stem taken root in the earth,
when he blows upon them, and they wither,
and the tempest carries them off like stubble.
To whom then will you compare me,
or who is my equal? Says the Holy One.
Lift up your eyes on high and see:
Who created these?
He who brings out their host and numbers them,
calling them all by name;
because he is great in strength,
mighty in power,
not one is missing.
Why do you say, O Jacob,
and speak, O Israel,
"My way is hidden from the LORD,
and my right is disregarded by my God"?

Have you not known? Have you not heard?
The LORD is the everlasting God,
the Creator of the ends of the earth.
He does not faint or grow weary;
his understanding is unsearchable.
He gives power to the faint,
and strengthens the powerless.
Even youths will faint and be weary,
and the young will fall exhausted;
but those who wait for the LORD shall renew their strength,
they shall mount up with wings like eagles,
they shall run and not be weary,
they shall walk and not faint.

Mark 1:29-39

Jesus left the synagogue at Capernaum, and entered the house of Simon and Andrew, with James and John. Now Simon's mother-in-law was in bed with a fever, and they told him about her at once. He came and took her by the hand and lifted her up. Then the fever left her, and she began to serve them.

That evening, at sundown, they brought to him all who were sick or possessed with demons. And the whole city was gathered around the door. And he cured many who were sick with various diseases, and cast out many demons; and he would not permit the demons to speak, because they knew him.

In the morning, while it was still very dark, he got up and went out to a deserted place, and there he prayed. And Simon and his companions hunted for him. When they found him, they said to him, "Everyone is searching for you." He answered, "Let us go on to the neighboring towns, so that I may proclaim the message there also; for that is what I came out to do." And he went throughout Galilee, proclaiming the message in their synagogues and casting out demons.

THE LAWYER'S TALE

I have been blessed throughout my life with mentors. We commonly think of a mentor as a teacher who imparts knowledge to a student, but the most important mentors are those who demonstrate wisdom in their very lives. From those I learn the most important things. One of my mentors tutors children in the art of creative writing. His position is that the public schools are neglecting the art of storytelling. He seeks to address that gap. In doing so, he quite often counsels those he teaches with these words, "Don't tell me. Show me." This is very good advice, both for school children learning to write effectively and for elderly preachers who sometimes wander in the woods. Don't tell me. Show me.

Last year, we read from Matthew. Matthew is the "tell me" Gospel. It is filled with sayings, parables and teachings of Jesus. This year, we read from Mark. Mark is the "show me" Gospel. Mark makes his case not on what Jesus said, but on what Jesus did. Where Matthew tells us of Jesus' genealogy, of a birth accompanied by heavenly signs showing that even nature is aware of the change in Creation, Mark shows us a woman with a fever.

Jesus left the synagogue at Capernaum, and entered the house of Simon and Andrew, with James and John. Now Simon's mother-in-law was in bed with a fever, and they told him about her at once. He came and took her by the hand and lifted her up. Then the fever left her, and she began to serve them.

In Mark's telling, Jesus isn't who he is because of his wise sayings, or his ability to argue points of Jewish law. His very actions speak of the existence of power unsuspected by the people of the time. Jesus' actions say, "Something big is happening. Your world is changing. Pay attention!" The power of Jesus' actions in Mark lies in mystery, just as do our lives. Our lives are such unlikely things for a universe to produce that we must acknowledge the mystery behind our existence or live stunted lives. Jesus brings the mystery to the house of Simon and his mother-in-law and demonstrates that it is no fantasy. Could such a demonstration find soil in which to grow in 21st Century America? We are very different people, with very different understandings, and a sadly atrophied appreciation of the power of mystery.

I just finished a very interesting book titled "The Swerve" by Stephen Greenblatt. The author proposes that the atomism of Epicurus, who lived in the 4th Century before Christ, informed the humanist movement in the 15th Century which lead to the Renaissance, and ultimately to us. I read a lot of fun stuff like that. Mr. Greenblatt is convinced that Epicurus won out and thus his view forms the soil from which we spring. In his words,

> And the enlightenment he [Epicurus] offered did not require sustained scientific inquiry. You did not need a detailed grasp of the actual laws of the physical universe; you needed only to comprehend that there is a hidden natural explanation for everything that alarms or eludes you. That explanation will inevitably lead you back to atoms. If you can hold on to and repeat to yourself the simplest fact of existence — atoms and void and nothing else, atoms and void and nothing else, atoms and void and nothing else — your life will change[15].

Atoms and void and nothing else. What an arid landscape, and how like our lives today! We don't need to know much about particle physics to comprehend that we, and everything else, are made of atoms. We don't need to know much about astronomy to comprehend that space is really, really empty for miles and miles and miles. You just wouldn't believe how many miles or how empty. We can acknowledge these things, but we have vastly more difficulty in grasping that all this wonder rests on a foundation of mystery of the deepest sort because at every turn, we are encouraged to glory in the human mind's unparalleled ability to unravel the big questions. So, we turn to atoms and void and nothing else since that sort of world and that sort of answer appears to us to be the only "real" answers there are. That is the soil in which we grow, and we have attempted, since at least the Enlightenment if not before, to graft the Gospel of Jesus Christ onto this barren vine, with mostly poor results.

Nevertheless, I am convinced that however we try to make the Gospel of Jesus Christ into atoms and void and nothing else, there remains the small voice within us acknowledging that our souls are born from mystery and into mystery we return.

The writer of Mark agrees with that. To Mark, we are like birds on a wire, contentedly settled in, while power hums beneath our feet, unnoticed and unacknowledged. Mark is showing us that power in the most direct way.

I am not so skilled as Mark and I don't have access to Simon Peter's mother-

---

15 Stephen Greenblatt, *The Swerve: How the World Became Modern*, W. W. Norton & Company; First Edition edition (September 26, 2011)

in-law, but I share his need to show you the wonder and mystery into which we are born for without wonder, we are left in dryness from which no life can come. I couldn't live in such a desert. I simply do not understand our existence in this way. I want to raise my voice with that of Isaiah and shout:

Have you not known? Have you not heard?
Has it not been told you from the beginning?
Have you not understood from the foundations of the earth?
It is he who sits above the circle of the earth,
and its inhabitants are like grasshoppers;
who stretches out the heavens like a curtain,
and spreads them like a tent to live in;
who brings princes to naught,
and makes the rulers of the earth as nothing.

How can I make that reality, that power beneath our feet, real to an Epicurean world of atoms and void and nothing else? There are many things of wonder and mystery in the world to which I could address your attention, but I have chosen a humble fungus known as Pilobolus[16]. I suppose I could start with something gigantic, as I did once before, showing you the relative sizes of the planets and stars and trying to grant you a perspective on how huge and complex is the universe, but the more I think about it, the wiser it seems to start small. Few things are smaller or more humble than a fungus. Yet, as smart as we are, we can learn from a lowly fungus.

I would suggest that the marvel that is the miracle of Pilobolus is impossible to grasp from the perspective of atoms and void and nothing else. How could such wonder be, if all is atoms and void and nothing else? It exceeds my capacity to imagine how something so wondrous as Pilobolus could come to be within the sort of intellectual desert in which Epicurus lived.

So, by now you are probably wondering what could be so fantastic about a fungus, and it is this: the miracle of Pilobolus lies in the manner in which it has resolved the problem of reproduction. Pilobolus, you see, lives in cow dung. I understand completely that this is a life style you would not readily embrace, but it seems to suit Pilobolus well. It thrives in cow pats.

A young Pilobolus spore, just starting out, must first find an agreeable cow pat

---

16 http://herbarium.usu.edu/fungi/funfacts/pilobfct.htm

— no easy task if you are a fungus. What must happen is that a cow must eat a Pilobolus spore, subsequently depositing the spore and its new habitat upon the meadow, from which Pilobolus will produce new spores. This is an enormous problem for a Pilobolus spore because cows, being mammals, have a built-in revulsion to their own waste, and do not graze near it. The problem is to get the spore far enough away from the home cow pat so another cow might by chance ingest it while nibbling grass, and start the process over.

Here is the miracle. Pilobolus has evolved a way to shoot its spores onto the grass quite a distance from its home cow pat. Its "shotgun" is a stalk swollen with cell sap, bearing a black mass of spores on the top. Below the swollen tip is a light-sensitive area. The light sensing region affects the growth of Pilobolus by causing it to face toward the sun. As the fungus matures, water pressure builds in the stalk until the tip explodes, shooting the spores into the daylight.

The spores fly away at 35 feet per second, at a height of 6 feet, and land as far away as 8 feet. Pilobolus, without knowing it, can shoot over a cow. Additionally, shooting the spores into the daylight gives them a better chance of landing in a sunny place where grass or other plants are growing. The cows that made the dung for the previous batch of Pilobolus will probably eat these spore-covered plants and start the process all over again.

To make this work, the spores must be indigestible so that they can pass through a cow unharmed. The Pilobolus fruiting body must have evolved a light-sensitive area which will keep the fungus "pointed" to the sun, whose heat will build the pressure in the stem of the fungus to sufficiently high pressure to propel the spore package over a cow. Then the spores must be able to cling to the plants where they land in order to re-enter a cow. This is a pretty impressive engineering problem for a fungus to undertake.

Biologists will tell you that the fungus evolved these characteristics as a result of random selection. I do not doubt that species evolve over time. What I **do** doubt, what I cannot get my mind to accept, is that Pilobolus came to this totally remarkable life cycle through purely random chance. Which is more difficult to believe? That Pilobolus randomly evolved into a shotgun with an aiming mechanism having spent countless generations stuck inside a cow with no way to reproduce, or that God himself, the ground of our being, the power in the wires beneath our feet, walked upon the earth to demonstrate that we are loved?

For me, it's no contest. Can I offer proof that the genius of the Pilobolus was arrived at by other than random forces? Of course not. If God could be the subject of investigation, He wouldn't be God. Nevertheless, does my heart reject the former and embrace the latter? Unquestionably. Will the biologists point out that I have only proved my faulty understanding of the power of random selection? Undoubtedly. Too bad for the biologists.

Welcome that which your heart hears as true, for there are more things in heaven and earth, Horatio, than are dreamt of in your philosophy.

J. STEWART SCHNEIDER

The Way Things Are

"Viewing God's Commandments as standardized tests for entrance to Heaven is much less likely to lead you in His ways than to simply accept them as expert advice for living a fulfilled life."

Deuteronomy 30:15-20

Moses said to all Israel the words which the Lord commanded him, "See, I have set before you today life and prosperity, death and adversity. If you obey the commandments of the LORD your God that I am commanding you today, by loving the LORD your God, walking in his ways, and observing his commandments, decrees, and ordinances, then you shall live and become numerous, and the LORD your God will bless you in the land that you are entering to possess. But if your heart turns away and you do not hear, but are led astray to bow down to other gods and serve them, I declare to you today that you shall perish; you shall not live long in the land that you are crossing the Jordan to enter and possess. I call heaven and earth to witness against you today that I have set before you life and death, blessings and curses. Choose life so that you and your descendants may live, loving the LORD your God, obeying him, and holding fast to him; for that means life to you and length of days, so that you may live in the land that the LORD swore to give to your ancestors, to Abraham, to Isaac, and to Jacob."

Matthew 5:21-37

Jesus said, "You have heard that it was said to those of ancient times, 'You shall not murder'; and 'whoever murders shall be liable to judgment.' But I say to you that if you are angry with a brother or sister, you will be liable to judgment; and if you insult a brother or sister, you will be liable to the council; and if you say, 'You fool,' you will be liable to the hell of fire. So when you are offering your gift at the altar, if you remember that your brother or sister has something against you, leave your gift there before the altar and go; first be reconciled to your brother or sister, and then come and offer your gift. Come to terms quickly with your accuser while you are on the way to court with him, or your accuser may hand you over to the judge, and the judge to the guard, and you will be thrown into prison. Truly I tell you, you will never get out until you have paid the last penny.

"You have heard that it was said, 'You shall not commit adultery.' But I say to you that everyone who looks at a woman with lust has already committed adultery with her in his heart. If your right eye causes you to sin, tear it out and throw it away; it is better for you to lose one of your members than for your whole body to be thrown into hell. And if your right hand causes you to sin, cut it off and throw it away; it is better for you to lose one of your members than for your whole body to go into hell.

"It was also said, 'Whoever divorces his wife, let him give her a certificate of divorce.' But I say to you that anyone who divorces his wife, except on the ground of unchastity, causes her to commit adultery; and whoever marries a divorced woman commits adultery.

"Again, you have heard that it was said to those of ancient times, 'You shall not swear falsely, but carry out the vows you have made to the Lord.' But I say to you, Do not swear at all, either by heaven, for it is the throne of God, or by the earth, for it is his footstool, or by Jerusalem, for it is the city of the great King. And do not swear by your head, for you cannot make one hair white or black. Let your word be 'Yes, Yes' or 'No, No'; anything more than this comes from the evil one.

You know what drives most women nuts? Men. We do everything wrong, we misinterpret their intentions, we make them work harder than they would otherwise do, and we get under foot. Why would any rational being tether themselves to such an infuriating entity?

And yet, one would be remiss to fail to point out the exertions women put themselves through in order to attract the attention of this most unsatisfactory of creatures. They walk about in shoes designed by a sadist, stuff themselves into preposterous clothing, cake makeup all over their faces and laugh at the male's pitiable attempts to be amusing as if whatever stupidity he just said was the most prescient and entertaining thing ever uttered. The differing perspectives of the two genders sometimes makes me wonder if they are separate species. Women are from Venus, Men are from Mars, as the book title has it.

Of course, they aren't separate species, and they don't inhabit separate planets. Women are from Earth and men are from Earth. As challenging as it is sometimes to make a life together, the truth is that men need women and women need men, and not just for automobile maintenance and yard work. It is the way the world works. During the Creation, the only thing that God proclaimed "not good" was the creation of Adam without an Eve. We walk through life most comfortably two-by-two. It's just the way things are for most people.

That's what I want you to do today — think about the way things are. I'd like you to mentally compare the way you think about the way things are with the way you think about the Commandments of God. Just for a few minutes today, I'd like you to stop viewing the Commandments of God as tests to get to heaven, and consider them as the way things are — instructions from the Creator on how to get the most out of our experience here, you might say.

I think there is something wrong in the relationship between us and God, and since I'm a minister of the Gospel, I bet you can guess who I think has the wrong end of the stick. What is it in our perception of God that leads us to believe that He delivered to Moses the Ten Test Questions, rather than the Ten Instructions? In particular, when we speak of God's commandments, why are we so insistent on having an explanation for them instead of just accepting that they are the way things are as we do with the complicated relations between men and women?

In the matter of instructions, Jesus has some decidedly queer things to say in our Matthew passage today. He affirms that it is a very bad idea to murder one another, then goes on and says it's a very bad idea to harbor anger against another. It's a very bad idea to insult another. It's not a good idea, when there is a dispute between you and another, to push it all the way to a court. Much better to resolve the matter before you get there.

Then Jesus stops preaching and really starts meddling. He starts talking about plucking out your eyeball and chopping off your hand. He says that a divorced woman can never again know the warmth of human love. This doesn't sound much like Jesus. What kind of a teaching is this?

I'd like to suggest that it isn't a teaching. I think we make a mistake to read Jesus' words here as a teaching, and I think we make a mistake when we view God as the rule-enforcer in the sky. Instead, I think we should view God not as a noun, but as a verb, and I think we should view Jesus' words not as teachings, but as revelations about the way things work.

I was taught, half a century ago, that God is the rule-maker who insists on His own way, for His own purposes. Do what God commands or else! The one thing I wasn't taught was this: we live in God's creation. God knows more about it than we do, and the commandments God gives us, far from being a manipulative effort to play us like puppets, lead to life — affirming, fulfilling, interesting, pleasurable life — because that's the way He put his creation together just as the need of a man for a woman is the way He put His creation together. It is the way the world works. It is what IS.

To understand this better, we need to keep in mind that God's instructions have just that purpose – to instruct us in the way to affirming, fulfilling, interesting and pleasurable life in God's Creation. Instead of viewing these words of Jesus as "or else!" words, we can read them as, "The world is put together in such a way that if you follow these instructions, you will have a fulfilling life. If you depart from these instructions, your life will get worse and worse until having your eye gouged out would be better, by comparison."

To enable us to approach this new way of viewing Jesus' words, we must first rid ourselves of the baggage we have hung on the word we use to refer to the Creator — "god."

There is a powerful statement about God in the story of the burning bush. I mentioned in passing recently that God's name isn't "God." God announced to Moses at the burning bush that Moses should tell the people, if they asked who he had spoken to, that he had spoken to YHWH, a name related to the Hebrew verb "to be." It might be translated as "I am who I am" or "I will be what I will be." God is the great "I AM." God is the way the world is.

Obviously, that's not really a name, like Bob or Ned. It is a statement which cannot be put up against other names, nor compared. I AM WHO I AM. It is not a noun. It is a verb, a statement of existence. It is a complete statement of the way things are. God isn't one of God's creatures, nor a part of His Creation to be distinguished from other parts. God is What IS. The name God gave Moses was "I AM REALITY." Cooperation with God's commandments amounts to whole-hearted cooperation with the inevitable.

When you get right down to it, I think that's what's wrong with the word "god." It's a noun. The world is full of nouns. Nouns are things. To refer to the creational and covenantal I AM as "God" makes him one of that world full of things. The rulebook of collegiate basketball is a thing. I can ignore it. And I do. I still don't know how many points you get if you kick a hole in one. Things can be accepted or not.

God is not a thing. Neither is YHWH any proper part of speech in Hebrew. It is related to the verb "to be" and is always explained in texts as "might be translated 'I am who I am' or 'I will be who I will be'" but it is not directly translatable. It is a word of such unapproachable holiness that the Jews of the time of Jesus did not pronounce it, substituting the word "Adonai," meaning "Lord." If you look in your First Testament, in most translations, the word "Lord" is set in small caps. The Hebrew behind this word is the name of God, and in Jesus' time, when such a passage was read the reader would speak the word Adonai, even though the name was printed. In fact, Orthodox Jews to this day refer to Him as "haShem" or "The Name." I really want you to dig into that statement. God's name isn't Fred. It isn't Dagon or Sin or Chumash.

That's probably more than you wanted to know about Jewish practice, but I want you to get a sharp sense of the difference between the word "god" which we toss around so carelessly, and the name of the creational and covenantal I AM, who is so holy that it would be an affront even to speak His name. God isn't a thing. God is the very essence of our existence. God is the reality in which we live, and that reality, we are instructed, is founded in love.

The trouble with god, then is that the word is a noun, whereas the great I AM is a state of being, a verb, the first cause, the unmoved mover, the Primus Movem. All things came into being through haShem, and without haShem not one thing came into being.

With that kind of pedigree, it's no wonder we put haShem on a pedestal in a far-away heaven and cower down before Him. I'm not even suggesting that such an approach to haShem is inappropriate. We might benefit from a little more of that. But however powerful and benign such a concept of the great I AM is, the concept as we perceive it is still little more than a dictator, and we aren't put together to be terrified into behaving. We rebel.

On the other hand, if we see the words of Scripture as the great I AM revealing to us what it takes to live healthy, prosperous, pleasant lives in the Creation He knows best, we'd be great fools not to listen.

It is as if we had been invited to live in a beautiful condominium. With the keys came the notation, "The hot water is on the left, and the cold water is on the right."

If we think of god as the landlord, that is, as a thing, we might think we could avoid the rules by sneaking around behind Him or claiming that we don't believe in Him. The reality is that if we insist, despite what the rules say, in turning the left handle for cold and the right for hot, we are dooming ourselves to uncomfortable showers for all time.

> But if your heart turns away and you do not hear, but are led astray to bow down to other gods and serve them, I declare to you today that you shall perish; you shall not live long in the land that you are crossing the Jordan to enter and possess.

If we think of the rules as simply the way things are, the state of being in the condominium, we see things differently. Now we keep the faucets straight and take comfortable showers.

> See, I have set before you today life and prosperity, death and adversity. If you obey the commandments of the LORD your God that I am commanding you today, by loving the LORD your God, walking in his ways, and observing his commandments, decrees, and ordinances, then you shall live and become numerous, and the LORD your God will bless you in the land that you are entering to possess.

The trouble with god, then, is that we have tried to collapse the great I AM into a short noun. And we have succeeded. God is optional for many, many people in the world today. The Old Man on television's "Pawn Stars" says "Oh my god!" to express disgust. We speak of wilderness as being "god-forsaken." We even call on this noun to damn things or people that annoy us. The trouble with god is that the word has lost all of its awe and power and become just another thing.

God is optional even among believers, who can so easily convince themselves that their selfish, self-centered desires and hopes are OK with this abstract noun located somewhere far, far away. When Jesus starts speaking of gouging out your eyeball, though, as being preferable to the trouble you will cause by chasing every skirt that crosses your path He moves the Great I AM up close and personal.

It is hard to grasp, particularly after a lifetime of thinking of God's Commandments as a standardized test for heaven, but it makes very good sense, I think. It's also dreadful hard to obey, because we're not very good at behaving peacefully, and we are awfully good at rationalizing acceptable reasons for doing unacceptable things. Suppose I'm very, very angry with someone. If I'm a civilized person, I won't murder them, and I can easily convince myself that this god person will overlook it because it's natural to be angry from time to time. "Not good enough," Jesus says. "You are off the rails. The anger you are cuddling in your breast will eat you from the inside out. There IS no god person you can flim-flam. There is haShem, the Name, the great I AM, the way things are, the creational and covenantal first cause, the reason and power that sustains you. You cannot avoid the way things are because they are the way things are. Go and make peace with your brother."

If I find my head turning because a pretty girl walked by, and I engage in a little fantasy, what's the harm in that? "Not good enough," Jesus says. "You are off the rails again. haShem has given you a wife and she is flesh of your flesh and bone of your bone. She is the way things are for you, and is not to be compared to others for to compare is to measure, to measure is to yearn, and you will burn with conflicted ideas. Go and take a cold shower. The cold faucet is the one on the right."

The trouble with seeing god as a thing is that we imagine that we have power over things. There is no other way to speak of God other than making Him a noun, but God is not a noun, though we live in His house. To kick against His explanation of how to live here comfortably, happily and in peace with your surroundings is both pointless and foolish.

To hammer that point home, the last thing Jesus says is:

> Do not swear at all, either by heaven, for it is the throne of God, or by the earth, for it is his footstool, or by Jerusalem, for it is the city of the great King. And do not swear by your head, for you cannot make one hair white or black. Let your word be "Yes, Yes" or "No, No."

To swear by something is to offer it as bond that your statement is true. There is nothing here, heaven, earth, Jerusalem, or even your own head, which is not haShem's. Listen to Him.

The End of the Beginning

The events of Holy Week, from Jesus' entry into Jerusalem until Golgotha, are often thought of in magical ways. Magical thinking about the Crucifixion is one way we protect ourselves from the horrors of the reality of the thing. A magical Jesus who meekly lays down His life which in some poorly understood way assuages the offended Father is more palatable than a political, rabble-rousing Jesus directly confronting the government and the authorities of the time, then being cruelly tortured, mocked and killed by those same authorities.

And yet … He was.

J. STEWART SCHNEIDER

Sunday

"It is not possible to consider Holy Week without also considering the political aspects of Jesus' actions. In them we find a condemnation of the systems and governments which we create, and which, inevitably, feed upon us in turn."

Zechariah 9:9-10

⁹Rejoice greatly, O daughter Zion!
Shout aloud, O daughter Jerusalem!
Lo, your king comes to you;
 triumphant and victorious is he,
humble and riding on a donkey,
 on a colt, the foal of a donkey.
¹⁰He will cut off the chariot from Ephraim
 and the warhorse from Jerusalem;
and the battle-bow shall be cut off,
 and he shall command peace to the nations;
his dominion shall be from sea to sea,
and from the River to the ends of the earth.

Mark 11:1-11

When they were approaching Jerusalem, at Bethphage and Bethany, near the Mount of Olives, he sent two of his disciples and said to them, "Go into the village ahead of you, and immediately as you enter it, you will find tied there a colt that has never been ridden; untie it and bring it. If anyone says to you, 'Why are you doing this?' just say this, 'The Lord needs it and will send it back here immediately.'" They went away and found a colt tied near a door, outside in the street. As they were untying it, some of the bystanders said to them, "What are you doing, untying the colt?" They told them what Jesus had said; and they allowed them to take it. Then they brought the colt to Jesus

*and threw their cloaks on it; and he sat on it. Many people spread their cloaks
on the road, and others spread leafy branches that they had cut in the fields.
Then those who went ahead and those who followed were shouting,*

> *Hosanna!*
> *Blessed is the one who comes in the name of the Lord!*
> *Blessed is the coming kingdom of our ancestor David!*
> *Hosanna in the highest heaven!*

*Then he entered Jerusalem and went into the temple; and when he had
looked around at everything, as it was already late, he went out to Bethany
with the twelve.*

For the Sundays of Lent, I thought we might do something a little different — I'm going to depart from the Lectionary texts, and turn to the
Gospel of Mark for a day-by-day account of the last week of Jesus' life.
We'll start today with Palm Sunday, the first day of the week, as Jesus arrives in
Jerusalem. My goal here is to allow us, as closely as we can, to walk in the
footsteps of the disciples and get a feeling for what the reality of this last week
must have been.

My fear is that the story of Easter has become little more than a fairy tale to
many of us, who treasure the images of children and hidden eggs and candy,
sometimes at the expense of the actual events. Archbishop Timothy Dolan
said:

> "Maybe the greatest threat to the Church is not heresy, not dissent, not
> secularism, not even moral relativism, but this sanitized, feel-good,
> boutique, therapeutic spirituality, that makes no demands, calls for no
> sacrifice, asks for no conversion, entails no battle against sin, but only
> soothes and affirms."

The story we will play out during the Lenten period is gritty and real and hor-
rifying and eye-opening and soul feeding if we will but listen to it. During
Transfiguration Sunday we heard the very voice of God ordering us to "listen
to him." God doesn't just mean "Listen to his teachings about how to treat

people decently and be an inoffensive person." God means listen to him even in what he is doing, and follow him. God means, "Go and do ye likewise," church.

So, if I haven't scared you half to death already, I will by the end of the service, because we are headed to Jerusalem in the spring of the year, sometime around 30 A.D. and Jerusalem is the most dangerous place in the world.

Jerusalem in 30 A.D. was the center of government in an occupied country. Rome had been the ruling authority in Judea for nearly a century. It is impossible for one nation to occupy another nation for so long a period without the aid of collaborators. The simple practicalities of the situation are that if you are a small country, overrun by a large country, you will either find a way to collaborate, or you will be exterminated from the face of the earth. Judea had found a way, and the way involved the collaboration of the Temple authorities. Think the Vichy France government collaborating with the Axis from 1940 to 1944.

The cost of collaboration came at a terrific price. They gave up their independence. From the time that Rome deposed Herod Archelaus in 6 A.D. to the outbreak of the great revolt in 66 A.D., Rome replaced the Kohen Gadol, the High Priest, 18 times. The Kohen Gadol, the only person permitted to enter the Holy of Holies, had become a political appointee of Rome.

The Temple was where the taxes to Rome were aggregated. The Temple was where the records of debt were kept. The Temple had become, not the house of God, but the locus of Roman power in Judea. Even worse, to save the country, the Temple authorities permitted the notion that Roman control of Judea was legitimated by theology. They permitted the thought that Rome's place in the system was given by God. It goes without saying that Rome was **very** jealous of its power, and **very** violently opposed to any interference with it. That's what made Jerusalem the most dangerous place on earth, but in the spring of the year, Jerusalem became even **more** dangerous. In the spring, the Jews remember their deliverance from another empire as they celebrate the Passover.

Perhaps 1,300 years earlier, the Jews were oppressed by the most powerful kingdom on earth. Pharaoh was deemed the son of a god, a god himself. What Pharaoh said was done, as soon as it cleared his mouth. The Jews cried out to their God, and God responded, reaching even into the household of Pharaoh himself to bring death to Pharaoh's own family. The only ones spared, or passed over, were the Jews and in the end, Pharaoh's power and supposed divinity were crushed.

Now, the Jews are in thrall to another man who fancies that he is son of a god. On coins and in inscriptions, Caesar is called Lord, son of god, savior, king of kings, lord of lords, bringer of peace on earth. His power is even greater than that of Pharaoh, for his empire stretches much farther and includes Egypt.

In 30 A.D. Rome rules Idumea, Judea and Samaria through an agent, currently a man named Pontius Pilate. Each year, in the spring, this dangerous holiday of the Jews is laid upon Pontius Pilate's plate. In Mark's telling of the story, Jesus has been traveling toward Jerusalem from Galilee, about 100 miles north, in order to arrive in Jerusalem just at the Passover.

Passover was a recurring problem for Pilate. His job was to assure that the residents stayed orderly, law-abiding, tax-paying clients of Rome, but the Passover stirred up all sorts of nationalistic emotions among the lower classes who were not invested in the Roman economy. The confounded thing couldn't be done away with without riots and bad reports back to Rome, and it couldn't be ignored lest the Jews get it into their heads that it might happen again. The best that can be made of it is for the governor and reinforcements to the garrison at the Antonia Fort in Jerusalem to leave their comfortable lodgings at Caesaria Maritima and make an impressive procession into the city, demonstrating to all in the city that Rome is there with enough strength to quiet any superstitious nonsense these accursed Jews might get into their heads. Pilate and his troops were **very** unhappy about this.

Happy or not, every spring, Pilate and his troops had to make the sixty-mile trip from their comfortable lodgings at Caesaria Maritima, "Caesar by the Sea" in English, and go to hot, fetid, noisy, uncomfortable Jerusalem to scare the blazes out of the local population. Caesaria Maritima was on the shores of the Mediterranean, so every spring, Pilate and his troops, horns blaring, leather armor creaking, feet tramping in time, the Roman eagles in plain display, made imperial procession into Jerusalem through the Western gate.

Meeting them at the Western gate would be a formal group of Temple authorities, the well-to-do of the city, anyone who was profiting from working with the Romans, anyone who benefited from a peaceful existence under Roman rule. Anybody who was anybody, in other words.

This year, there would be another procession. None of the rich and famous would see this procession. This other procession would approach Jerusalem at the same time, but from the east. In place of a show of Roman force, would be a man on a donkey. In place of heavily armed soldiers would be a rabble of Galileans and religious fanatics who had heard the man's message. In the place of implied violence at the western gate was a display of submission at the eastern gate. When Jesus rode into that eastern gate, he was riding to his death in the most dangerous place on earth. It had all been most carefully planned.

Jesus told his disciples

> Go into the village ahead of you, and immediately as you enter it, you will find tied there a colt that has never been ridden; untie it and bring it. If anyone says to you, "Why are you doing this?" just say this, "The Lord needs it and will send it back here immediately."

Prior arrangements had been made. The deadly serious confrontation Jesus had walked from Galilee to cause, was about to be set in motion.

I want you to set aside all the notions in your head of a doe-eyed Jesus innocently approaching Jerusalem to the cheering of children. This was no children's parade. In his long walk from Galilee to Jerusalem, Jesus had predicted his death no fewer than three times. The image I want you to substitute for that is the photograph on the front of our bulletin, of the lone Chinese protester in Tienanmen Square in 1989, his groceries in his hand, facing down a column of tanks. Jesus knew exactly what he was doing. And the most critical symbol of His entrance was that colt. In our passage from Zechariah today, we read

> Lo, your king comes to you;
>   triumphant and victorious is he,
> humble and riding on a donkey,
>   on a colt, the foal of a donkey.

Can you get hold of the drama here? On the West side of the city, Pilate and his troops, showing the eagles of Rome, enter the city in Imperial procession, proclaiming Tiberius Caesar, son of god, prince of peace, the divine Caesar to the cheering of everybody in the city of any substance. On the other side of the city, a man proclaims himself the fulfillment of Zechariah's prophesy, the king of the Jews, the destroyer of empires to the cheering of the marginalized, the poor and the powerless. It is Tienanmen Square.

We are not accustomed to think of the death of Jesus as having any political component, but unless we squeeze our eyes very tightly shut, that conclusion is inescapable. Jesus was killed by the Romans. Rome did not kill for issues of Jewish cultic practice. Rome killed for attacks upon Rome, and this was what that was. If Jesus is king of the Jews, Lord and Savior, then Tiberius Caesar is not.

The message is not lost on the people observing the counter-procession, for they shout

Hosanna!
Blessed is the one who comes in the name of the Lord!
Blessed is the coming kingdom of our ancestor David!
Hosanna in the highest heaven!

On the West side of the city, a demonstration of the kingdom of Tiberius Caesar. On the East, a demonstration of the kingdom of God.

I know that you have been taught since you were this high that the same crowds that welcomed Jesus into Jerusalem later called for his crucifixion, I've even preached it myself, but I've come to believe that it is not so. The crowd which welcomed Jesus into Jerusalem were his followers, proclaiming the coming of the kingdom of God. Those who later called for his crucifixion were the response of the status quo, trying to protect itself from this attack.

I know also that you have been taught that Jesus came to Jerusalem to confront the Jewish worship system and to establish a little white Presbyterian church in the wild wood in its place. I believe that this is also false. Jesus' entry into Jerusalem was infinitely more important than doctrinal differences over worship practices.

I believe that the tension, no, the opposition, between the kingdom of God and the systems we have put in place to run our societies is inevitable. I believe that because I believe that God speaks to the human heart, but never to corporations or governments. Nevertheless, if we put aside for a time the need to demonize Rome, and let her sins and successes stand on their own, we have to acknowledge that as empires go, Rome wasn't all that bad. The Pax Romana, the peace of Rome, lasted for a millennium. For a thousand years, people could go about their business on Roman roads, resolve their disputes in Roman courts and live their lives protected by Roman security. By any measure but one, that is a successful system. The dimension in which it failed was that with Rome as their protector, who needs God? The money said, "In Caesar we trust." The Emperor was treated as a god, the prince of peace, the savior. This Roman system, which brought many good things, was legitimated by displacing God with the Emperor.

Church, it is my belief that any society, corporation, group or culture will, inevitably, substitute its values for the voice of God and legitimate itself by claiming loyalty to itself as tantamount to godliness. Not just Rome. ANY system, including this wonderful land in which we live.

If, when you sing "God Bless America" you are praying that God's people will stand up for God's values in our country, and that America will then be blessed, you are on the right track. If you are praying that God blesses America because God agrees with the American form of government, or that God blesses America because America is where the good guys live, or even that God blesses America because it's a safe, secure place to live, you have gone over to the dark side. Singapore is a safe, secure place to live, unless you like to chew gum. Then, not so much. That's a criminal offense in Singapore.

The lesson that is going to be taught to the Roman empire at the close of the week, and which will resound through history to our time, is that it is the kingdom of God which sustains and protects us. It is the kingdom of God which has the power, no matter how many horns you toot, how many soldiers you have, how many eagles you display, whether you believe it or not. God is inevitable.

Lent is a time of severe self-examination. It is a time when we ask ourselves if we are any more faithful than the disciples who ran and hid when the going got scary. When Jesus entered Jerusalem on that colt of a donkey, he was directly confronting the status quo, the rule of Rome, the collaboration of the very Temple, all the things that lead God's people to look to Rome for that which they should seek from God. All the people in Jerusalem with a vested interest in continuation of the Temple, who were making money from the Romans, who had been raised to respect the government, would see him as a rabble-rousing trouble-maker.

Knowing what you now know about the background of Palm Sunday, the question posed by these two processions into Jerusalem is this: had you been there, at which gate would you have been standing?

"We must never confuse the Way of
Christ with something as trivial as just being an inoffensive
person. Following the Way of Christ may well lead you into
confrontation with authority. Celebrate that opportunity, for
you are sharing it with the Lord."

Jeremiah 7:1-7,11

*The word that came to Jeremiah from the Lord: Stand in the gate of the
Lord's house, and proclaim there this word, and say, Hear the word of the
Lord, all you people of Judah, you that enter these gates to worship the Lord.
Thus says the Lord of hosts, the God of Israel: Amend your ways and your doings, and let me dwell with you in this place. Do not trust in these deceptive
words: "This is the temple of the Lord, the temple of the Lord, the temple of
the Lord."*

*For if you truly amend your ways and your doings, if you truly act justly one
with another, if you do not oppress the alien, the orphan, and the widow, or
shed innocent blood in this place, and if you do not go after other gods to
your own hurt, then I will dwell with you in this place, in the land that I gave
of old to your ancestors for ever and ever. Has this house, which is called by
my name, become a den of robbers in your sight? You know, I too am watching, says the Lord.*

Mark 11:12-19

*On the following day, when they came from Bethany, he was hungry. Seeing
in the distance a fig tree in leaf, he went to see whether perhaps he would
find anything on it. When he came to it, he found nothing but leaves, for it
was not the season for figs. He said to it, "May no one ever eat fruit from you
again." And his disciples heard it.*

Then they came to Jerusalem. And he entered the temple and began to drive out those who were selling and those who were buying in the temple, and he overturned the tables of the money-changers and the seats of those who sold doves; and he would not allow anyone to carry anything through the temple. He was teaching and saying, "Is it not written, 'My house shall be called a house of prayer for all the nations?' But you have made it a den of robbers."

And when the chief priests and the scribes heard it, they kept looking for a way to kill him; for they were afraid of him, because the whole crowd was spellbound by his teaching. And when evening came, Jesus and his disciples went out of the city.

In the morning as they passed by, they saw the fig tree withered away to its roots. Then Peter remembered and said to him, 'Rabbi, look! The fig tree that you cursed has withered.' Jesus answered them, 'Have faith in God. Truly I tell you, if you say to this mountain, "Be taken up and thrown into the sea," and if you do not doubt in your heart, but believe that what you say will come to pass, it will be done for you. So I tell you, whatever you ask for in prayer, believe that you have received it, and it will be yours.

Monday's Jerusalem Times, sometime around 30 A.D. had two interesting items on the front page. Above the fold was a large story about the annual imperial procession through the West gate by Pontius Pilate and the reinforcements to the Antonia Fort. It was quite an event. Anyone of note in the city made a point to be there to welcome in the Imperial Eagles.

Below the fold was a much smaller story of a disturbance at the East gate. Apparently some of the lower classes had made a disturbance about a man on a donkey. Authorities promised a prompt investigation. What the Jerusalem Times didn't know was that what began at the East gate was about to spread all over the world.

Today Jesus returns to confront the Temple. What I want us to think about today is this: "What was so wrong about the cooperation between the Temple and Rome – the church and state – that it would be necessary for Jesus to symbolically destroy it?"

Notice that I didn't say Jesus cleansed the Temple. He destroyed it. All through my childhood, the events of Monday were explained to me as Jesus cleansing the Temple to correct what had gone wrong in Jewish worship practice. The Jews had become too legalistic. The Jews had 5,000 laws and no one could keep them all. God was through with blood sacrifices. The Jews were making money in the Temple by changing money and selling birds for sacrifice. As I've gotten older, I've come to believe that Mark's account of Jesus' actions on Monday had nothing to do with correcting Jewish worship forms or ending blood sacrifice. Jesus' actions on Monday were much, much more important than that. Jesus symbolically destroyed the Temple on Monday, just as Jeremiah had prophesied. Why would He do that?

Perhaps a thousand years earlier, King David announced his plan to build a grand temple for God, who, at the time, was living in a tent. David didn't think it was appropriate for God to live in a tent when David had a grand house to live in, and thought he would do God a favor — extend a little charity to God, you might say, by sprucing up His digs.

> Now when the king was settled in his house, and the Lord had given him rest from all his enemies around him, the king said to the prophet Nathan, "See now, I am living in a house of cedar, but the ark of God stays in a tent."

The prophet Nathan initially gives him the go-ahead, but the next day he returns with a much different message:

> Thus says the Lord: Are you the one to build me a house to live in? I have not lived in a house since the day I brought up the people of Israel from Egypt to this day, but I have been moving about in a tent and a tabernacle. Wherever I have moved about among all the people of Israel, did I ever speak a word with any of the tribal leaders of Israel, whom I commanded to shepherd my people Israel, saying, "Why have you not built me a house of cedar?"

David announced to Nathan that he's had this great idea to build a fine house for God, and God answered David saying, "Nu? And who asked you?" David's plan to build a house for God was really David's attempt to take ownership of God's house for his own purposes. If David builds a great house for God it would be called David's Temple and David, the king, would have great influence over what happens in it. Taking ownership of the things of God to legitimate the things we want will never work. We can't slap a coat of God on our lives to make them look better. That was the problem in Jesus' time as well – the Romans had taken ownership of the Temple.

David's son, Solomon, did build the Temple at God's command, and by all accounts it was a wonder of the world. It became for the Jews the virtual navel of the world, the holiest place on earth, the actual dwelling place of God. It stood for about 400 years until it was completely destroyed by Babylon in the year 586 B.C., but in 518 B.C., the returning exiles rebuilt a much more modest structure which we call the Second Temple. Although it failed to recapture the grandeur of Solomon's Temple, it became for the Jews just as important, and just as much the dwelling place of God on earth. It stood until just before Jesus' time.

At this point, Herod the Great, one of history's nastiest people, enters the picture. Herod's family was from Idumea (the Bible's Edom) and had been forced to convert to Judaism when Israel conquered Edom. Nonetheless, by careful maneuvering, he became a client king of Rome. So, when Jesus was born, the guy on David's throne was a political appointee of Rome without even a proper pedigree as a Jew.

To curry favor and to build himself up, Herod started an ambitious building program and one of the projects was to remodel the Second Temple, though "remodel" is a terrific understatement. He rebuilt it completely, and, sure enough. it was known as "Herod's Temple."

The first thing he did was to clear an enormous platform containing 40 acres. At the center of the Temple was a building containing the Holy of Holies, where one would have found the Ark of the Covenant if it hadn't gone missing six hundred years earlier. The Holy of Holies was so sacred that the High Priest, the Kohen Gadol, also a political appointee of Rome, could enter there only on Yom Kippur, the Day of Atonement.

Outside the building containing the Holy of Holies were a series of four concentric courts. The outer court was open to all, including non-Jews. Only male and female Jews could go into the second court. The third court was for Jewish men only. Finally the fourth court was restricted to priests. The closer you got to the Holy of Holies, the holier the ground upon which you walked and the smaller the group of people who were admitted.

To top off the cake he had built, and to re-assure Rome that he was faithful to them, Herod installed a large golden eagle atop one of the gates, symbol of Rome and its supreme divinity, Jupiter Optimus Maximux. Herod had done just what David had proposed — he had built a Temple for his own purposes and slapped a coat of God on it.

As you can imagine, the eagle did not go down a treat with the locals and two Jewish teachers told their students to hack the thing off the Temple. They were burnt alive for their troubles. On Monday, Jesus is going to accomplish what they attempted.

There's one other thing you need to know to understand Mark's account of Monday. That is the word "intercalation." An intercalation is a technique that Mark uses a lot. He starts a story, but doesn't finish it, then he starts a second story and tells it to the end. Then he finishes the first story. The first story becomes a frame around the main story. We are to use the first story to interpret the inner story.

The two stories Mark tells us today are, first, a puzzling story about a petulant Jesus cursing a fig tree, and, second, Jesus' well-known temple tantrum. The notion that Jesus threw hissy fits at fig trees or at the Temple doesn't sound very much like the Jesus we know from the rest of the Gospel. With what we know about the Temple and Mark's use of frames, what exactly is Mark telling us?

Let's start with the outer story.

> On the following day, when they came from Bethany, he was hungry. Seeing in the distance a fig tree in leaf, he went to see whether perhaps he would find anything on it. When he came to it, he found nothing but leaves, for it was not the season for figs. He said to it, "May no one ever eat fruit from you again." And his disciples heard it.

Passover happens in the month of Nissa, March-April to us. There is no way a fig tree could have figs that early in the year. We can either ignore this passage as meaningless, take from it that Jesus had a petulant streak we hadn't seen before, or we can use our new word, "intercalation," to see it for what it is — a frame around the main story. Jesus approached the fig tree seeking fruit, and, when he found none, he cursed it. Next, in the same way, Jesus moves to the

Temple. What fruit is He expecting there?

> And he entered the Temple and began to drive out those who were sell-
> ing and those who were buying in the Temple, and he overturned the
> tables of the money-changers and the seats of those who sold doves;
> and he would not allow anyone to carry anything through the Temple.
> He was teaching and saying, "Is it not written,
>
> > 'My house shall be called a house of prayer for all the nations?'
>
> > But you have made it a den of robbers."

We need to be careful here. The problem wasn't the Temple, or Rome, nor
less Jewish worship forms. The problem was that, in order to exist as an occupied country, the Temple leadership had forged a partnership with Rome in
which the High Priest became a political appointee, and the Temple spread
the message that Rome's rule was legitimate. The same Rome that minted
coins calling Tiberius Caesar "Lord of Lords," "King of Kings," and "son of
god" got to hire and fire the High Priest who was supposed to lead the people
in God's ways. What could possibly go wrong with this arrangement?

This is not about a rejection of the blood sacrifice system and it is most certainly NOT about replacing the Temple with a little white Presbyterian church
in the wild wood. It is about the collaboration of God's Temple with a Roman
system that benefited the well-to-do at the expense of the poor. It was the sub-
stitution of worship for justice, and to understand that, we have to look at the
passage from Jeremiah that Jesus referred to and we need to be precise with
the phrase "den of robbers."

Jeremiah spoke in the Sixth Century B.C. Babylon was the problem then, and
Jeremiah's message was clear, "Surrender. God is punishing you for your re-
fusal to abide by His demand that you act justly." You can just imagine how
popular that made Jeremiah. The people told Jeremiah that God would protect them because the Temple was located there, and God would never allow
His Temple to be destroyed, so they were safe. They were taking ownership of
God's Temple as a shield against Babylon, who Jeremiah was telling them was
God's agent to punish them for departing from God's commandment of justice! Jeremiah told them that God demanded more from them than worship —
He wanted them to do justice — and that God would most certainly punish
them if they failed to do so.

The word that came to Jeremiah from the Lord: Stand in the gate of the Lord's house, and proclaim there this word, and say, Hear the word of the Lord, all you people of Judah, you that enter these gates to worship the Lord. Thus says the Lord of hosts, the God of Israel: Amend your ways and your doings, and let me dwell with you in this place. Do not trust in these deceptive words: "This is the Temple of the Lord, the Temple of the Lord, the Temple of the Lord."

As the First Testament Prophets constantly remind us, God never rejects justice for lack of worship, but often rejects worship for lack of justice. You can't go to church regularly, put in your tithe, pray before meals, then spend the rest of your time being a jerk and expect God to overlook that. If the church is used as a place where worship is substituted for justice, God will, indeed, abandon that church. As Jeremiah predicted, that is just what happened.

Jeremiah continues:

For if you truly amend your ways and your doings, if you truly act justly one with another, if you do not oppress the alien, the orphan, and the widow, or shed innocent blood in this place, and if you do not go after other gods to your own hurt, then I will dwell with you in this place, in the land that I gave of old to your ancestors for ever and ever. Has this house, which is called by my name, become a den of robbers in your sight?

And there's our phrase, "den of robbers."

If you think about it a minute, you'll realize that a den of robbers isn't a place where robbers rob. It's a place where robbers hide **after** the robbery. It's a sanctuary for robbers. The problem wasn't with people selling pigeons and exchanging money in the Court of the Gentiles. That was a necessary part of the worship form. You couldn't offer Roman coins in the Temple — they bore an image on the Emperor, and the second commandment forbids graven images. You had to be able to buy animals for sacrifice, because otherwise how would pilgrims and city-dwellers come by an animal for sacrifice? Jesus prevented anyone from carrying anything through the Court of the Gentiles. Surely carrying something in the least holy part of the Temple complex isn't a problem. None of these things happening in the Court of the Gentiles was the problem. The problem was that the Temple had become a part of the Roman system and the Roman system was all about making the rich richer at the expense of the poor and helpless. This system was robbing the people, then hiding in the Temple. Jesus didn't cleanse it. He destroyed it. He ran off those who were necessary to its operation, thereby symbolically shutting it down, just as Jeremiah had said He would, for God cannot live in an unjust house.

Now the framing story of the fig tree makes sense. The next day, the disciples find it withered to the root. Mark wants us to understand clearly that the fig tree is the Temple, and Jesus has destroyed it.

On Sunday, the entrance into Jerusalem said to the Roman authorities, "You have no power and no legitimacy." This demonstration on Monday said to the Temple, "The threat issued by Jeremiah has come to pass, and I have shut it down for your failure to act justly."

Jesus' actions aren't about cleansing the Temple by removing commercial transactions from the Court of the Gentiles. They are about turning the house of God into a refuge in which one hides from one's own sins. You cannot escape confession that you are a sinner and have fallen short of the grace of God by running to the church house and crying "The Temple of the Lord! The Temple of the Lord!" And you can't drag the Temple of the Lord into your secular enterprise without staining it with your own sin.

To those who cry out that the United States is a Christian nation, I would ask, "Does this country truly act with the love of God toward those who need? Does this country love her enemies? Do we make our rain to fall upon the just and the unjust alike?"

God requires of us to act justly toward one another. God forbids that we should act unjustly, then use His Temple as a sanctuary from our sins, a den of robbers. The question I want you to take is this: Are we, as a country, acting justly?

Tuesday

"The Word of God comes only to the human heart — never to groups or governments. Those who have heard the Word may join together for God's purposes, but we must always be on guard not to mistake the good of the group for the Word of God."

Deuteronomy 6:4-10

Hear, O Israel: The Lord is our God, the Lord alone. You shall love the Lord your God with all your heart, and with all your soul, and with all your might. Keep these words that I am commanding you today in your heart. Recite them to your children and talk about them when you are at home and when you are away, when you lie down and when you rise. Bind them as a sign on your hand, fix them as an emblem on your forehead, and write them on the door posts of your house and on your gates.

Mark 12:28-34

One of the scribes came near and heard them disputing with one another, and seeing that he answered them well, he asked him, 'Which commandment is the first of all?' Jesus answered, 'The first is, "Hear, O Israel: the Lord our God, the Lord is one; you shall love the Lord your God with all your heart, and with all your soul, and with all your mind, and with all your strength." The second is this, "You shall love your neighbor as yourself." There is no other commandment greater than these.' Then the scribe said to him, 'You are right, Teacher; you have truly said that "he is one, and besides him there is no other"; and "to love him with all the heart, and with all the understanding, and with all the strength," and "to love one's neighbor as oneself,"—this is much more important than all whole burnt-offerings and sacrifices.' When Jesus saw that he answered wisely, he said to him, 'You are not far from the kingdom of God.' After that no one dared to ask him any question.

Report from the Jerusalem Times, Tuesday, sometime in the spring around 30 A.D.

> A small group of religious radicals entered the Court of the Gentiles Monday, causing a near riot. The leader, believed to be a Galilean named Yeshua ben Yoseph, drove out a number of Temple-authorized vendors and bankers and caused minor damage by overturning vendors' seats and tables.
>
> Authorities believe that this is the same group behind a demonstration at the East gate which coincided with the Imperial Procession of the noble Pontius Pilate and the reinforcements to the Antonia Fort on Sunday.
>
> Authorities are treating it as a potential trouble-spot during the Passover, due to the presence of so many pilgrims in town and promise quick action to restore order within the City.

I keep going on about how the voice of God speaks only to the human heart, never to corporations or teams or governments. It is something I truly believe. The way laid out by Jesus is hard and scary and potentially deadly. We're only human, and when faced with something as challenging as the teachings of Jesus, it's just like us to try and find a way to tell ourselves that we're doing good without actually undertaking the hard work Jesus demands. We make groups, then become good team players and hope that staying within the rules of the group will be good enough. It's not, of course, but that's our hope.

To show you how that works, I will tell you the story of a charity called "Doing Good Inc." The charity's purpose was to locate needs in the community and meet them. Doing Good Inc. would feed the hungry, clothe the naked, cure the sick. It will only do good things.

At the first meeting the founders realized that they needed a phone so that people with needs could call them. The phone would need to sit on something, so they needed a desk, and the desk needed to be somewhere. What they needed was an office. For that, they needed some money. As they polled the community for funding for the office, one of them remembered that his brother-in-law worked for Acme Chemicals.

Acme was something of an embarrassment locally because it billed itself as "Improving life through chemicals" but they really made mustard gas for sale to third world dictators. They employed a lot of people though, so the community looked the other way. What are you going to do? Throw all those good people out of work? Acme was excited to join with them and provided a lot of money and banners and handouts, all of which carried the phrase, "Provided for the good of the world by Acme."

At a board meeting, Father Flannigan, one of the founders, brought up the point that Acme, though the biggest, and truthfully, only, donor had goals inconsistent with the purpose of Doing Good Inc. to do only good. Father Flannigan pointed out that Acme's mustard gas caused thousands of casualties world wide, and that that is not "doing good" by anyone's measure.

Fortunately, cooler heads prevailed and it was noted that a position on the board is to be used to find ways to succeed, not ways to fail. Furthermore, however lamentable the use other people put Acme gas products to, Acme had assured them that they were selling it as an air freshener. It was suggested that Father Flannigan didn't have the needs of the poor foremost in his priorities. He resigned, and the brother-in-law who initially thought of Acme took his place on the board.

Over time, Doing Good Inc. became Acme's major charitable outreach, and it appeared prominently in Acme's advertising. The board itself, with its increased responsibilities resulting from the funds Acme provided, voted to compensate itself for its work and Acme agreed to underwrite the cost of the compensation. There was general celebration that Doing Good Inc. was now a great success and a large party was had with congratulatory speeches and a new slogan, "You're Doing Good when you're doing Doing Good!" The actual work of Doing Good Inc., the face-to-face dealing with the poor, was put in the hands of employees provided by Acme.

If we substitute the Temple for Doing Good Inc. and Rome for Acme Chemical, we have a pretty good idea of the situation in 30 A.D. To exist in an occupied land, the Temple had compromised with Rome, but Rome's objectives were inconsistent with the objectives of the Temple. The problem here is that politics is the art of compromise. God ... not so much into compromise. Forgiveness can be had. Compromise cannot. Jesus crashed the party and kicked the leg out from under the buffet table.

I really want to press you on this. It's absolutely critical to understanding our lives as Christians. On Sunday, Jesus staged a counter-procession into

Jerusalem, fulfilling the prophesy of Zechariah that the true power, God the king, would arrive, humble and seated on a colt. On Monday, Jesus symbolically shut down the Temple by running off the people necessary to its operation in fulfillment of the prophesy of Jeremiah that this would happen if the Temple substituted worship for justice. On Tuesday, today, we see the reaction of the authorities.

Notice that I said "the authorities," not "the Jews." Mark is crystal clear throughout that the people are with Jesus.

> [18]And when the chief priests and the scribes heard it, they kept looking for a way to kill him; for they were afraid of him, because the whole crowd was spellbound by his teaching.

> [32]they [the chief priests, the scribes, and the elders] were afraid of the crowd, for all regarded John as truly a prophet.

> [12] When they realized that he had told this parable against them, they wanted to arrest him, but they feared the crowd. So they left him and went away.

> [37] ... And the large crowd was listening to him with delight.

It's those on the board of directors of Doing Good Inc. who are confronting Him, not the crowd of the Jews. It's the Board of Directors that has the sweet deal.

Trying to report on everything that happened to Jesus on Tuesday would take a lot of sermons. Mark dedicates nearly three chapters to it. As I was going through those three chapters, one exchange jumped out at me.

> As he was walking in the temple, the chief priests, the scribes, and the elders came to him and said, "By what authority are you doing these things? Who gave you this authority to do them?"

There's real irony here. In the first verse of his Gospel, Mark tells us, "The beginning of the good news of Jesus Christ, the Son of God." Mark knows that Jesus is the Son of God. We, his readers, know that Jesus is the Son of God, but the chief priests, the scribes and the elders, the board of directors of Doing Good Inc. don't recognize him. I immediately thought of the opening to John's Gospel.

He was in the world, and the world came into being through him; yet the world did not know him. He came to what was his own, and his own people did not accept him.

The irony of the question is amusing, but the drama is deadly. The priests, scribes and elders want to know what grant of authority Jesus has from the Romans or Temple, the only source of power they know. The Temple authorities, who are there to lead the people in God's ways, have, over the course of the past century, become functionaries of the Roman Empire. They are political appointees, beholden to Rome for their position and their income. For them, being righteous is being a good team player – someone who works for the good of the Temple and the Empire. For them, doing good is doing Doing Good. Jesus is urging an entirely different view, and it's threatening. Jesus, on Sunday, told anyone willing to listen that true power lies only with God. On Monday, Judgment Day arrived for the Temple. Jesus convicted the Temple for its failures to proclaim God's word uncompromisingly and its failure to act justly and He shut it down.

Everybody wake up now! This is the thing I want you to remember, if you forget every thing else I said. In the view of the Temple authorities, and in our view as well, if we want to be honest about it, sin is often understood as stepping out of bounds of the systems in which we live, <u>but the systems themselves remain beyond question</u>. That is a truly wicked idea. Sin is not merely about how we individually hurt ourselves and others, but also about how our institutions, societies, churches, families and communities can also become corrupted and hurtful. We want to equate being a good American with being a good Christian, or being a good Republican with being a good Christian. Or being a good Democrat, or a good PTA member. We want to measure ourselves against a human standard of behavior which values above all, the good team player.

Sin has nothing whatsoever to do with being a bad team player. Jesus was quite a bad team player. Being aware of sin is being aware that every last thing we do is going to be composed of mixed motivations, pride and compromise because we are composed of mixed motivations, pride and compromise. Sin has very little to do with bad things people do. Bad things people do are the **result** of sin, not its definition. Sin is that quality of being human which causes us always to fall short of the Grace of God.

Over and over again, we define doing good as doing Doing Good because that's easier and more agreeable than doing what Jesus is doing — insisting that God's people act in God's way. When the systems in which we live are contrary to God's way, then we, as Christians, **must** rise up against them and that means doing what Jesus did and kicking the leg out from under the buffet table if the table is laden with unjust riches. It is not enough for us, as Christians, to comfort the afflicted. We must also afflict the comfortable when those within the system allow themselves to be led into acting unjustly.

I saw something this week that truly shocked me. I picked up my taxes from my tax guy, who I know to be a thoroughly nice man — someone you'd be pleased to spend time with. But he works within a system — one of the big tax preparer companies — and they have a business plan that includes refund anticipation loans. That always seemed a little goofy to me, since you're going to get your money pretty quickly anyway, but this is part of their plan, and for the poor, money now may be the difference between eating now or not. The thing that shocked me, though, was the fine print — the APR for these loans is nearly 125%. Nicest guy in the world. Good family man. ONE HUNDRED TWENTY FIVE PERCENT INTEREST!?!?

Can he change that? No. Was it his idea? No. But he lives within a system that measures righteousness by the bottom line on an accounting sheet. The Temple authorities and the population of occupied Palestine lived within a system that measured righteousness by Roman standards of a peaceful, orderly, profitable Roman province. Realizing this is what made that question by the Temple authorities to Jesus, "By what grant of authority do you do these things?" jump out at me. These were probably nice guys and good family men, too. There's nothing to suggest that they were villains. These people served God, but served Him from within a system that did not recognize God's authority so that the Temple came to be all about worship and nothing to do with justice. No matter how much money it makes for the big tax preparer company, charging poor people 125% interest isn't just.

Pretty gloomy, huh? Every system devised by human hands winds up taking ownership of our souls and bending them to the will of the system, substituting the goals of the group for the will of God. What's a poor Christian to do?

That's the question the scribe asks Jesus in today's passage, "Which commandment is the first of all?"

Jesus answered, "The first is, 'Hear, O Israel: the Lord our God, the Lord is one; you shall love the Lord your God with all your heart, and with all your soul, and with all your mind, and with all your strength.'"

Jesus is quoting the S'hma, the prayer recited morning and night by Jews then and now. We Christians want to read it as a commandment – LOVE GOD OR ELSE. But can you, by an act of your will, force yourself to love something? Of course you can't, yet God loves you, even though you don't love God with all your soul and with all your mind, and with all your strength.

In contrast, the Talmud understands these words to be a promise, not a command. You WILL love the Lord your God when you remind yourself, morning and night, that it is by the love of God that you are sustained, even in the face of your inability to reciprocate. You WILL act in gratitude once you remind yourself that God is one, the only power, and that it is God who sustains you.

Jesus isn't done. He turns to Leviticus 19:18 and quotes, "The second is this, 'You shall love your neighbor as yourself.' There is no other commandment greater than these." If God loves us even though we can't reciprocate, the least we can do is love our neighbors, even those who call us enemy, and we can love ourselves, even though we are flawed and fall short of the Grace of God. If God sees something lovable in both us and our neighbor, who are we to disagree?

Then the scribe said to him, "You are right, Teacher; you have truly said that 'he is one, and besides him there is no other'; and 'to love him with all the heart, and with all the understanding, and with all the strength,' and 'to love one's neighbor as oneself,' — this is much more important than all whole burnt-offerings and sacrifices." When Jesus saw that he answered wisely, he said to him, "You are not far from the kingdom of God."

Go ye and do likewise, church.

"We are tribal people and unless we confess that, we will become lost in our own tribe to such an extent that we can no longer hear the Word of God."

Romans 12:1-3

I beseech you therefore, brethren, by the mercies of God, that ye present your bodies a living sacrifice, holy, acceptable unto God, which is your reasonable service.

And be not conformed to this world: but be ye transformed by the renewing of your mind, that ye may prove what is that good, and acceptable, and perfect, will of God.

For I say, through the grace given unto me, to every man that is among you, not to think of himself more highly than he ought to think; but to think soberly, according as God hath dealt to every man the measure of faith.

Mark 14:1-11

It was two days before the Passover and the festival of Unleavened Bread. The chief priests and the scribes were looking for a way to arrest Jesus by stealth and kill him; for they said, 'Not during the festival, or there may be a riot among the people.'

While he was at Bethany in the house of Simon the leper, as he sat at the table, a woman came with an alabaster jar of very costly ointment of nard, and she broke open the jar and poured the ointment on his head. But some were there who said to one another in anger, 'Why was the ointment wasted in this way? For this ointment could have been sold for more than three hundred denarii, and the money given to the poor.' And they scolded her. But Jesus said, 'Let her alone; why do you trouble her? She has performed a good service for me. For you always have the poor with you, and you can show kindness to them whenever you wish; but you will not always have me. She has done what she could; she has anointed my body beforehand for its burial. Truly I tell you, wherever the good news is proclaimed in the whole world, what she has done will be told in remembrance of her.'

Then Judas Iscariot, who was one of the twelve, went to the chief priests in order to betray him to them. When they heard it, they were greatly pleased, and promised to give him money. So he began to look for an opportunity to betray him.

The Jerusalem Times, Wednesday, sometime around the year 30 A.D.

> Temple Authorities continue to be close-lipped about their investigation into the Galilean group believed to be behind a demonstration on Sunday and a serious disturbance in the Court of the Gentiles on Monday. When asked about the status of the investigation as the Passover rapidly approaches, High Priest Caiaphas would say only, "We are continuing to pursue all available investigative leads. It is imperative that God's City and God's Temple be protected from disturbance particularly at this time of the year."

We are Christians, but we are also tribal people. We belong to the Greenup Tribe or the Boyd Tribe and the American Tribe. During Lent, we have talked quite a lot about the human desire to find compromise between our tribal loyalties and the Word of God. Today we'll see just how pernicious that desire can be. On Palm Sunday, Jesus confronted Rome. On Monday, he convicted the Temple. On Tuesday, he brought His message directly to the chief priests, the scribes and the elders, and they did not like it. On Wednesday, the treachery begins.

When I say "the treachery," I don't mean just the betrayal by Judas, although that is bad enough. I mean the stubborn, insidious, baneful and deadly drive we all have to re-interpret God's word into something less threatening, less disruptive of our tribal loyalties, less personally involving of ourselves.

Mark's story of Jesus' journey to Jerusalem starts in Caesaria Philippi. On this long journey, Jesus instructs His Disciples on what is to occur and tries to prepare them for their participation in the events. That turns out to be as hard then as it is now, and that is the reason we view Lent as a penitential season. We want to avoid the horrible events of Good Friday, and we particularly want, just as did the Disciples, to avoid the suggestion that as a follower of Jesus, we have a personal and participatory role to play. The story of the Disciples' failure to understand and participate in Jesus' death and Resurrection is our story as well. We would much prefer to avoid the implications of Jesus' teaching. We'd be happier if Lent was about internal change, and nothing about changes to our external life that might be noticed by others and open us to criticism, ridicule or worse. We would like, in short, to approach the Gospel of Jesus in the same way I approach dieting — by changing my internal view of food to a healthier one while still being able to eat an entire pie.

It was our tendency to favor a faith free of sacrifice, risk and personal commitment that Archbishop Timothy Dolan spoke about when he said:

> "Maybe the greatest threat to the Church is not heresy, not dissent, not secularism, not even moral relativism, but this sanitized, feel-good, boutique, therapeutic spirituality, that makes no demands, calls for no sacrifice, asks for no conversion, entails no battle against sin, but only soothes and affirms."

This is precisely the approach taken by the Disciples as well — internal change to ourselves is praise-worthy. Involving ourselves in the external world, confronting its injustices is suicide. Yet, look at how carefully Jesus laid out their itinerary.

> Then he began to teach them that the Son of Man must undergo great suffering, and be rejected by the elders, the chief priests, and the scribes, and be killed, and after three days rise again. He said all this quite openly. And Peter took him aside and began to rebuke him.
>
> **Mark 8:31-32**

> ... for he was teaching his disciples, saying to them, "The Son of Man is to be betrayed into human hands, and they will kill him, and three days after being killed, he will rise again."

> Then they came to Capernaum; and when he was in the house he asked them, "What were you arguing about on the way?" But they were silent, for on the way they had argued with one another about who was the greatest.
>
> **Mark 9:31-34**

"See, we are going up to Jerusalem, and the Son of Man will be handed over to the chief priests and the scribes, and they will condemn him to death; then they will hand him over to the Gentiles; they will mock him, and spit upon him, and flog him, and kill him; and after three days he will rise again."

Mark 10:33-34

James and John, the sons of Zebedee, came forward to him and said to him, "Teacher, we want you to do for us whatever we ask of you." And he said to them, "What is it you want me to do for you?" And they said to him, "Grant us to sit, one at your right hand and one at your left, in your glory."

Mark 10:35-37

Just in case we haven't been paying attention, Mark even places the story of the restoration of sight to blind barTimaeus right after that last exchange as if to say, "They are blind, these disciples." I would add, "And so are we." We would like to compromise with Jesus' clear journey toward death and Resurrection and turn it into something much less personal and participatory, only to be met with the words of Jesus, "If any want to become my followers, let them deny themselves and take up their cross and follow me."

The story of Wednesday is the story of failed discipleship. Jesus tells his disciples that he will be killed in Jerusalem, and Peter rebukes him. A second time Jesus tells them that he will be killed and rise again, and the disciples go off and get into an argument with one another about who is the greatest disciple. A third time, Jesus tries to focus them on the job at hand, and is met by a request from James and John to seat them in places of honor in what they imagine to be a coming temporal kingdom.

It is only this unnamed woman, a person I would call "the First Christian" who truly hears what Jesus is saying and responds to it with appropriateness and even exuberance. While the inner group of the Disciples are avoiding the question or involving themselves in loony speculation about who sits where and who is the greatest, the First Christian anoints Jesus for burial because burial is where they have been headed since they left Caesaria Philippi.

This is the part of the Gospel that we fail Jesus in every day of our lives, just as the disciples did. We imagine that the Gospel of Jesus Christ is about being decent, inoffensive people. If the Gospel of Jesus Christ were about being in-offensive, Paul wouldn't have had to preach about not being ashamed of the Gospel. The Gospel IS offensive. This cross is offensive. We should be offend-ed by it, and any attempt to change it into Easter Bunnies and jelly beans is an attempt to do just what the disciples are doing — denying and rebuking Jesus for being offensive. There is only one way to the Resurrection and that is through the cross, and there is only one way to the cross, and that is the way that Jesus is demonstrating to us — the way of confrontation of injustice in ourselves, our relationships, our cultures and our communities, firmly but non-violently.

It is this that Paul speaks about when he says

> I beseech you therefore, brethren, by the mercies of God, that ye present your bodies a living sacrifice, holy, acceptable unto God, which is your reasonable service.

> And be not conformed to this world: but be ye transformed by the re-newing of your mind, that ye may prove what is that good, and accept-able, and perfect, will of God.

We've seen that every group we invent, every tribe we involve ourselves in, in-evitably is found to be composed of mixed motivations, pride and compro-mise because we are composed of mixed motivations, pride and compromise. When we confess the realities of sin in personal and common life each Sun-day, this is what we are talking about. There is a constant pushing match be-tween the world and the demands of the Gospel, each trying to conform the other to its plan. We are not to be conformed to the way of the world, howev-er comfortable that may be. Rather, we are to seek to conform the world to the Gospel standard, presenting our very bodies as a living sacrifice.

So, what is that Gospel standard? If I told you that Jesus' ministry was about restoring justice to the world, I believe a large number of you would hear me preaching that Jesus came to punish wrong-doers. For us, justice means pun-ishment. God's word of justice, however, as we heard it at the beginning of this sermon from the great First Testament prophets, speaks of rescuing the oppressed, defending the orphan, pleading for the widow. Our tribal under-standing of justice is quite different from God's demand for justice.

In my experience, our idea of justice has more to do with making our lives more comfortable by removing troubling people than it has to do with restoring troubled people to health. When we think of justice, we think of the bad guy getting caught. But God's idea of justice is one of restoration. When God speaks of justice, He speaks of restoring the community to a state of wholeness and healing by seeking justice, rescuing the oppressed, defending the orphan, and pleading for the widow. God's justice doesn't speak of excising people from the community, but of restoring them, new and whole, into the community. God's justice is about fixing what is wrong. Mere words and good intentions were not going to change that state of affairs. And so, Jesus goes willingly to his death in Jerusalem.

I said at the beginning that our drive to compromise God's way with our desire to see ourselves favorably and to protect what we see as our entitlements is pernicious. We want to live in a decent society, which we think would be one where the good guys are never troubled and the bad guys are locked up. Jesus' way was not a decent way. It was scandalous. Jesus actually became a criminal. Jesus intended to allow the Roman and Temple authorities to do just what groups like that always do — act violently to protect the status quo and their own tribal existence. Jesus was going to put them on trial in front of the population and history and show them for just what they are and then, when the sin that is in personal and common life had expended its violence upon him, broken and destroyed him, drained the very life from him, Jesus' way was to show that however bad we can be, God's grace is sufficient. Jesus would rise from the grave.

Jesus was more than a prophet, but prophet he also was. The way taught by Jesus was revolutionary and prophetic. In the three hundred years between his Resurrection and Constantine's declaration that Christianity was the state religion of Rome, it persisted as revolutionary and prophetic. Then, it became something different. As a state religion, it became protective of our tribal ways and that is the world in which we live now. In that sort of a world, we dearly want to substitute worship for justice. The word of God, in the person of Jesus of Nazareth, urges us to resist that temptation.

Our way now is the same as Jesus' was then. You, as Christians, are charged to remember that the Word of God comes only to the human heart, and never to governments, clubs, groups or tribes, however well-intentioned. You, as Christians, are charged with the responsibility of challenging sin in personal and common life, presenting your bodies a living sacrifice, holy, acceptable unto

God.

Go ye and do likewise, church.

J. STEWART SCHNEIDER

Thursday

"The notion that "Jesus did it all"
leads us to a passive, self-congratulatory Christianity
which makes no demands, calls for no sacrifice, asks for
no conversion, entails no battle against sin, but only
soothes and affirms."

Exodus 12:1-14

The Lord said to Moses and Aaron in the land of Egypt: This month shall mark for you the beginning of months; it shall be the first month of the year for you. Tell the whole congregation of Israel that on the tenth of this month they are to take a lamb for each family, a lamb for each household. If a household is too small for a whole lamb, it shall join its closest neighbor in obtaining one; the lamb shall be divided in proportion to the number of people who eat of it. Your lamb shall be without blemish, a year-old male; you may take it from the sheep or from the goats. You shall keep it until the fourteenth day of this month; then the whole assembled congregation of Israel shall slaughter it at twilight. They shall take some of the blood and put it on the two doorposts and the lintel of the houses in which they eat it. They shall eat the lamb that same night; they shall eat it roasted over the fire with unleavened bread and bitter herbs. Do not eat any of it raw or boiled in water, but roasted over the fire, with its head, legs, and inner organs. You shall let none of it remain until the morning; anything that remains until the morning you shall burn. This is how you shall eat it: your loins girded, your sandals on your feet, and your staff in your hand; and you shall eat it hurriedly. It is the passover of the Lord. For I will pass through the land of Egypt that night, and I will strike down every firstborn in the land of Egypt, both human beings and animals; on all the gods of Egypt I will execute judgments: I am the Lord. The blood shall be a sign for you on the houses where you live: when I see the blood, I will pass over you, and no plague shall destroy you when I strike the land of Egypt.

This day shall be a day of remembrance for you. You shall celebrate it as a festival to the Lord; throughout your generations you shall observe it as a perpetual ordinance.

Mark 14:12-25

On the first day of Unleavened Bread, when the Passover lamb is sacrificed, his disciples said to him, 'Where do you want us to go and make the preparations for you to eat the Passover?' So he sent two of his disciples, saying to them, 'Go into the city, and a man carrying a jar of water will meet you; follow him, and wherever he enters, say to the owner of the house, "The Teacher asks, Where is my guest room where I may eat the Passover with my disciples?" He will show you a large room upstairs, furnished and ready. Make preparations for us there.' So the disciples set out and went to the city, and found everything as he had told them; and they prepared the Passover meal.

When it was evening, he came with the twelve. And when they had taken their places and were eating, Jesus said, 'Truly I tell you, one of you will betray me, one who is eating with me.' They began to be distressed and to say to him one after another, 'Surely, not I?' He said to them, 'It is one of the twelve, one who is dipping bread into the bowl with me. For the Son of Man goes as it is written of him, but woe to that one by whom the Son of Man is betrayed! It would have been better for that one not to have been born.'

While they were eating, he took a loaf of bread, and after blessing it he broke it, gave it to them, and said, 'Take; this is my body.' Then he took a cup, and after giving thanks he gave it to them, and all of them drank from it. He said to them, 'This is my blood of the covenant, which is poured out for many. Truly I tell you, I will never again drink of the fruit of the vine until that day when I drink it new in the kingdom of God.'

Follow-up report from the Jerusalem Times, Thursday, sometime in the spring around 30 A.D.

The office of High Priest Caiaphas continues to refuse to comment on the investigation into the activities of the Galilean group suspected to be behind the disturbances this week at the East gate and in the Court of the Gentiles. Sources near the Temple, however, speaking on condition of anonymity, hint that a break in the case may be imminent.

It is Maundy Thursday. The cards are laid. The hand is played. Judas has covertly gone to the Temple authorities and agreed to hand over Jesus in a place where there will not be a riot when he is taken. The matter is delicate. The crowds who have heard the message of Jesus are "spellbound" in the words of the Temple authorities. Any attempt to arrest him in public will cause even more disorder. The plans laid in secret must be played out in secret. Now, as evening falls and the twelve sit down with Jesus to the *Seder*, the shadow of the cross rises silently beyond the walls of the upper room.

Why do you think this meal was so important that we remember it still, two thousand years later? Jesus went to a lot of trouble to make sure that He could share this meal with his disciples. Jesus knew that he was betrayed, but it is absolutely critical that no one be allowed to interrupt this time with his disciples so His preparations involve a lot of secret stuff. He sends two disciples to find the room where they will eat the meal, so that any enemy following would not know which disciple to follow. He entrusts them with a secret sign: they are to search for a man carrying water and follow him. What is to happen in that room is that important.

In the Gospels of Matthew, Mark and Luke the last supper is described as a *Seder*, the meal God declared as a day of remembrance to the Israelites.

> You shall celebrate it as a festival to the Lord; throughout your generations you shall observe it as a perpetual ordinance.

What is being remembered is the salvation of the Israelites from oppression by Pharaoh. Just as their ancestors were freed from slavery, Jesus is inviting His disciples to join him in a new Exodus in which they will be freed from slavery to the oppression systems of their time − the ways of darkness − and introduced to a life directed by obedience to God − the way of light. Jesus is actually inviting the disciples to participate with him in His journey through death to Resurrection.

All through our discussion of Holy Week we have emphasized that Christianity anticipates an individual's participation even when the demands of Christ run counter to every other thing in the culture. The notion that "Jesus did it all" leads us to a passive, self-congratulatory Christianity which makes no demands, calls for no sacrifice, asks for no conversion, entails no battle against sin, but only soothes and affirms.[17]

---

17 Archbishop Timothy Dolan

Individual participation is critical because it is only the human heart which can be touched by the death of Jesus. We've talked a lot the past three Sundays about the Word of God speaking always in protest to culture. We are tribal people, and the tribes we create, because they come from our hands, are tainted with our sinfulness and inevitably come to dominate us. If you doubt that, ask yourself why college ball, begun with the purest of intentions to teach young men and women sportsmanship and discipline, so often suffers recruiting scandals. People do loony things "for the good of the team" that we'd be unable to explain otherwise.

Because doing what Jesus demands — loving the Lord with all your heart, soul, mind and strength and your neighbor as yourself — is hard, but doing what everybody else is doing is easy, we come to believe that acting for the good of the group is the highest good we can do. Our way of doing things — our tribe, if you will — must be protected at all costs:

> So the chief priests and the Pharisees called a meeting of the council, and said, 'What are we to do? This man is performing many signs. If we let him go on like this, everyone will believe in him, and the Romans will come and destroy both our holy place and our nation.'

We lose sight of the harm to God's children such a focus inevitably causes and to protect the group, we say

> But one of them, Caiaphas, who was high priest that year, said to them, 'You know nothing at all! You do not understand that it is better for you to have one man die for the people than to have the whole nation destroyed.'

I described this idea, that the good of the group is the highest good for all, as pernicious, and that it is. It enslaves us by dividing us into "us" and "them," then shortens our view to only "us," preventing us from seeing "them" and their relationship to God. How are we to love our neighbor as our selves if we see our neighbors always as the enemy? Dividing the world up into "us" and "them" is the way civilization works, but in this last meal, Jesus is going to demonstrate to the disciples that they are a community set apart, for the good of "us" AND "them," and that they are saved from the oppression of the domination groups that make up our civilization.

It would be hard to overstate the importance of this shared meal but if we would walk in the steps of the disciples, we have to enter the meaning of that meal just as they did, with their understanding of what was happening.

One of my students asked me once when Jesus became a Christian. His question reveals just how important to us it is to decide who is "in" and who is "out." He needed to hear that Jesus was a Christian, and hence one of us. He was very disappointed to learn that Jesus lived and died a Jew. The need to separate us from them even affects our churches. Jesus includes in this last shared meal those who will abandon him as well as the one who will betray him.

Jesus and His disciples would approach this last meal as Jews, with Jewish understanding rooted in the account from Exodus. There is no other event in Jewish history so foundational to the Jewish people than this, and these thoughts and associations would be in their minds throughout. Consequently, it is impossible to separate the accounts in Exodus of the institution of the Passover meal from the events of Maundy Thursday.

In the passage from Exodus for today, the Passover meal is laid out for the Israelites in detail. First, it is to be a shared meal just as the Last Supper is to be a meal shared by the entire community, even Judas.

> Tell the whole congregation of Israel that on the tenth of this month they are to take a lamb for each family, a lamb for each household. If a household is too small for a whole lamb, it shall join its closest neighbor in obtaining one; the lamb shall be divided in proportion to the number of people who eat of it. Your lamb shall be without blemish, a year-old male; you may take it from the sheep or from the goats. You shall keep it until the fourteenth day of this month; then the whole assembled congregation of Israel shall slaughter it at twilight.

With the blood of the lamb, they are to identify themselves as a community set apart just as Jesus is setting the disciples apart as the nucleus of the post-Easter community.

> They shall take some of the blood and put it on the two doorposts and the lintel of the houses in which they eat it.

They are to remind themselves of the bitterness of the slavery in Egypt from which God is about to free them.

They shall eat the lamb that same night; they shall eat it roasted over the fire with unleavened bread and bitter herbs.

The meal is to be eaten hurriedly, in anticipation of the salvation of God from their slavery.

This is how you shall eat it: your loins girded, your sandals on your feet, and your staff in your hand; and you shall eat it hurriedly. It is the Passover of the Lord.

We think about the loaf and cup. This is the meal they ate, lamb and unleavened bread and bitter herbs and salt water, their sandals on their feet and their staffs in their hands. The key to understanding the importance of this last meal lies in the concepts of shared meal and community set apart. To be a Christian is to declare yourself part of a community set apart, and obedient to the will of God. To declare yourself a Christian is to participate in the death and Resurrection of Christ.

What does that mean, that Christianity is participatory? It means that following Christ is not a spectator sport. It is active, not passive. We go to church on Sunday to hear the Word proclaimed, to sing praises to God for his Grace, to learn the teachings of the church, but we ACT as Christians when we leave here to confront the reality of sin in personal and common life. We are fed as a community, but, inevitably, we act individually.

When Jesus gathered His disciples in that upper room, all twelve, including Judas, He was gathering His community about him, re-enacting the Exodus story, identifying them as a community apart and granting a new meaning to the shared meal so that after the terror of Good Friday, they would be equipped to act as Christians in the post-Easter world in which they would find themselves. He was calling them to participate with him in his death and Resurrection. Look at the verbs Mark uses:

While they were eating, he took a loaf of bread, and after blessing it he broke it, gave it to them, and said, "Take; this is my body." Then he took a cup, and after giving thanks he gave it to them, and all of them drank from it. He said to them, "This is my blood of the covenant, which is poured out for many."

He took. He blessed. He broke. He gave. He is inviting them into his experience. He still does. When we share Communion, we participate with Christ in

His death and Resurrection.

Of course, **we** know that before they set out on their post-Easter missions, they all ran and hid. It was Jesus alone who faced Pilate. And this is the other big piece we have talked about: The church strengthens, and teaches, blesses and sustains, but it is the individual Christian who acts. With few exceptions, the Disciples, after the Resurrection, embarked upon individual ministries and, with the exception of John, suffered individual martyrdom. Church tradition teaches that Andrew was crucified in Greece. Peter was crucified upside down in Rome. James the son of Zebedee was killed in Judea but his brother John apparently escaped. Phillip was martyred in Hierapolis either by beheading or by crucifixion upside down. Nathaniel was skinned alive and crucified in Armenia. Thomas was killed with a spear in India!

When you read a life of the saints and see all this violence, you have to admit that there are only two alternatives: these guys were crazy as bedbugs, or something had gotten into them that drove them to these extremes. That something is the Word of God. If you don't believe in the indwelling, uncompromising, empowering Spirit of God, then you have to see each of these men as crazy people, an embarrassment. Do you? If the answer is "No," then we are left with the Holy Spirit driving these men even to extremes of suffering horrible death. Where did this come from? I would say clearly from the Word of God indwelling in them, strengthened by their participation in a community set apart.

Can we still speak of Christians as a community set apart? I think unquestionably that we can, and must. As I look back over my long memory of churches in this area, from the '50s and '60s, when the church truly informed the culture, to the present, when the church has become a minority voice in the conversation that is our people, I think of Jesus on his long journey to Jerusalem. The crowds that attended to Him on his journey became the smaller crowd that welcomed him into the East gate on Palm Sunday, became the smaller crowd that followed him to convict the Temple, became the group of twelve who now meet with him for the *Seder* on Maundy Thursday. Even of this small group, one has already abandoned their fellowship, though he is still present. Soon, Peter will deny him. The remainder will scatter, and Jesus will stand before the Roman prefect alone.

Why is this, do you think? All of us here remember the crowds that filled our sanctuaries when we were younger. We remember fondly youth programs, and ice cream socials and large choirs, and when we look around our sanctuaries today at the empty pews, it hurts us to our hearts. Where did the crowds go? Has the church become irrelevant in our time, a quaint holdover from an earlier age?

You could hold that thought only if you also think that Jesus, standing alone before Pilate, was irrelevant. God acts most visibly when we are weakest. When the church informed the culture in our childhood and the pews were filled, the church actually became a secular force to be dealt with, and if you were in politics you knew you had better appeal to "the church vote" if you wanted to hold on to your job. Many of us earnestly yearn for a return to that state of being. I'm skeptical. Large churches and heavy influence minimize the need for each of us to respond to God's Word individually. When we lived in a time of plenty, it was easier to say, "The church will take care of it." But that which is everyone's job is no one's job. In the smaller church, we see our position as individuals and our individual responsibility to be Christ's disciples more clearly.

In Mark's Gospel, Jesus' ministry appears to extend only one year, but during that year, Jesus strengthened, taught and prepared His disciples for their task in the post-Easter world. It is that task that the church, the Bride of Christ, has undertaken in our time. The church strengthens, teaches and prepares us for our individual time of testing, our individual time to stand before Pilate. When we understand the church in that role, we can be strengthened. We can be taught. We can be prepared for the time of testing.

Lest you think that you can cruise through this life without coming to a time of testing, let me pose some questions to you. No matter how much you love UK ball, what if the athletic program were about to embark upon a recruiting violation and you knew about it? Would you stand up to protest? What if America, saying that it was protecting us, undertook to torture people. Would you then speak up? Could you speak up? What if America's demand for cheap goods insured that children in third world countries would have to labor to produce them. Would you buy?

It should be no surprise to learn that I think the church, the Bride of Christ, exists on earth not to seek secular power for itself, but to raise, train and empower the saints who will stand, alone, before Pilate at their time of trial. I believe this, church, because I believe that the Word of God speaks always in protest to tribal loyalties and that each Christian will, at some time or another, come to a time of testing when he or she must say to his or her culture, his or her tribe, "What you are doing is contrary to the Word of God and I cannot go with you."

It All Comes Down to an Empty Tomb

"The empty tomb, a thoroughly unhistorical event, is the thing that separates Christians from other worthy people."

John 20:1-18

Early on the first day of the week, while it was still dark, Mary Magdalene came to the tomb and saw that the stone had been removed from the tomb. So she ran and went to Simon Peter and the other disciple, the one whom Jesus loved, and said to them, "They have taken the Lord out of the tomb, and we do not know where they have laid him." Then Peter and the other disciple set out and went toward the tomb. The two were running together, but the other disciple outran Peter and reached the tomb first. He bent down to look in and saw the linen wrappings lying there, but he did not go in. Then Simon Peter came, following him, and went into the tomb. He saw the linen wrappings lying there, and the cloth that had been on Jesus' head, not lying with the linen wrappings but rolled up in a place by itself. Then the other disciple, who reached the tomb first, also went in, and he saw and believed; for as yet they did not understand the scripture, that he must rise from the dead. Then the disciples returned to their homes.

But Mary stood weeping outside the tomb. As she wept, she bent over to look into the tomb; and she saw two angels in white, sitting where the body of Jesus had been lying, one at the head and the other at the feet. They said to her, "Woman, why are you weeping?" She said to them, "They have taken away my Lord, and I do not know where they have laid him." When she had said this, she turned around and saw Jesus standing there, but she did not know that it was Jesus. Jesus said to her, "Woman, why are you weeping? Whom are you looking for?" Supposing him to be the gardener, she said to him, "Sir, if you have carried him away, tell me where you have laid him, and I will take him away." Jesus said to her, "Mary!" She turned and said to him in Hebrew, "Rabbouni!" (which means Teacher). Jesus said to her, "Do not hold on to me, because I have not yet ascended to the Father. But go to my brothers and say to them, `I am ascending to my Father and your Father, to my God and your

God.'" Mary Magdalene went and announced to the disciples, "I have seen the Lord"; and she told them that he had said these things to her.

What makes Christians so peculiar? Well, maybe "different" would be better, but what is it, exactly, that makes Christians unique? It's not just that we try to live moral, other-directed lives. We all know non-Christians who do that. Mahatma Gandhi comes to mind, or the Dalai Lama, a man who strikes me as most decent. It would be awfully flattering to think of Christians as the decent people and everybody else as indecent, but we all know that won't do.

So, what makes Christians special? Keep that question in the back of your mind while we take a walk in some detail through today's text. To keep you awake during such a thing, I'll start by making you mad. You just can't doze off if you're mad, so I'm going to provoke you right at the start.

The Resurrection of Jesus is not a historical event.

There! That should get you stoked up.

Now, let me tell you what I mean. The battle of Waterloo was a historical event. The assassination of President Lincoln was a historical event. The destruction of the Towers in New York, the war in Iraq, the American Revolution, the kidnapping and rescue of Elizabeth Smart – all historical events. A "historical event" is an event which you can reconstruct from the varying accounts of witnesses. There are records from which you can formulate theories about how this event or that happened and test those theories against the observable facts.

The Resurrection of Jesus of Nazareth, called the Christ, crucified upon order of Pontius Pilate, is not a historical event because we know nothing about how it happened. Jesus was the only witness we can name, and He didn't tell us anything about the event.

We know what happened before. We know what happened after, but the event itself is undocumented. There are no photographs, unless you accept the Shroud of Turin. Individuals can spin endless theories about how it happened, but there is no evidence to support one theory over another.

Since there were no witnesses to the actual event, from the very first there were attempts to explain away what happened after without recourse to the fairly preposterous idea of reanimation of a very dead man. His disciples came in and stole the body away, somehow getting around the Roman guards. He wasn't really a man. He was a spirit being who only appeared to die. It wasn't really Jesus on the cross, but a substitute. The theories were endless, and continue to this very day. In the end, there is no evidence whatsoever as to what happened. It all comes down to an empty tomb.

That makes the Resurrection of Jesus Christ a totally unique event in all of history. I cannot think of another undocumented event that has caused such a sweeping change in the story of man as has this one, very strange, event in this one, very small country.

It's not enough to just say "It's a miracle." Ancient literature is chock-a-block with miracle stories. Elijah is credited with raising the widow's son from the dead, for one example. The ancients knew so little about the natural world that they saw miracles everywhere. All those miracles put together did not cause a decimal place's difference in the history of the world, but this one did. That, alone, should put us on notice that we're dealing with something remarkable – something very different from the other miracle stories.

The problem for us is that we have heard this story every Resurrection Sunday for all our lives, and we know how it comes out, so, for us, it has all the drama of a favorite movie we've seen time and again. It did **not,** I'd like to point out, hit the people of the time that way. It was absurd. It was an enormous intervention into life as they knew it. It was an affront to their dignity, logic and understanding. It was a world tipping event. That's why John reveals it so slowly and carefully. Getting it all at once, as we do from our perspective two thousand years later is just too much.

The first witness to the Resurrection, Mary Magdalene, on seeing the stone rolled away, leaped to the obvious conclusion:

> They have taken the Lord out of the tomb, and we do not know where they have laid him.

Even though Jesus told his disciples what was going to happen, even unto telling them he would be raised from the dead, that's not the first explanation that's going to come to Mary's mind when she sees the stone rolled away. The first explanation that will occur to her is that someone has stolen Jesus' body. If you didn't know the story so well, that's what you would think, too. Since you do know the story so well, there's a tendency to say "Hallelujah! Lent is over! Christ is raised! Glory to God! Where you wanna eat?" Mary Magdalene and the other first witnesses don't know how the story ends. That's how I want you to hear this story today. I want you to take this last Lenten walk with these people at the same pace that they walked it. I want you to feel the dread of the tomb that Mary felt. When she saw the stone rolled away, she ran for it!

Mary runs for help without looking inside, undoubtedly scared to death about what she would find. In Judea, exposed bodies were often preyed upon by wild dogs. Someone having stolen Jesus' body might well be the best outcome she can imagine, and she doesn't dare think of what she might find in the tomb. She runs and tells Peter and the other disciple, and together they run back to the tomb. The other disciple gets there first, and, screwing up his courage, bends down and peers into the grave.

This is hard, church. This is a grave. This is a fresh grave. We can imagine the disciple, his face contorted with fear, looking in to see ... he doesn't know what he's going to see, but his imagination can provide sufficient disquieting possibilities. Jesus' body dismembered by dogs? The Romans have been in and desecrated the corpse? Some other horror? He sees only the linens. He doesn't dare go in. Is he, perhaps, holding his breath? Is the grave filled with the stench of death? There are the linens. Where is the body?

Next, Peter, all out of breath, does what Peter always does – he blunders right into the grave, and now, we can take in the entire scene. There are the linens that wrapped the body, but no body! No signs of violence. The cloth that covered Jesus' face is neatly wrapped up, in a place away from the linens. There has been no ravaging of the grave. Whatever has happened has been orderly, respectful. Fearfully, the other disciple enters the grave with Peter, sees, and understands that the tomb is empty.

John tells us that the two disciples then returned home because "for as yet they did not understand the Scripture, that he must rise from the dead." They still didn't know what had happened.

Mary lingered behind. I don't know where she got that courage. Something very, very frightening had happened in the graveyard. Her heart must have still been pounding, and now she was left alone in the graveyard, weeping, while the men went home to try to understand what had happened. She didn't just linger in the graveyard, though. She actually looked into the grave!

What was she expecting to see? Surely the two disciples had told her what they found, so she knew what was in there. What need forced her to see it through her own eyes? That is, for me, the most human of moments. It's all well and good to hear from an elderly preacher that Christ is raised, all mixed up with childhood memories of bunnies and baby ducks and colored eggs, but what we want, what we thirst and hunger for, is the evidence of our own senses. That's what Mary sought as well, and when she did ... she saw angels.

Mary has all the evidence there is to have at this point. She knows that Jesus was crucified. She knows that He was nailed to the cross. She knows that He was incontrovertibly dead when he was taken down from the cross, prepared for burial, and placed in the tomb. THIS tomb. This empty tomb.

Even so, Mary's still stuck on her original conclusion: Someone stole His body.

The angels ask, "Woman, why are you weeping?"

She answers, "They have taken away my Lord, and I do not know where they have laid him."

This first witness to the most remarkable undocumented event of history couldn't get it, even faced with angels. There are a lot of explanations that fit what came after that don't involve such a preposterous idea as the Resurrection. But evidence? It all comes down to an empty tomb.

Now we know what makes Christians peculiar. The door to the empty tomb is the very place where Christians meet the decent people of all other faiths, and those of no faith. It all comes down to that empty tomb.

You see, the non-Christian sees an empty tomb. The non-Christian interprets the empty tomb to mean that someone has taken the body. No mystery here. No reason to reach for any other explanation. The tomb is empty.

The Christian, like Mary, looks into the same empty tomb and sees angels. The Christian sees what the non-Christian, however decent, cannot. We see angels.

I know exactly what you're thinking. You're thinking, "I must not be a Christian. I never have seen an angel."

How in blazes would you know that? The writer of Hebrews reminds us not to forget to entertain strangers, for by so doing some people have entertained angels without knowing it. A Christian is one who looks into emptiness and sees it filled with the Word of God. A Christian is one who looks beyond the evidence of his senses for the presence of that which exceeds all he knows. In a very real way, when Mary looked into the tomb, and saw the angels, it was then that she became a Christian.

When all is said and done, it truly comes down to an empty tomb. What do you see?

Bookends

"Taking the Gospel of Jesus Christ and removing it from the here and now to some fantastic place in the sky, outside our day to day lives, is a tragedy."

Acts 2:1-21

When the day of Pentecost had come, the disciples were all together in one place. And suddenly from heaven there came a sound like the rush of a violent wind, and it filled the entire house where they were sitting. Divided tongues, as of fire, appeared among them, and a tongue rested on each of them. All of them were filled with the Holy Spirit and began to speak in other languages, as the Spirit gave them ability.

Now there were devout Jews from every nation under heaven living in Jerusalem. And at this sound the crowd gathered and was bewildered, because each one heard them speaking in the native language of each. Amazed and astonished, they asked, "Are not all these who are speaking Galileans? And how is it that we hear, each of us, in our own native language? Parthians, Medes, Elamites, and residents of Mesopotamia, Judea and Cappadocia, Pontus and Asia, Phrygia and Pamphylia, Egypt and the parts of Libya belonging to Cyrene, and visitors from Rome, both Jews and proselytes, Cretans and Arabs — in our own languages we hear them speaking about God's deeds of power." All were amazed and perplexed, saying to one another, "What does this mean?" But others sneered and said, "They are filled with new wine."

But Peter, standing with the eleven, raised his voice and addressed them, "Men of Judea and all who live in Jerusalem, let this be known to you, and listen to what I say. Indeed, these are not drunk, as you suppose, for it is only nine o'clock in the morning. No, this is what was spoken through the prophet Joel:

> *'In the last days it will be, God declares,*
> *that I will pour out my Spirit upon all flesh,*
> > *and your sons and your daughters shall prophesy,*
> *and your young men shall see visions,*

and your old men shall dream dreams.
Even upon my slaves, both men and women,
    in those days I will pour out my Spirit;
    and they shall prophesy.
And I will show portents in the heaven above
    and signs on the earth below, blood, and fire, and smoky mist.
The sun shall be turned to darkness
    and the moon to blood,
    before the coming of the Lord's great and glorious day.
Then everyone who calls on the name of the Lord shall be saved.'"

Numbers 11:24-30

Moses went out and told the people the words of the LORD; and he gathered seventy elders of the people, and placed them all around the tent. Then the LORD came down in the cloud and spoke to him, and took some of the spirit that was on him and put it on the seventy elders; and when the spirit rested upon them, they prophesied. But they did not do so again.

Two men remained in the camp, one named Eldad, and the other named Medad, and the spirit rested on them; they were among those registered, but they had not gone out to the tent, and so they prophesied in the camp. And a young man ran and told Moses, "Eldad and Medad are prophesying in the camp." And Joshua son of Nun, the assistant of Moses, one of his chosen men, said, "My lord Moses, stop them!" But Moses said to him, "Are you jealous for my sake? Would that all the LORD's people were prophets, and that the LORD would put his spirit on them!" And Moses and the elders of Israel returned to the camp.

John 7:37-39

On the last day of the festival, the great day, while Jesus was standing there, he cried out, "Let anyone who is thirsty come to me, and let the one who believes in me drink. As the scripture has said, 'Out of the believer's heart shall flow rivers of living water.'" Now he said this about the Spirit, which believers in him were to receive; for as yet there was no Spirit, because Jesus was not yet glorified.

I'm ashamed to say it, but when I look back on my time at First Presbyterian as a child, my memories are sort of … well … foggy, I guess you would say. We affirmed with the Creed every Sunday and I recited it with the congregation, but it was quite a long while before anyone bothered to explain to me why I believed in the Catholic church when we were Presbyterians, and the Holy Ghost thing totally creeped me out. As a kid, I did **not** like ghosts.

You see, the problem wasn't only that nobody was bothering to tell my brother and me what all this mysterious stuff was about. The more serious problem was that I don't think my mom and dad knew, either. This was the 1950s. Folks went to church because that's what folks did, and it would do you a world of good if you'd pay attention, as my grandmother used to say. My problem was that nobody was explaining to me what I ought to pay attention to, or what good it might do me.

I really don't mean to be critical of people now long dead. It was the understanding at the time, that churches sort of oozed good medicine, and if you sat in the church you'd soak it up, like a sink sponge. The Trinity, in particular, left me baffled. The Father-Son-Holy-Ghost was somewhere … up there … and didn't seem to have much to do with me, other than to spy on my every thought and action and make lists of what I did and thought, which were then passed on to Santa Claus. Really. I was that confused.

I also don't have any clear memories of the church acknowledging Lent in anything like the detail we did this year, or of Easter either, beyond wearing new clothes and being given a dyed chick, which became a dead dyed chicken within a week. Nothing about Pentecost, to my memory.

And I mourn this. Taking the Gospel of Jesus Christ and removing it from the here and now to some fantastic place in the sky, outside our day to day lives, is a tragedy. I don't want that to happen here.

That's why we went through Lent with so much detail, handling each and every element of the story, so that we would come to know the crown of thorns as a real thing that can hurt you; so we would see the bowl and pitcher and recall that Jesus washed the feet of the disciples with just such things; so that we could come face to face with the weight and the splinters and the full horror of the cross.

All through the Sundays of Easter, I have shown you that the stories of the new church aren't things that happened to people long dead in a place far away and a time turned to dust, but represent the path of all believers as they move from unschooled disciples to Apostles, ready to go about their Master's work. Now we come to the climax of that believer's journey in the time of Pentecost for Easter and Pentecost form bookends of our journey.

We celebrate Pentecost as the birthday of the church, and it is that, but it's an awful lot more. It's an integral part of Easter, to my mind. Resurrection Sunday and Pentecost are intimately connected. Easter is not complete until the gift of the Holy Spirit at Pentecost.

The synoptic Gospels, Matthew, Mark and Luke, describe the Last Supper as a Passover meal. John puts it the day before. Either way, the events of the Crucifixion and Resurrection were at the time of the Passover.

The Passover, of course, is the Jewish celebration of the delivery of the children of Israel from slavery in Egypt. The next Jewish observation is Shavu'ot. It falls 50 days after Pesach and is also called Pentecost. (Pentecost, of course, means "the fiftieth day.") When Luke tells us in our passage from the book of Acts that, "When the day of Pentecost had come," he is speaking of Shavu'ot. It is both a harvest festival, celebrating the first, early barley harvest, and a celebration of the giving of the Torah, the law of the Jews.

The Jews see the same intimate connection between Pesach and Shavu'ot, Passover and Pentecost, as I am urging us to see between Resurrection Sunday and Pentecost Sunday. To remind themselves of the connection Orthodox Jews "count the Omer" between Pesach and Shavu'ot. An Omer is a unit of measure, and they count each day, giving a blessing and saying, for instance, "Today is sixteen days, which is two weeks and two days of the Omer." Just as Pesach celebrates liberation from slavery, Shavu'ot celebrates the giving of God's law to them, and they are reminding themselves that their redemption from slavery was not complete until they received God's law.

The Jewish understanding is that the children of Israel, leaving the slavery of Egypt, were just a confused mass of people, following their leader, Moses. Not too different from the Lion's Club, but with livestock. They had no identity. They had no God calling. They were just a mob, out in the desert. And if you read the stories of their wandering, you can see what a mess they were. They rebelled, they complained, they had mutinies. They drove Moses, and God, half nuts. In Jewish understanding, it was the gift of Torah, God's law, that organized the people into a God-led people, a people with a purpose. For that reason, Pesach and Shavu'ot have to remain connected. The one without the other is unthinkable.

However, there still was something missing. Listen again to our passage from the Hebrew Scriptures.

Moses went out and told the people the words of the LORD; and he gathered seventy elders of the people, and placed them all around the tent. Then the LORD came down in the cloud and spoke to him, and took some of the spirit that was on him and put it on the seventy elders; and when the spirit rested upon them, they prophesied. But they did not do so again.

Later, when Joshua becomes alarmed that two men in the camp are prophesying, Moses answers him and says:

Would that all the LORD's people were prophets, and that the LORD would put his spirit on them!

Something is missing. Torah has been given. A covenant between God and his people has been made. Still, something is missing, something is yet to come. John, in his Gospel, tells us what:

"Let anyone who is thirsty come to me, and let the one who believes in me drink. As the scripture has said, 'Out of the believer's heart shall flow rivers of living water.'" Now he said this about the Spirit, which believers in him were to receive; for as yet there was no Spirit, because Jesus was not yet glorified.

What is missing is the indwelling Holy Spirit, and because Jesus was not yet glorified, there was no Spirit.

As a child at First Presbyterian, I understood my role as requiring me to sit quietly in the pew and listen to what Rev. Curry said from the pulpit, raised above the congregation on the chancel. In other words, I saw myself in just the way the children of Israel arrayed themselves behind Moses. Moses was God-led, and the people followed him because of that. That was, apparently,

185

good enough for them, and it was certainly good enough for me. I would have been horrified to hear anything about the Holy Ghost dwelling in me. As I said, I did <u>not</u> like ghosts, indwelling or otherwise.

If my childish understanding of my role as a Presbyterian had been accurate, how would we come to understand the story of Pentecost? Luke describes it in dramatic terms:

> When the day of Pentecost had come, the disciples were all together in one place. And suddenly from heaven there came a sound like the rush of a violent wind, and it filled the entire house where they were sitting. Divided tongues, as of fire, appeared among them, and a tongue rested on each of them. All of them were filled with the Holy Spirit and began to speak in other languages, as the Spirit gave them ability.

I wonder if mainline denominations shy away from words like spirit-filled or spirit-led because they feel uncomfortable with that drama? Have the more charismatic churches laid claim to these phrases so powerfully that we no longer are willing to claim them as our own? I hope not because Resurrection Sunday without Pentecost is as unthinkable as Pesach without Shavu'ot. They are bookends. Our redemption is not complete until we have received the Holy Spirit, and accepted God as the leader of our lives. Until then, we're just a mob, wandering in the wilderness. Our redemption is not complete until we receive the Holy Spirit, and that is what we celebrate on Pentecost.

Church, I want you to hear this. If you don't remember anything else I have told you during the Easter season, I want you to remember this: If you celebrate Resurrection Sunday as the day our Lord was resurrected, and Pentecost as the birthday of the church, and don't live out the connection between the two, accepting the gift of the Holy Spirit into your own lives as the completion of Jesus' sacrifice, you will wander in the wilderness until you do. You will be like the children of Israel following Moses, complaining, mutinying, griping, wandering. If you see your role as sitting in a pew while the minister delivers speeches from the chancel, rather than accepting the Holy Spirit, tongues of fire, great wind, drama and all, into your own heart, you will wander in the wilderness until you do.

Coupla Biscuits

"The question I would pose is this: in the 21st Century, is Christianity on the path of Babel or the path of Pentecost? Are we scattered or are we in communion one with the other? The answer I'd like to propose is this: We are precariously seated atop the Tower of Babel."

Genesis 11:1-9

Now the whole earth had one language and the same words. And as they migrated from the east, they came upon a plain in the land of Shinar and settled there. And they said to one another, "Come, let us make bricks, and burn them thoroughly." And they had brick for stone, and bitumen for mortar. Then they said, "Come, let us build ourselves a city, and a tower with its top in the heavens, and let us make a name for ourselves; otherwise we shall be scattered abroad upon the face of the whole earth." The LORD came down to see the city and the tower, which mortals had built. And the LORD said, "Look, they are one people, and they have all one language; and this is only the beginning of what they will do; nothing that they propose to do will now be impossible for them. Come, let us go down, and confuse their language there, so that they will not understand one another's speech." So the LORD scattered them abroad from there over the face of all the earth, and they left off building the city. Therefore it was called Babel, because there the LORD confused the language of all the earth; and from there the LORD scattered them abroad over the face of all the earth.

Acts 2:1-11

When the day of Pentecost had come, the disciples were all together in one place. And suddenly from heaven there came a sound like the rush of a violent wind, and it filled the entire house where they were sitting. Divided tongues, as of fire, appeared among them, and a tongue rested on each of them. All of them were filled with the Holy Spirit and began to speak in other languages, as the Spirit gave them ability.

Now there were devout Jews from every nation under heaven living in

Jerusalem. And at this sound the crowd gathered and was bewildered, because each one heard them speaking in the native language of each. Amazed and astonished, they asked, "Are not all these who are speaking Galileans? And how is it that we hear, each of us, in our own native language? Parthians, Medes, Elamites, and residents of Mesopotamia, Judea and Cappadocia, Pontus and Asia, Phrygia and Pamphylia, Egypt and the parts of Libya belonging to Cyrene, and visitors from Rome, both Jews and proselytes, Cretans and Arabs — in our own languages we hear them speaking about God's deeds of power." All were amazed and perplexed, saying to one another, "What does this mean?" But others sneered and said, "They are filled with new wine."

But Peter, standing with the eleven, raised his voice and addressed them, "Men of Judea and all who live in Jerusalem, let this be known to you, and listen to what I say. Indeed, these are not drunk, as you suppose, for it is only nine o'clock in the morning. No, this is what was spoken through the prophet Joel:

> *'In the last days it will be, God declares,*
> *that I will pour out my Spirit upon all flesh,*
> *and your sons and your daughters shall prophesy,*
> *and your young men shall see visions,*
> *and your old men shall dream dreams.*
> *Even upon my slaves, both men and women,*
> *in those days I will pour out my Spirit;*
> *and they shall prophesy.*
> *And I will show portents in the heaven above*
> *and signs on the earth below,*
> *blood, and fire, and smoky mist.*
> *The sun shall be turned to darkness*
> *and the moon to blood,*
> *before the coming of the Lord's great and glorious day.*
> *Then everyone who calls on the name of the Lord shall be saved.'"*

The older I get, the worse my hearing gets, and the more amused I become by what I think I heard people saying. For me, the world is composed of a lot of misunderstandings. The father of one of my friends was even more hard of hearing than I am, and, like me, had come to accept the fact that he was never going to hear anything said to him properly on the first go-around.

Two young men knocked on his door one evening. They explained to him that their car had broken down, and asked politely to use his telephone. The old man listened patiently to the explanation, and when the young men finished speaking, he sighed and said, "You say you're a couple a biscuits?"

No matter how clearly you speak, chances are I'm going to hear something different from what you thought you were imparting to me. Really, given the differences in understanding, background, experience and degree of distraction that is currently living inside your head, it's a marvel to me that we manage to understand ANYTHING we say to one another.

Even so, it's important for us to speak in a way in which we will be understood. I was at 13th and Winchester at the light, preparing to turn left to go to the Chapel of St. Starbuck the other day. On the street corner was a gentleman in a short-sleeved white shirt and tie, holding a Bible and shouting at the passing cars. Of course, everybody had their windows up (it was hot outside) and the radio on, and nobody could make out anything he had to say. I only heard him because I thought he was in some distress from the way he was flailing about, so I cracked my window a bit. He was shouting about hell fire and damnation, and trying to scare people into church.

Not very effective, but I did feel a small twinge of kinship with him. Sometimes, during the sermon, I look down at your peaceful faces, and I think "They're so precious when they're asleep ... "

We have two stories today about talking and understanding. In the story of the Tower of Babel, that which was thought to be understood was confused. In Luke's account of Pentecost, that which was thought to be confused was understood. Taken together, these stories tell us WHAT to tell a contemporary congregation, and HOW to tell it.

We need that advice, because people of the time and place in which we live find it very difficult to hear what we are saying. We live a culture in which the name of God has become only an expression of delight and the name of Jesus an expression of dissatisfaction. "Oh God! He's right! Jesus! I hadn't thought of that!"

It's tough enough to talk about a God no one has seen and a Savior who walked the earth two millenia ago to people who imagine they are smart enough to drill holes in the bottom of the ocean a mile down without consequences. Add into it that some of what we talk about was originally written to Bronze Age people who thought they lived in a three-leveled Creation with heaven beyond a sphere just up there and hell below our feet, and it's no wonder some people wind up yelling at cars at 13th and Winchester.

So, should we ignore the stories from the Bible because they were written to people with a different understanding than we have? Absolutely not. What we must do, instead, is to dig into the stories to find the truths that are in them. And there are such truths, church. There are.

What is the truth in this story of the Tower of Babel which makes it Scripture instead of an archaeological exhibit in a museum somewhere along with cuneiform tablets from Nineveh? I'd like to suggest that the story of the Tower of Babel is about the impossibility of reaching a relationship with God by our own efforts. No matter how many rocket ships, telescopes and large hadron colliders we build, we are not going to wind up with God in our test tube. Science can teach us wonderful things about God's creation, but nothing about God. I think that's the scriptural truth behind the story of the Tower of Babel: You cannot raise yourself to the level of heaven. You must be lifted by the grace of God.

To the credit of the very smart people working in the scientific fields, they are beginning to admit as much. Karl Popper once suggested that there may not be an ultimate theory for physics – that, rather, every explanation may require a further explanation. A rival possibility is that such knowledge may simply be beyond us. Well … duh … we religious people could have told him that, if he only asked.

The Good News is that although we can't build a tower to God by our own efforts, God sent his Son unto the earth in order that the world be saved by Him. The Good News has nothing to do with building very tall towers. It has everything to do with God's great love which moves Him to reach out to us. Imagining that we can get there by tower, step ladder or Mentos and Diet

Coke rocket is our mistake.

The question I would pose is this: in the 21st Century, is Christianity on the path of Babel or the path of Pentecost? Are we scattered or are we in communion one with the other? The answer I'd like to propose is this: We are precariously seated atop the Tower of Babel.

If you spend some time with the account of Pentecost I think it will start to sound surprisingly familiar to you. Peter is speaking. Many devout Jews understand what he is saying, but others scoff and say, "They are filled with new wine." They can understand the WORDS because all heard him in their native language. It's the SENSE of what he is saying that makes him sound like a drunk. Some of the people just cannot accept the things Peter is saying. This sounds an awful lot like what is taking place in our society today. The Christian community speaks of God and Jesus, and the secular community says, in effect, "They're off their heads."

I suppose that the Christian community could respond, as Peter did, by saying "Nu-uhn either! We're not drunk!" but I don't think we'd have any more luck than Peter had. To those untouched by the Holy Spirit, talk of God and Jesus is always going to be heard as babble about being a coupla biscuits. Our job is to speak in a way that keeps the number of people who reject what we say out of hand to as small a number as we can. That means we have to speak in a way that makes sense to 21st Century understanding while still communicating that the ineffable, transcendent God is beyond 21st Century understanding and always will be.

So, here we sit in the beginning of the 21st Century, talking past each other. The religious faithful hear the Gospel in their own tongues, and the rest of the population hears incredible stories from an ancient time, and can only respond, "You must be drunk or crazy." That's why I think we're in the Tower of Babel era. Our understanding is confused. To quote my mentor, Brother Kit Hathorn, "We don't understand half of what we know."

You and I stand in the shoes of Peter. It's our job to preach to the world the Gospel of Jesus Christ. But we must do so in a way that permits those to whom we are speaking to hear more than "you say you're a coupla biscuits," and I think we're not doing that.

The most visible Christians today – the ones that appear in the press or on TV

— are the ones screaming about "evil-ution," or chasing up mountains in Turkey trying to find Noah's Ark. It's no wonder that the world at large comes to think of Christians as soft-headed do-gooders or hell fire fundamentalists. To a 21ˢᵗ Century world, we sound like drunks! We are not talking to them in terms they can understand, and when we do talk to them, we often offer them things they reject out of hand.

So … what SHOULD we tell them? How SHOULD we spread the Good News to a 21ˢᵗ Century audience? Jesus told his Disciples,

> "A new command I give you: Love one another. As I have loved you, so you must love one another. By this all men will know that you are my disciples, if you love one another."

HOW we express ourselves is as important as WHAT we say. In Peter's first Epistle, he reminds us:

> Whoever speaks must do so as one speaking the very words of God; whoever serves must do so with the strength that God supplies, so that God may be glorified in all things through Jesus Christ.

If your words are not guided by the teaching of Jesus, just don't say anything. You aren't helping. If the best you can do is to speak hatred toward Islam, for God's sake, just stuff a sock in it! You're making it worse.

If you speak in love, you will be heard in love, and that is the first step.

The second step is just as simple: don't choke the baby. I was talking to an evangelical the other day. He was quite sure that I don't know what I am talking about, and equally sure that he did. To demonstrate this, he deluged me with passages from all over the Bible, ignoring context, time or Testament. I felt I had been hit by an avalanche of Scripture. I could hardly breathe. Do you think this gooey morass of Biblical quotes convinced me of anything? No, it did not.

The Good News is that this world had a Creator. This Creator didn't walk away, but sustains His creation every second of every minute of the day. Our Psalm for today reminds us:

> You hide your face, and they are terrified;
> you take away their breath,
> and they die and return to their dust.

Our very existence is conditional upon Him, and He offers us a relationship with Him. It is so important to Him that this relationship be offered that He took on human form and came to us to tell us about it, even suffering an agonizing death for our sake. That's quite enough. If you get that much across in love and respect for the other person, you have done quite a bit.

The Good News is counter-intuitive to a modern audience. It is often expressed in images that were ideal for ancient people, but which sound hopelessly naïve to modern ears. Somehow, we have failed to notice that we don't understand half of what we know. In such a world, the story of God's evangelism toward us begins to sound like a coupla biscuits. It is up to us, faithful disciples, to make it not so – to make it intelligible to the modern world, and that is our task.

J. STEWART SCHNEIDER

The Lamed Vovniks

"A willingness to confront the issue of undeserved suffering is a milestone on the path to awareness."

Job 23:1-9, 16-17

Then Job answered:

"Today also my complaint is bitter;
*   his hand is heavy despite my groaning.*
Oh, that I knew where I might find him,
*   that I might come even to his dwelling!*
I would lay my case before him,
*   and fill my mouth with arguments.*
I would learn what he would answer me,
*   and understand what he would say to me.*
Would he contend with me in the greatness of his power?
*   No; but he would give heed to me.*
There an upright person could reason with him,
*   and I should be acquitted forever by my judge.*

"If I go forward, he is not there;
*   or backward, I cannot perceive him;*
on the left he hides, and I cannot behold him;
*   I turn to the right, but I cannot see him.*
God has made my heart faint;
*   the Almighty has terrified me;*
If only I could vanish in darkness,
*   and thick darkness would cover my face!"*

Hebrews 4:12-16

The word of God is living and active, sharper than any two-edged sword,
piercing until it divides soul from spirit, joints from marrow; it is able to

judge the thoughts and intentions of the heart. And before him no creature is hidden, but all are naked and laid bare to the eyes of the one to whom we must render an account.

Since, then, we have a great high priest who has passed through the heavens, Jesus, the Son of God, let us hold fast to our confession. For we do not have a high priest who is unable to sympathize with our weaknesses, but we have one who in every respect has been tested as we are, yet without sin. Let us therefore approach the throne of grace with boldness, so that we may receive mercy and find grace to help in time of need.

Job is not an easy book to love. It's not even an easy book to read. I'd be a lot happier if I could bring you a Bible stuffed with rainbows, puppy dogs and unicorns from one end to the other, but that's not the Bible we have. There are difficult, troubling books in the Bible – books that make you re-examine what you always thought. Job is one of them.

If you haven't read Job in a while, let me remind you of the beginning. Heavenly beings are presenting themselves before God in the Holy court. One of these beings is "ha-satan" which means "the accuser." In English, we often understand that this character is Satan, but I want to warn you against that reading. In Hebrew, the identification of this heavenly being clearly is "ha," meaning, "the" and "satan," meaning "accuser" or "advocate." In other words, it's a title, not a name.

This is the first place where we modern people have a problem with the Book of Job — it lacks a villain, and I want a villain in my stories, particularly those dealing with the suffering of the innocent. Every last thing I saw on television from the time I was old enough to turn on Hopalong Cassidy presented to me as a law of nature that innocent suffering occurs because of the actions of the guy in the black hat. The villain does bad stuff because that's what villains do, and the bad stuff inflicts suffering on the innocent town's folk. As a corollary, suffering may be ended by removing the villain.

With my apologies to my Buddhist friends, the Four Noble Truths of the town's folk, as preached in the B westerns, are:

1. All life is suffering

196

2. The cause of suffering is the presence of a villain
3. Cessation of suffering is attainable.
4. The path to cessation of suffering is to put a .45 caliber bullet in the villain.

It sounds stupid when I put it this way, but this is the underlying assumption of many, many of our brothers and sisters. Suffering comes because of villains, and can be removed from the human condition by simply removing the villains.

As I look around God's Creation, I cannot escape innocent suffering. It is everywhere. I was reading a book the other day depicting, just in passing, the suffering of starving children in India. It's overwhelming! If the English characters in the book reserved a train and filled it with bananas, there would be too few bananas to feed the children pushing their hands through the windows crying, "Ma! Ma!" The surfeit of bananas would simply draw more children until there was an end to the bananas, to the world's supply of bananas!

We don't have to travel so far as India, though. Innocent suffering aplenty is arrayed before us here, though we are often as blinded to it by its commonness as the riders on Indian trains become to the begging children. The young family who suffer from homelessness. The father who has lost his job because the corporation he worked for "consolidated" to improve the bottom line. The young people who wait on you at the big-box stores or in fast food lines. Do you imagine their families are well-fed and cared for on minimum wage? Have you tried to put together a budget based on minimum wage? Take-home pay after Social Security and Medicare payments, not counting state taxes, is about $242.00 for a 40-hour week. IF you get 40 hours. Go ahead. Make a budget and get back to me.

How do we square so much misery with the idea of a good, loving God? How do we view this misery without becoming angry? What keeps us from screaming, "All right, God! Get on this. Starving children offend me!"

Most commonly, we try to separate God from the misery by giving the bad stuff to Satan, or blaming the victim. We need our villains to make sense of innocent suffering, and if we cannot find one readily to hand, we are shockingly willing to cede God's sovereignty, or a portion of it, to a villain of our own creation. We describe the misery arrayed before us as the work of the devil or we allow ourselves to entertain the thought that poverty, malnutrition and unemployment are the fault of those suffering from them. The poor are welfare frauds. They are lazy. They are addicted. The good God I worship offers them hope, but they turn their backs.

This is why Job is such an infuriating book. Job won't let you get away with any of these excuses. The holy being described, ha-satan, is not an opponent of God. Ha-satan is clearly under the control of God. He can do nothing without God's approval. If the devil is the source of suffering, he is so only because God approved it.

Neither will Job allow us to blame the victims of suffering for their experience. God, Himself, proclaims that Job is righteous. All the bad stuff that happens to Job isn't his fault, however much his friends later try to make it so. The Book of Job insists that we confront God's sovereignty with our eyes open. There is only one God, not some sort of dualistic perversion of monotheism in which the forces of good and evil battle to the death for possession of God's Creation. This character, ha-satan, is more like "the District Attorney" – a heavenly being whose job it is to uncover unrighteousness — than he is like the Prince of Darkness, God's opponent.

God asks the District Attorney where he's been. The DA relates that he has been walking about on the earth, and that seems to remind God of Job. "Have you considered my servant Job? There is no one like him on the earth, a blameless and upright man who fears God and turns away from evil."

And so we have it, from the lips of God. All that we will hear of Job's suffering is through no fault of Job's. God proclaims that Job is blameless and upright. Not only is he blameless, but there is no one like him on earth. He is the only blameless and upright person on the face of the earth. In a rainbow, puppy dog and unicorn Bible, this is the man who should be blessed, and he was. His barns overflowed. He lived surrounded by loving family and in successful comfort. That's the way things work in a puppy dog and unicorn world – the good do well, the evil get theirs. God smiles upon those who fear Him, and destroys those who do not. Virtue is not its own reward, virtue is rewarded.

The District Attorney, though, doesn't buy it, and I can readily relate to this. After a quarter century as a district attorney, I came to believe that everyone is guilty, and this heavenly being has come to the same conclusion. Job isn't righteous because he is a righteous man. He is righteous because God has treated him so well. To settle the matter, God permits the District Attorney to take everything from Job – his flocks, his herds, his barns, even his children, and, in the end, to afflict Job with horrible boils from his head to his foot. All to settle, in effect, a bet between God and the District Attorney.

The important thing to remember here is that Job has done nothing to deserve this sort of treatment. Worse yet, when his "friends" come to comfort him, they instead wind up trying to blame him for what happened, as if his misery wasn't already more than a man could bear, insisting that God wouldn't have inflicted such pain on him if he hadn't sinned in some awful way. Listen to the conversation on the street about the homeless, the unemployed, those on welfare. Whose fault? Who is blamed? Whose words?

But Job was blameless, and God did expose Job to undeserved suffering. We know that because we're reading the story and we are party to the discussions in the heavenly realms, about which Job knows nothing. We know that Job is blameless and upright, and that his suffering has nothing to do with anything he has done. Job doesn't. Job suffers in order to teach the District Attorney something about a blameless man!

How is this fair? How are we to relate to this turn of events? If you do what is right, should you not succeed? Should not pain and suffering fall upon only the evil ones? If we live right-directed lives, are we not entitled to a comfortable retirement?

Except, as any fool knows, it doesn't work that way. Innocent suffering surrounds us. Children die of horrible diseases. Elderly people fall, are forgotten by their neighbors and die on their floors. Young people unselfishly serve their country and are killed in Afghanistan. We're up to our knees in undeserved suffering. We're drowning in it! What kind of unfair, messed up world is this? We're offended. I'm offended by the Book of Job telling me that God inflicts all these horrors on Job just to prove a point to the District Attorney, and I'm offended at the sight of Job, suffering these horrors without the first clue why – baffled, frightened, and angered. My heart is with Job when he cries out

God has made my heart faint;
    the Almighty has terrified me;
If only I could vanish in darkness,
    and thick darkness would cover my face!

How **do** we approach such a book? How do we understand a book that seems to make God the author of all miseries? When God inflicts undeserved suffering on Job, who is blameless, it's like trying to shift gears without using the clutch – it grinds our mental gears.

When people share with me their ideas of what heaven is like, it usually involves a place where there are no tears, where no one wants for anything, where everything is as we would have it be. In the heavenly realms, they tell me, the virtuous receive their reward, and the evil ones their punishment. Virtue is rewarded. Transgressions are punished. It is as we want this world to be.

But this world is not that way. This is a world in which Job suffers, though he is a blameless man. How can God permit that? The Book of Job won't even let us off the hook in the usual way – that suffering enters this world because we are all sinners. God himself declares Job to be "blameless." Job's friends bend heaven and earth to blame Job for his suffering, but we know that Job suffers because of a debate between God and the District Attorney. Blaming the victim won't work here.

The only way to make any sense of this is to come to a deeper understanding of suffering. We have to draw a line between undeserved suffering and unnecessary suffering. And when we do, the story of Job opens for us the story of Jesus, for the suffering of Jesus was undeserved, but not unnecessary.

Not to state the obvious, but when we suffer, we bear it better if we know that it is necessary. If a child were trapped in a burning car and bystanders rushed to save the child, burning their hands in the process, as happened recently, that suffering would be much easier to bear than the burns received through some unforeseen accident. If we can see the reason for our suffering, we can be content. Job cannot see why he is suffering, and his anguished cry sears my heart because we are all Job – if we suffer, and that suffering serves a greater purpose, we cannot see it, and we become overwhelmed by the inequities of our undeserved suffering.

But, isn't the problem less one of a sinful world, which is, after all, the work of God's hands, than it is the aching need we all feel to see only deserved or necessary suffering? Isn't the problem a reflection of our limited perceptions, and our frustrations from living in a world which we cannot understand? What is the value of necessary suffering? How are we to weigh it, in what

200

scale, against what standard?

Jewish tradition teaches that there are, at any one time, thirty-six righteous men in the world, called the Lamed Vovniks, or the Pillars of the Universe. The tradition holds that if even one of them were to disappear, the world would collapse upon itself. No one knows who they are. The Lamed Vovniks themselves do not know who they are. They are simply righteous people who receive the suffering of the world upon themselves, and thereby sustain it. In a portion of a longer poem[18] my friend Rabbi Cohen of Memphis sent me, we learn:

> It snows on one of them; rains on another.
> Both are without shoes.
> Another is schlepping a heavy box and not complaining; another is stroking the sodden fur of a blind cat.
> . . .
> In their own sight they are small as mesons; to most of us they are smudges on the sills of the world, schmutz on the discarded shmattas of the quotidian.
> But when one of them has goose flesh, the universe trembles; when one of them sneezes, there is a momentary brownout throughout the Milky Way.

The universe is sustained and has its being upon the unknowing suffering borne by the righteous. Crazy, huh? Where do the Jews come up with these mishuginah ideas? Surely nothing is gained by the suffering of the innocent. Job was treated unfairly, that's that, and I'm offended.

It always puzzles me the way we have taken the death of Jesus and slapped a coat of very good varnish over the instrument of His torture, so that we may easily toss of "He died for our sins," but when it comes to Job, everybody gets their knickers in a twist. Jesus was tortured and killed, and that's all right because He was just doing his Jesus thing, but Job got psoriasis and that's awful!

The difference between Jesus and the Lamed Vovniks is that Jesus knew that his suffering, though undeserved, was necessary. How else is the world to know that God himself has come to walk among us? How else are we to look upon Jesus and know He was not just one more poor bit of schmutz on the

---

18 Mikhail Horowitz, *Thirty-six Sentences on the Lamed Vovniks,* used by permission

discarded shmattas of the life of Palestine under the Romans? And if we couldn't see Jesus as something unique, how could we hear the words of the writer of Hebrews

> For we do not have a high priest who is unable to sympathize with our weaknesses, but we have one who in every respect has been tested as we are, yet without sin. Let us therefore approach the throne of grace with boldness, so that we may receive mercy and find grace to help in time of need.

We are incomplete creatures, church, unable to see the effect of our suffering on the universe. There is a mathematical theory that tells us that the flap of a butterfly's wing in Brazil, though we cannot trace the path of cause and effect, will change the path of a tornado in Tulsa. By the carefully developed mathematics of chaos theory, our world is described, at any one moment, as if it were a wire coat hanger which had been unbent, straightened out and somehow come to be balanced on its very end, standing upright on a table. We can't begin to imagine how something as improbable as this moment came to be, but it is so fragile that the closing of a door in a neighbor's house or the wind from a passing insect would be enough to topple it.

The universe as God created it is just such a delicate balancing act, a spider's web in which your stubbed toe, in ways that you cannot comprehend, affects you know not what else in God's plan. Each of us, like the Lamed Vovniks, is unaware how our suffering may make God's creation infinitesimally better. Job suffered to further a discussion between God and the District Attorney. Who is to say that this purpose was not important? God does not dole out unnecessary suffering. For us, short sighted creatures that we are, faith demands that we know that God is still involved with us and His Creation.

> The word of God is living and active, sharper than any two-edged sword, piercing until it divides soul from spirit, joints from marrow; it is able to judge the thoughts and intentions of the heart. And before him no creature is hidden, but all are naked and laid bare to the eyes of the one to whom we must render an account.

Who knows? Perhaps there is a Lamed Vovnik with us in this room, and we don't know it. From the same poem:

> I thought I sussed one out, once, at a soup kitchen in Minneapolis.

He was doling out stew to a bunch of losers, not the beautiful kind but the other kind, whose dreams have been flattened by steamrollers of neglect, . . .

But he was beaming, beaming at each of the stubby shadows as they shuffled in front of him, rekindling the dead light in their eyes with the light in his, if only for a moment.

. . .

Suppose for a moment that they could know themselves, and not immediately combust, or crumble to dust.

How then would it be?

Such was the life of our Lord, church. Such was the life of our Lord.

J. STEWART SCHNEIDER

What Everyone Knows

"The guidance of the group, our cultural expectations, lead us astray from the Way of Jesus when we confuse them with the Gospel."

Genesis 12:1-9

The Lord said to Abram, "Go from your country and your kindred and your father's house to the land that I will show you. I will make of you a great nation, and I will bless you, and make your name great, so that you will be a blessing. I will bless those who bless you, and the one who curses you I will curse; and in you all the families of the earth shall be blessed."

So Abram went, as the Lord had told him; and Lot went with him. Abram was seventy-five years old when he departed from Ur. Abram took his wife Sarai and his brother's son Lot, and all the possessions that they had gathered, and the persons whom they had acquired in Ur; and they set forth to go to the land of Canaan. When they had come to the land of Canaan, Abram passed through the land to the place at Shechem, to the oak of Moreh. At that time the Canaanites were in the land. Then the Lord appeared to Abram, and said, "To your offspring I will give this land." So he built there an altar to the Lord, who had appeared to him. From there he moved on to the hill country on the east of Bethel, and pitched his tent, with Bethel on the west and Ai on the east; and there he built an altar to the Lord and invoked the name of the Lord. And Abram journeyed on by stages toward the Negeb.

Matthew 9:9-13, 18-26

As Jesus was walking along, he saw a man called Matthew sitting at the tax booth; and he said to him, "Follow me." And he got up and followed him.

And as he sat at dinner in the house, many tax collectors and sinners came and were sitting with him and his disciples. When the Pharisees saw this, they said to his disciples, "Why does your teacher eat with tax collectors and sin-

ners?" But when he heard this, he said, "Those who are well have no need of a physician, but those who are sick. Go and learn what this means, 'I desire mercy, not sacrifice.' For I have come to call not the righteous but sinners."

While he was saying these things to them, suddenly a leader of the synagogue came in and knelt before him, saying, "My daughter has just died; but come and lay your hand on her, and she will live." And Jesus got up and followed him, with his disciples. Then suddenly a woman who had been suffering from hemorrhages for twelve years came up behind him and touched the fringe of his cloak, for she said to herself, "If I only touch his cloak, I will be made well." Jesus turned, and seeing her he said, "Take heart, daughter; your faith has made you well." And instantly the woman was made well. When Jesus came to the leader's house and saw the flute players and the crowd making a commotion, he said, "Go away; for the girl is not dead but sleeping." And they laughed at him. But when the crowd had been put outside, he went in and took her by the hand, and the girl got up. And the report of this spread throughout that district.

Think back to when you were a kid, and cooked up some hare-brained scheme that would likely get you killed, and presented it to your mother, and she said, "No." What was the very first argument you offered to your mother?

"Everybody else is doing it," right? And, just what did your mother say to that?

"If everybody else was jumping off the roof, would you do that, too?" That's what <u>everybody's</u> mother said.

Now, be honest. You can lie to your mother, but you can't lie to me. If everybody else was jumping off the roof, you'd jump off the roof, too, wouldn't you? Of course you would. We're social animals. Sometimes, however, that very need for social confirmation can interfere with the sort of intimate relationship God has in mind for us, because it can drag us away from God into the more comfortable arms of societal approval. The Second Testament isn't an offer of a relationship with a people. It's an offer of a relationship with a person. YOU.

I want very much to share with you from these two stories the way in which God calls us out from the group mentality that so often substitutes for righteousness into a committed relationship with Him which is true righteousness. I want you to know just how counter-cultural the call of Jesus Christ is.

In a bit more than six weeks, I'll go to the Archabbey of St. Meinrad – a community of men who have committed themselves to a life apart – for the Spiritual Life Retreat. This year, to my great surprise, I find they even quote me in the advertising for the retreat. I said:

It would be hard to describe how important the retreat to St. Meinrad's Archabbey is to me in my spiritual life. The Archabbey seems to me to be under a special dispensation of silent meditation from which the word of God emerges with unusual clarity. The fellowship, the time away, all empower me in a way nothing else I do during the year does.

I didn't describe it as being under a special dispensation of silence because the monks are silent – they are not under an oath of silence – but because the sounds and distractions of life seem to have no power to penetrate the walls of St. Meinrad. At St. Meinrad, it is possible to come into closer contact with God. It is a very special place, and the place from which I gained the courage to refuse a death penalty case, which got me fired, which brought me here to you. I think we both owe the monks of St. Meinrad a thank-you.

I get a tremendous kick in the spiritual pants from my annual trip there. I come back from a simple weekend with the monks empowered and enlivened, but as much as I am spiritually lifted by approaching the cathedral church at 5 a.m. to hear the monks chant the psalter, I would not gladly live there. God has not called me to withdraw from the world, but to live in it.

Here's the surprising thing you might not have thought about: Each of you is similarly called to live in the world, obeying the teachings of Jesus Christ, doing the work of the church in your daily lives, however mundane you may think your life is.

Which brings up the entire question of call. What do we mean by call, and are "regular" people called, or only clergy?

Easily the most famous call in Scripture is our passage from Genesis. Those who took the Jewish History class will remember that I went into it in some detail and included an ancient Rabbinic story about how the call of Abraham came about. To refresh your memory, Abram's father (Abram didn't become Abraham until later), Terah, was a maker of idols. Had a little shop in downtown Ur where he made all sorts of idols. It was a pretty good living, and Abram could look forward to more of the same when his father died.

Things looked good in Ur not just because Abram stood to be financially secure, but also because the occupation in which his father toiled was a respected one. Everybody, and I mean everybody, knew and believed how vitally important it was to honor the gods that ruled everything they did. The gods, after all, kept the society of Ur together. The ruled the harvest, without which there would be famine. They ruled the fertility of the livestock, without which there would be no clothes, or milk, or oxen with which to plow. They governed the fertility of wives, without which there would be no sons to carry on the father's name. There simply was no more important thing, nothing with such life-and-death potential, than a careful observation of the rites associated with the various gods.

And Terah provided the images for those rites.

I'm guessing that if you got yourself a clay clipboard and a writing stylus, and went into the streets of Ur to question people on their beliefs, you would get a pretty consistent answer. These people were *henotheistic*. They held a major relationship with one or two gods, while still accepting the reality and power of other gods. That is to say, in your survey, you'd find some people favoring this god, and some that, but none who would offer up the idea that there was but one great God who created everything, and that the images that Terah made were nothing but trinkets. That was just not on the map.

Here's the meat of the matter – the nut of the controversy. Everyone in Ur knew about the power of the gods to affect their lives, for better or worse, even unto things like bringing on famine. Church, there is no more dangerous thing than something "everybody knows." This is the group mentality that sometimes masquerades as righteousness that I was talking about. What "everybody knows" is what we fall back on when we're too lazy or tired or misdirected to respond to a committed relationship with God. After all, if you go with the group, nobody's going to criticize you. You're just like everybody else. Things that "everybody knows" are dangerous because we substitute the group understanding for what we should be understanding personally after deep prayer. We get distracted and abdicate our personal relationship with God to follow the crowd.

Worse than that, because all of us want to think we're doing the right thing, we come to see those things that "everybody knows" to be the right things, and we get a lot of reinforcement in that because everybody else is doing exactly the same thing. We all want to feel that we're doing the right thing, and we all look to what "everybody knows" for confirmation that we're doing the right thing.

This is what was going on in Ur. Everybody knew the gods ran things, and everybody confirmed what everybody knew. And if you wanted to say something different, you were just wrong, that's all.

If you can get a grip on that, you have the perspective you need to see just how counter-cultural and upsetting Jesus' actions in calling a tax collector and eating with him and his friends would have appeared to the people of the time. Everybody knew that the tax collectors were corrupt pawns of Rome. What in the world does this Jesus, who everybody is holding out as this great do-gooder, doing with a bunch of tax collectors and sinners? Jesus' actions in actually calling a tax collector as a disciple is as upsetting as what is about to happen in our story in Ur.

One day, the story goes, Terah came home to find every idol in his shop smashed with the exception of the largest idol, who was holding a hammer.

I can't even begin to imagine Terah's fury when he returned to find all his stock, his livelihood, smashed, not to mention his fear at the sort of retribution the gods would bring to him for this desecration. Think of the revulsion we feel when we read that some screwball has desecrated a Jewish synagogue, or that some wingnut set fire to a church. That's the kind of fury Terah was feeling.

He immediately asked his son, Abram, what had happened. "The larger idol became jealous and smashed all the others," Abram replied.

"What?" Terah roared. "You know these idols are made of wood and metal, that I fashioned them myself. They can't move!"

"Then, why do you worship them?," asked Abram. "If they can't protect themselves, how can they protect you?"

The teachings of Jesus were corrective of an existing understanding of God, but this one came out of the blue. Where in all of Ur would Abram have come across such an idea? This is 700 years before Moses. There is no Ten Commandments. There is no First Covenant. Where would he get such an idea? The answer, I think, is, "He wouldn't." There is no archaeological evidence for bronze age monotheism in Ur of which I am aware.

Instead, out of all the Third Millennium B.C.E. Mesopotamians wandering around eastern Iraq 2,000 years before Jesus, God called this one, and told him, "I know everybody in town thinks these idols are real, but they are not, and you are not to have anything to do with them."

Think of the kind of upset that would cause. In the years after the Resurrection, one of the complaints Rome offered against Christians was that they were atheists – they refused to admit the reality of the Roman gods. When Abram smashed the idols in this story, he was doing more than making a speech about his understanding of religion. He was following the relationship God had forged with him, even though it meant parting with <u>everything</u> that "everybody knows." He made of himself an outcast, a rebel without a clue in the eyes of everyone around him. This is the sort of thing that happens when an informed Christian listens to the voice of God within him and acts upon it.

I know you are tired of hearing about that single death penalty case of mine, but it's the only time in my entire life I have acted on the word of God which lead me so far from what everybody knows, so it's the only example I have. Most of the time, I stop at stop lights, and fuss about politicians and fudge a little with the speed limit on the Interstate, just like everybody else. This one time, the voice of God said one thing, and the law said another, and I made a spectacle of myself by listening to God. <u>That's</u> the sort of thing Abram was doing, and it was all the more amazing because where in all of Ur would Abram have heard about God?

It wasn't so much a question of Abram choosing God from the shelf in his father's store. It was that God chose Abram, in the same way that the Presbyterian Church teaches that God chooses us.

Moving from the Rabbinic story to the actual text of Genesis, the family moved from Ur to Haran, maybe because of the scandal. Who knows? In Haran, God told Abram, "Go from your country and your kindred and your father's house to the land that I will show you."

And Abram went.

God chose Abram, and again Abram responded in faith, leaving behind everything he ever knew to go somewhere he didn't know and undertake something he hadn't been told about. In the same way, when Jesus chose Matthew the tax collector and said, "Follow me," Matthew responded in faith and he went.

Abram's faithful response to God's call drew him out of the group understanding of righteousness into true righteousness. Jesus' call to a tax collector moved Jesus outside of what was deemed proper in Palestine. No man can serve two masters. We either follow the indwelling spirit of God to a committed relationship with Him, or we follow the crowd.

Our time here in God's creation isn't a dry run for a life of perfection in heaven when we die. It is a feast of blessings, a bounteous table to which we are invited by a gracious God who chooses us. Our job is to commit our every moment to listening for the invitation and responding to it in faith, even if to do so means leaving the group and exposing ourselves to the criticism of the society in which we live.

God's call is counter-cultural. It is to a one-on-one relationship with each of us, a dance with God in which God always, <u>always</u>, must lead. Those who have ears will listen, Jesus said. If you listen, you will hear. If you pay attention to God, at the expense of the group, you will feel his hand upon your arm. Follow Him, Church!

J. STEWART SCHNEIDER

Ceci n'est pas une pipe

"Those who claim a name obligate themselves to act in accordance with it. It is one thing to represent yourself as a first baseman. It is another to be able to catch a line drive."

Job 42:1-6, 10-17

Then Job answered the LORD:
"I know that you can do all things,
and that no purpose of yours can be thwarted.
`Who is this that hides counsel without knowledge?'
Therefore I have uttered what I did not understand,
things too wonderful for me, which I did not know.
`Hear, and I will speak;
I will question you, and you declare to me.'
I had heard of you by the hearing of the ear,
but now my eye sees you;
therefore I despise myself,
and repent in dust and ashes."

And the LORD restored the fortunes of Job when he had prayed for his friends; and the LORD gave Job twice as much as he had before. Then there came to him all his brothers and sisters and all who had known him before, and they ate bread with him in his house; they showed him sympathy and comforted him for all the evil that the LORD had brought upon him; and each of them gave him a piece of money and a gold ring. The LORD blessed the latter days of Job more than his beginning; and he had fourteen thousand sheep, six thousand camels, a thousand yoke of oxen, and a thousand donkeys. He also had seven sons and three daughters. He named the first Jemimah, the second Keziah, and the third Keren-happuch. In all the land there were no women so beautiful as Job's daughters; and their father gave them an inheritance along with their brothers. After this Job lived one hun-

213

dred and forty years, and saw his children, and his children's children, four generations. And Job died, old and full of days.

Mark 10:46-52

Jesus and his disciples came to Jericho. As he and his disciples and a large crowd were leaving Jericho, Bartimaeus son of Timaeus, a blind beggar, was sitting by the roadside. When he heard that it was Jesus of Nazareth, he began to shout out and say, "Jesus, Son of David, have mercy on me!" Many sternly ordered him to be quiet, but he cried out even more loudly, "Son of David, have mercy on me!" Jesus stood still and said, "Call him here." And they called the blind man, saying to him, "Take heart; get up, he is calling you." So throwing off his cloak, he sprang up and came to Jesus. Then Jesus said to him, "What do you want me to do for you?" The blind man said to him, "My teacher, let me see again." Jesus said to him, "Go; your faith has made you well." Immediately he regained his sight and followed him on the way.

The story of blind barTimaeus in our text today made me think about names. My surname, Schneider, comes from the German verb "schneiden" which means to cut. A Schneider, in German, is a "tailor." We can be pretty sure, then, that somewhere, back in my family tree before surnames were being used, was a tailor. Not only that, but that far back in the mists of history, a son was expected to follow in the trade of the father, and my family must have had a long tradition of tailoring. It must have defined the family so firmly that, as surnames came into use, people started referring to my family as "the tailors," or "die Schneider," in German.

One of my cousins, arriving in New York, set up his business on the Lower East Side. He put up a sign saying "Schneider." No business. Nothing. His family was starving. He went to God in prayer.

"What should I do? My family is starving!" he prayed.

"Use my name," God replied. And so, my cousin took down his sign that said "Schneider" and put up another one in good high German reading "Gott und Schneider."

Business boomed! My cousin could hardly handle the work. He had to hire more people. Eventually, he bought a building uptown and proudly hung his sign "Gott und Schneider."

Nothing. Not the first job. He faced bankruptcy. In prayer, he begged God what to do.

"Schneider," God replied. "You're uptown. These people have no German. You have to speak so they can understand. Take down the sign that says 'Gott und Schneider' and put up one that says 'Lord and Tailor'"

OK, that story works better when spoken than read. I started musing about names as I was praying my way through the story of blind barTimaeus in Mark because we don't know what his name was. "barTimaeus" isn't a name. It's two words in Aramaic – "bar" meaning "son of" and "Timaeus," the father's name. All we know about blind barTimaeus is that he is the son of someone named Timaeus and that he is a blind beggar.

What would it be like, I wonder, to be without a name? What would it be like not to be known in your community as Ron or Linda, but as "that guy with the shopping cart," or "the guy that sleeps under the bridge?" What would it be like to be known, not by the positive things you contribute to your community, but by your handicap, "blind barTimaeus?" What would such a thing do to your idea of yourself? When I was growing up, the neighbor of my grandmother had a Downs syndrome adult son who lived with her. He was always referred to as "poor little Kent Earl." What would something like that do to you?

We are the animals who name things, but we're also the animals perpetually confused by the relationship of a thing and its name. We confuse the name of a thing with its reality. My surname came about because of the relationship between my ancestors and the trade of tailoring, but I am by no means a tailor. I am different from my name, and in the same way, the individual who begged Jesus for his sight had a name, and a sense of self. For all we know, he was a talented singer. Maybe he thought great thoughts. He recognized Jesus as his teacher. All we know of him, though, is that he's a blind beggar and the son of Timaeus. He is more than that, but all we know about him is his title – blind barTimaeus!

In a famous painting by René Magritte, the painter portrayed a tobacco pipe realistically, then wrote below it, "Ceci n'est pas une pipe" which means, "This is not a pipe." And it isn't. It's an <u>image</u> of a pipe. We're trapped by our language into thinking an image of a pipe is a pipe and we're also trapped by our language into thinking that the name of a person IS the person.

And what of the names we take on later – butcher, baker, candlestick maker – and particularly, "Christian?" That's the other side of names – the names we take on define us, but we also define the names themselves because we become an example of them. If a stranger arrived in town, and did not know what a blind beggar looked like, the people of the time would have pointed to poor Timaeus' blind son as defining what a blind beggar looks like. If the only Muslim you ever saw was an intolerant and violent jihadist, then, as far as you know, Muslims are intolerant, violent jihadists and the enemies of Christians. It isn't so, but that's exactly the conclusion you would reach from the media. In the same way, if you were an Iranian, living in a theocracy where the religion and the government are intimately entwined, you would equate western culture with Christianity. If the only contact you had with Western culture was in the form of JDAM bombs from Predator drones, you would have a pretty grim notion of what a Christian is. We're as trapped by our flawed understanding as blind barTimaeus is by his handicap.

I'll probably get kicked out of the preacher's club for saying this, and banned from St. Starbuck for life, but since the things we do while calling ourselves "Christian" define what non-Christians believe Christians to be, I wish people would be a little more circumspect about calling themselves Christian. There are an awful lot of people who take on the name Christian only to act in ways that are as foreign to the teaching of our Lord as could be imagined. In the same way that nutcase Muslims do a disservice to the memory and teaching of the Prophet by using their religion for violent ends, there are people who hide behind the name of our Lord to do unconscionable things. How did Jesus of Nazareth, who came to comfort the afflicted and afflict the comfortable, who lived the life of a servant, opposing the institutions of power and privilege which impeded the path of God's people to a relationship with Him come to be the patron saint of the comfortable and the powerful? How did Jesus of Nazareth who hung upon the cross the very institutions which, in the name of God, operated to benefit the powerful at the expense of the poor come to be the rallying cry of the institutions which operate to benefit the powerful? How did the name of Christ become so intimately associated with the American way of life that it is sometimes difficult to unravel the two?

Glad you asked. It is because those who lightly take on the name "Christian" have defined it as such. If Warren Jeffries "marries" girl children in the name of the Fundamentalist Church of Latter Day Saints, he contributes to the perception that Mormons are all about marrying girl children. If a priest of the Catholic church abuses boy children, he contributes to the idea that the Roman Catholic Church is all about pederasty. If a Baptist congregation in the wilds of North Carolina decides to burn all copies of the Bible except the King James, proclaiming them to be "Satan's books" then they contribute to the perception that Christians are blockheads. And, as much as it pains me to say it, if we, in the Presbyterian Church, wall ourselves off from contact with those who live in the non-Presbyterian world, and offer worship services that appeal to our sense of tradition, but which bore the brains out of those not raised in this tradition, then we contribute to the perception that organized religion is an archaic holdover from the last century, on the order of buggy whips and corset hooks.

We are as trapped as blind barTimaeus.

The story of blind barTimaeus isn't about the power of Jesus to restore sight. The world of Jesus' time was filled with blind beggars. We have no stories of Jesus, the miraculous optometrist, restoring sight to all in Palestine. This story is about a man trapped by his past, trapped by his name, or lack of it, being granted the ability, through his faith, to see a future when none existed before. With his restored sight, he has a new name, "Christian" for we are told

> Jesus said to him, "Go; your faith has made you well." Immediately he regained his sight and followed him on the way.

An encounter with Jesus inevitably changes you. The question I would raise is whether we have substituted an encounter with a church for an encounter with Jesus. My dad told me something once with great candor. Dad was a committed churchman his entire life, a member of the Christian Church (Disciples of Christ), but when he told me of his baptism, he confessed that it wasn't anything special. It was just something everybody his age did to join the church. Joining a church isn't the same thing as having an encounter with Jesus and taking on the name "Christian" isn't the same as joining a church. The relationship between you and the church is an image of the relationship between you and Jesus, not a substitute for it. Ceci n'est pas une pipe.

I want you to contrast my dad's confession with the experience of blind barTimaeus. I'm sure Dad felt good about being baptized, and I'm sure his family made a big deal out of it, but he confessed to me no experience of leaving a past which had entombed him and moving into a new future. He told me nothing that compares with the experience of blind barTimaeus. Nothing about sinking beneath the waters of baptism to rise anew, nothing about sharing the death and Resurrection of our Lord. For Dad, it was something all the kids his age did.

Dad traded no old name for a new. He had been raised in a family in which church attendance was enforced, as was I. There was no "ah HAH" moment for Dad at his baptism. It was a continuation of what had always been his family's expectations.

Not so blind barTimaeus. He pursued Jesus even though those around him, voices in the darkness of his sightless world, ordered him not to. Still, he cried out and Timaeus' son's life was changed forever. He left his meeting with Jesus with a new name and a new life. We have lost that, church. We have substituted a relationship with a church and a tradition of worship for a relationship with Jesus, and those on the outside, looking in, see no compelling reason to join us.

I think, because this is Reformation Sunday, that it is a good time to think about the ways we might be ready to break with the past, and move into a new future. I'll be criticized by my colleagues for over-simplifying something that is much more complex than this, but here goes, anyway. When Jesus walked upon the earth, the people believed that a relationship with God could only be obtained through the intercession of the Temple and adherence to the traditions of Jewish life. Jesus spoke for the disenfranchised, for the excluded, for those for whom a path to God had been pre-empted by the experts and held out the possibility of encountering God on a dusty street. When, in the 16th Century, the people believed that a relationship with God could only be obtained through the intercession of the Roman Catholic church, which even asserted the power to sell heavenly favor, Martin Luther pounded 95 thesis into the wood of the church door and insisted that the only relationship which God valued was that between the individual and Himself. We remember the beginnings of the Reformation on this Sunday to remind us that when the emphasis of organized religion falls too strongly on the "organized" part and too little on the "religion" part, that we have become as blind as the son of Timaeus.

The only relationship that counts, church, is the relationship between you and God. Your relationship with the church must never intrude into that essential, intentional and constitutional unity. Instead, the role of the physical church, the singing, the preaching of the word, is to further your personal, intimate relationship with God. The relationship with the church must be ancillary and supportive to your relationship, rather than a substitute for it. As in Magritte's picture, we are in danger of confusing the image of a pipe with a pipe by mistaking our relationship with a church for our relationship with God.

Ceci n'est pas une pipe. This is not a pipe. It is an image of a pipe. Water your garden, church, by attending to your relationship with God. When you take the name "Christian" mean by it a commitment to live by the teachings of our Lord, and to show that commitment in all you do.

J. STEWART SCHNEIDER

There is None Like Him

"God is not one of many. He is not comparable to others for there is no others with which to compare Him. This is a very difficult teaching. It is, nonetheless, central."

Genesis 18:1-15

The LORD appeared to Abraham by the oaks of Mamre, as he sat at the entrance of his tent in the heat of the day. He looked up and saw three men standing near him. When he saw them, he ran from the tent entrance to meet them, and bowed down to the ground. He said, "My lord, if I find favor with you, do not pass by your servant. Let a little water be brought, and wash your feet, and rest yourselves under the tree. Let me bring a little bread, that you may refresh yourselves, and after that you may pass on — since you have come to your servant." So they said, "Do as you have said." And Abraham hastened into the tent to Sarah, and said, "Make ready quickly three measures of choice flour, knead it, and make cakes." Abraham ran to the herd, and took a calf, tender and good, and gave it to the servant, who hastened to prepare it. Then he took curds and milk and the calf that he had prepared, and set it before them; and he stood by them under the tree while they ate.

They said to him, "Where is your wife Sarah?" And he said, "There, in the tent." Then one said, "I will surely return to you in due season, and your wife Sarah shall have a son." And Sarah was listening at the tent entrance behind him. Now Abraham and Sarah were old, advanced in age; it had ceased to be with Sarah after the manner of women. So Sarah laughed to herself, saying, "After I have grown old, and my husband is old, shall I have pleasure?" The LORD said to Abraham, "Why did Sarah laugh, and say, `Shall I indeed bear a child, now that I am old?' Is anything too wonderful for the LORD? At the set time I will return to you, in due season, and Sarah shall have a son." But Sarah denied, saying, "I did not laugh"; for she was afraid. He said, "Oh yes, you did laugh."

Matthew 9:35-10:8

Jesus went about all the cities and villages, teaching in their synagogues, and proclaiming the good news of the kingdom, and curing every disease and every sickness. When he saw the crowds, he had compassion for them, because they were harassed and helpless, like sheep without a shepherd. Then he said to his disciples, "The harvest is plentiful, but the laborers are few; therefore ask the Lord of the harvest to send out laborers into his harvest."

Then Jesus summoned his twelve disciples and gave them authority over unclean spirits, to cast them out, and to cure every disease and every sickness. These are the names of the twelve apostles: first, Simon, also known as Peter, and his brother Andrew; James son of Zebedee, and his brother John; Philip and Bartholomew; Thomas and Matthew the tax collector; James son of Alphaeus, and Thaddaeus; Simon the Cananaean, and Judas Iscariot, the one who betrayed him.

These twelve Jesus sent out with the following instructions: "Go nowhere among the Gentiles, and enter no town of the Samaritans, but go rather to the lost sheep of the house of Israel. As you go, proclaim the good news, `The kingdom of heaven has come near.' Cure the sick, raise the dead, cleanse the lepers, cast out demons. You received without payment; give without payment. Take no gold, or silver, or copper in your belts, no bag for your journey, or two tunics, or sandals, or a staff; for laborers deserve their food. Whatever town or village you enter, find out who in it is worthy, and stay there until you leave. As you enter the house, greet it. If the house is worthy, let your peace come upon it; but if it is not worthy, let your peace return to you. If anyone will not welcome you or listen to your words, shake off the dust from your feet as you leave that house or town. Truly I tell you, it will be more tolerable for the land of Sodom and Gomorrah on the day of judgment than for that town.

"See, I am sending you out like sheep into the midst of wolves; so be wise as serpents and innocent as doves. Beware of them, for they will hand you over to councils and flog you in their synagogues; and you will be dragged before governors and kings because of me, as a testimony to them and the Gentiles. When they hand you over, do not worry about how you are to speak or what you are to say; for what you are to say will be given to you at that time; for it is not you who speak, but the Spirit of your Father speaking through you.

Brother will betray brother to death, and a father his child, and children will rise against parents and have them put to death; and you will be hated by all because of my name. But the one who endures to the end will be saved. When they persecute you in one town, flee to the next; for truly I tell you, you will not have gone through all the towns of Israel before the Son of Man comes.

Matthew 9 is a great ordination sermon. Jesus grants power to his disciples to cast out evil spirits and cure diseases, but then instructs them to take nothing with them, relying on the kindness of strangers, if you will, perhaps to keep them humble. They are not going out as powerful men, but as servants to those who suffer. Then he tells them what their ministry is going to be like, and it is not going to be fun. It's going to involve arrests and flogging.

That's something we don't always focus on about Jesus – the powerful Jesus, the Imperial Jesus, if you will. We like to think of the Jesus we learned about as children – the one that loves us and protects us. Jesus in Matthew 9 is something different – the giver of power, the general directing his army.

The Rev. Larry Paul Jones, who taught me apocalyptic, said the most remarkable thing about Jesus. We were referencing a passage in the first chapter of Revelation:

> I turned around to see the voice that was speaking to me. And when I turned I saw seven golden lampstands, and among the lampstands was someone "like a son of man,"dressed in a robe reaching down to his feet and with a golden sash around his chest. His head and hair were white like wool, as white as snow, and his eyes were like blazing fire. His feet were like bronze glowing in a furnace, and his voice was like the sound of rushing waters. In his right hand he held seven stars, and out of his mouth came a sharp double-edged sword. His face was like the sun shining in all its brilliance.[19]

Larry Paul read the passage, looked at the class and said, "Jesus ain't your

---

19 Revelation 1:12-16

fishin' buddy."

Larry Paul has the gift of finding just the right words to make a concept stick in your mind, and he found it there. "Jesus ain't your fishin' buddy."

Because the church teaches and we believe that God is love, that Jesus sacrificed Himself for our sins, and that Jesus loves us, it is easy to come to a mental image of Jesus as sort of a divine nanny. Larry Paul didn't say this, but I could easily imagine him saying, "This is not a great idea." It makes us forget that God is the sovereign creator of all that is, the one, the unique, the alpha and omega. There is none like Him.

Jesus loves me, this I know, not just because the Bible tells me so, but because every day, every minute of the day, I can sense Him directing me, caring for me, buoying me up, giving me words for these sermons. Nobody would take that much time and trouble with somebody as hard-headed as I am if they didn't love me. I know this, right down to my shoe laces.

Knowing that God the Son extends His Grace to me, that God the Father loves me, that God the Holy Spirit communes with me tempts me to project off onto God the characteristics of other people who love me. How else am I to think about it? There's the rub, as the barbecue chef said to the chicken. God isn't at all like your grandmother, or your earthly father, or your second grade teacher. It's quite possible that your grandmother or your earthly father or your second grade teacher had godly qualities that supported and protected you, and, indeed, I think they must have done, because look how well you turned out, but that's not the same thing. Just as soon as you make a mental picture of God as the guy with the white beard on the big throne, you've missed the point. God isn't just like us, only bigger. God is God. There is none like Him. That's what Larry Paul was talking about when he said "Jesus ain't your fishin' buddy." Jesus, the Lamb, can be a scary thing indeed. That's why there's so much talk in the Bible about fearing God.

We run into Abraham in today's story sitting in front of his tent in the heat of the day. Interestingly, he doesn't seem to be in a desert. He's by the oaks of Mamre, and oaks don't grow in the desert. Wherever he is, it's too hot to work. The only sensible thing to do is to conserve strength, and that's what Abraham was doing. Anyway, he's older than Ned Johnson. He <u>deserves</u> to sit down and rest his bones.

To his surprise, he finds three men standing near him.

This is a mysterious passage. We don't know how the men got there. We don't know that they got there by walking down the road, but we also don't know that they didn't. We don't even know that there <u>was</u> a road. Abraham is a nomadic herder. His tent is out in the middle of nowhere. He's just suddenly confronted with three men.

The text tells us, "The LORD appeared to Abraham by the oaks of Mamre ..." Many Christians want to identify the three with the Father, Son and Holy Spirit, but I don't much like that interpretation because it portrays God as three separate beings.

However we understand the three men, it is clear that Abraham is having a *theophany*, an appearance of God. It's also clear that he knows that something important is happening, because he reacted in the most singular way.

> When he saw them, he ran from the tent entrance to meet them, and bowed down to the ground. He said, "My lord, if I find favor with you, do not pass by your servant. Let a little water be brought, and wash your feet, and rest yourselves under the tree. Let me bring a little bread, that you may refresh yourselves, and after that you may pass on — since you have come to your servant."

Abraham, aged 99 years, <u>ran</u> to them. He <u>bowed</u> down to the ground. He <u>addressed</u> them as "My Lord." He <u>acknowledged</u> that he might not be worthy for them to even notice. He <u>begged</u> to be permitted to serve them. This is all the more remarkable because Abraham, remember, isn't a simple shepherd. Genesis tells us, "Now Abram was very rich in livestock, in silver, and in gold." Abraham was an important man, a force to be dealt with in his area. Important as he was, though, he responded to the appearance of the Lord with the body language and speech of a servant.

This would be a good place to sort of mentally scoot our own, personal approach to prayer up next to Abraham's actions and see if we might learn something. Prayer is the place where the Lord meets us. And when He does, when we begin to pray, how is our approach to a meeting with God different than Abraham's?

American Protestants bring a lot of baggage to this business of prayer. We're not all that shot in the head about bowing. We're fiercely protective of our notions of equality and like nothing so well as catching somebody who has gotten above his raising, and helping him down from that perch. We've been big shots on the world stage so long, we find it enormously difficult to see ourselves in a subservient position.

But Abraham, rich and powerful as he was, did. His every word, his every action spoke of his acknowledgement of his inferiority to these visitors. That's not so easy for an American Protestant to pull off.

When our daughter Kat was a little girl, she made friends with another little girl in her preschool whose family did not very often go out to eat. One weekend, we took both girls to Jenny Wiley for a show and dinner. The little girl had never visited a buffet before, and was mightily impressed. We loaded up our plates and headed back to our table where she announced that we had to pray first. We said grace and, after a bit, went back for seconds. To our surprise, she insisted on praying a second time. When we said that was not really necessary, she insisted, explaining that praying over your food makes the food taste better.

Now, after you get over the initial reaction to just how cute that is coming from a preschooler, there's an important lesson here. The little girl did not understand prayer as a time of meeting with God. She understood prayer as something one did to make the food taste better. That's the baggage American Protestants bring to prayer. If we are not very, very careful, we'll come to see prayer as something one does to make life better, instead of as a time of communing with God.

Abraham knew he was in the presence of the divine, and he buried his face in the dust, unwilling to even look at the Lord. His every action was to find ways to please the Lord, to serve him. There was no thought of how it might benefit him. His only desire was to serve the Lord.

Abraham's protestations aren't the false modesty of a very rich man, or mere hospitality. They are exactly the response that we should have in the presence of God, and God's reaction confirms it. "Do as you have said."

You would think, in contemporary America, that the guests would say something like, "Oh, no! Don't go to any trouble for us," but that is pointedly **not** what happened. Their response to Abraham's offer was a command. "Do as you have said." God is God. There is none like Him.

Abraham doesn't bring a little water for their feet and some bread, though. He goes to enormous pains to bring only the best.

> And Abraham hastened into the tent to Sarah, and said, "Make ready quickly three measures of choice flour, knead it and make cakes." Abraham ran to the herd, and took a calf, tender and good, and gave it to the servant, who hastened to prepare it. Then he took curds and milk and the calf that he had prepared, and set it before them; and he stood by them under the tree while they ate.

That's a lot of running and hastening for a 99-year-old man. Let alone standing in the heat of the day, unwilling to even sit in the presence of his divine visitors while they ate.

This imperial aspect of God is one so unfamiliar to us that even though we know it to be so, it feels a little "wrong." I would be much happier with the brown-haired, blue-eyed loving Jesus portrayed on the famous painting hanging on the wall in the education building. That's the Jesus that just might go fishing with me. I'm happy and comfortable with that Jesus, and I'm uncomfortable with the view of God given me in this story.

Of course, we have no business demanding that God appear in ways we would prefer. God is God. There is none like him. We cannot reconstruct him in ways we find more comfortable. We must relate to him as he is, sharp double-edged sword and all.

When next you pray, church, be aware of how you approach God. Are you hastening to bring the best, and begging to be permitted to serve Him? Are you praying to make the food taste better? Which do you think represents true prayer? Or do both? What do you think about prayer, church?

J. STEWART SCHNEIDER

A Negotiable God

"The people of Moses' time saw God as so awesome, so holy, that they couldn't bear to approach him. They asked Moses to do so on their behalf. The God of the 21st Century is much more approachable, more tractable, more open to negotiation, you might say. Except there is and always has been only one God."

Exodus 32:1-14

When the people saw that Moses delayed to come down from the mountain, the people gathered around Aaron, and said to him, "Come, make gods for us, who shall go before us; as for this Moses, the man who brought us up out of the land of Egypt, we do not know what has become of him." Aaron said to them, "Take off the gold rings that are on the ears of your wives, your sons, and your daughters, and bring them to me." So all the people took off the gold rings from their ears, and brought them to Aaron. He took the gold from them, formed it in a mold, and cast an image of a calf; and they said, "These are your gods, O Israel, who brought you up out of the land of Egypt!" When Aaron saw this, he built an altar before it; and Aaron made proclamation and said, "Tomorrow shall be a festival to the LORD." They rose early the next day, and offered burnt offerings and brought sacrifices of well-being; and the people sat down to eat and drink, and rose up to revel.

The LORD said to Moses, "Go down at once! Your people, whom you brought up out of the land of Egypt, have acted perversely; they have been quick to turn aside from the way that I commanded them; they have cast for themselves an image of a calf, and have worshiped it and sacrificed to it, and said, 'These are your gods, O Israel, who brought you up out of the land of Egypt!'" The LORD said to Moses, "I have seen this people, how stiff-necked they are. Now let me alone, so that my wrath may burn hot against them and I may consume them; and of you I will make a great nation."

But Moses implored the LORD his God, and said, "O LORD, why does your wrath burn hot against your people, whom you brought out of the land of Egypt with great power and with a mighty hand? Why should the Egyptians say, 'It was with evil intent that he brought them out to kill them in the mountains, and to consume them from the face of the earth'? Turn from your fierce wrath; change your mind and do not bring disaster on your people. Remember Abraham, Isaac, and Israel, your servants, how you swore to them by your own self, saying to them, 'I will multiply your descendants like the stars of heaven, and all this land that I have promised I will give to your descendants, and they shall inherit it forever.'" And the LORD changed his mind about the disaster that he planned to bring on his people.

Matthew 22:1-14

Once more Jesus spoke to the people in parables, saying: "The kingdom of heaven may be compared to a king who gave a wedding banquet for his son. He sent his slaves to call those who had been invited to the wedding banquet, but they would not come. Again he sent other slaves, saying, 'Tell those who have been invited: Look, I have prepared my dinner, my oxen and my fat calves have been slaughtered, and everything is ready; come to the wedding banquet.' But they made light of it and went away, one to his farm, another to his business, while the rest seized his slaves, mistreated them, and killed them. The king was enraged. He sent his troops, destroyed those murderers, and burned their city. Then he said to his slaves, 'The wedding is ready, but those invited were not worthy. Go therefore into the main streets, and invite everyone you find to the wedding banquet.' Those slaves went out into the streets and gathered all whom they found, both good and bad; so the wedding hall was filled with guests.

"But when the king came in to see the guests, he noticed a man there who was not wearing a wedding robe, and he said to him, 'Friend, how did you get in here without a wedding robe?' And he was speechless. Then the king said to the attendants, 'Bind him hand and foot, and throw him into the outer darkness, where there will be weeping and gnashing of teeth.' For many are called, but few are chosen."

The story of Aaron and the golden calf comes up in the Lectionary texts once every three years, and it's greeted by preachers with a mixture of gratitude and dread. The dread part comes from the recognition that it's been preached to death and it's going to be real hard to come up with something that will keep God's children awake for the full 17 ½ minutes. The gratitude part comes from the realization that when you finally give up and preach the same sermon that's always preached about this passage – the one about not letting yourself get distracted by the golden calves of the world – that absolutely no one in the congregation is going to be mad at you. Everybody's going to say to themselves, "Yep! I got it. No golden calves. That's easy, preacher. What's for lunch?"

Personally, I'd just as soon you not be mad at me, but I have this compulsion to press you a bit on this passage, and on the discussion we had recently about how you can't enlist God in the furtherance of your own plans, which will probably make you mad at me. Fortunately, I'm such an intriguing character that I'm gambling you will forgive me sooner rather than later.

First, you need to know what I mean when I say you can't enlist God in the furtherance of your own plans. I said that it isn't about you — it's about God. I suspect that shocked some of you, since that's not how we usually think of things. I'm convinced, though, that as children of God it is our proper role. As a follower of the way taught and illustrated by Jesus, I am convinced that our role is the way of a servant, and that means that we can't shove God around to suit our purposes.

I suspect most of you will agree with that, but here's where I want to press you a bit beyond your comfort zone because if we're going to get anything out of this passage beyond, "Don't make golden calves." we have to do a little scholarly work. Every time I suggest this at the Chapel of St. Starbuck, Mrs. Wintersheimer hands me a bumper sticker that reads, "God said it, I believe it, and that ends it." My impression, however, is that this congregation is not offended by the need to involve our scholar's skills in reading Scripture, so I'm going to risk it. Let's dig into a real Di Vinci code mystery.

First, we need to understand Aaron's behavior a little better. Moses went up the mountain, leaving the people in the charge of his brother, Aaron. When Moses didn't come directly back, the people panicked and looked to Aaron for leadership, as they should do. But what they asked him for are gods. They demanded:

Come, make gods for us, who shall go before us;

Well, of course they did. They have lived in Egypt for 430 years. They are accustomed to idols they can look at, and they derive great comfort from them. Too, you have to be a little sympathetic with Aaron's plight. The people are rebelling. Moses has apparently disappeared into a volcano. If he doesn't give the people what they want, Aaron may be the next one into the volcano. So Aaron takes the course of compromise, ignores the commandment about making graven images, and graves himself the image of a calf which he offers up as the means to worship God.

That's the vital point. Our passage notes that after making the calf, Aaron told the people, "Tomorrow shall be a festival to the Lord." The underlying Hebrew is the name of God. Perhaps he thought, "I have to keep these people focused on God, but right now they want something to look at, so I'll make them an idol, and use that as a way to build worship to God as I ween them off idols." In other words, contrary to what you might think at first, Aaron isn't setting up a new god. He's setting up a alternative way to worship YHWH, and he's assuming unto himself the role of Moses. Aaron is suggesting that the people worship the right God in the wrong way. The problem, of course, is that nobody told him to do that. He's doing it on his on authority, for his own reasons, and in the face of God's commandment not to make graven images.

This is a pretty good description of us in the 21st Century. The people of Moses' time saw God as so awesome, so holy, that they couldn't bear to approach him. They asked Moses to do so on their behalf. The God of the 21st Century is much more approachable, more tractable, more open to negotiation, you might say. Indeed, it's almost impossible to recognize this God of thunder and fear in our modern concept of God. The fly in that ointment is that there is only one God. If the perceptions are different, if people of Moses' time understood God to be ineffable and people of our time have to look up the word "ineffable." it isn't God who changed. It is our perceptions of God.

The text has another surprise: Aaron cast A calf. Singular. But the people replied "These are your gods." Plural. Why would they do that? When the Bible says something inconsistent like that, we can either shrug our shoulders and say, "Oh well. It's not important." then proceed to re-write the Bible, just as Aaron re-wrote God into a more manageable golden calf, or we can take the text seriously, and investigate the meaning of this odd phrase. Let's do that.

The Book of Exodus, scholars tell us, was put in its final form by an anony-
mous editor or editors either during or shortly after the exile to Babylon. That
puts it in the 6th Century BC or perhaps later. If we look 400 years earlier
than that, we find Solomon, the third king of the United Monarchy of Judah
and Israel, and the builder of God's First Temple. Solomon died about 931
BC, and he was succeeded by his his idiot son, Rehoboam.

I call Rehoboam an idiot because the United Monarchy fell apart over a bit of
stupidity from him. On his father's death, the northern ten of the twelve tribes
came to Rehoboam and said, "Your daddy has taxed our brains out. You want
us with you, you got to work with us."

Rehoboam replied, "You think Daddy's taxes were high, wait until you see
what I got in store for you." and the northern 10/12's of the country took a
hike, choosing Jeroboam I as their king. The Temple, however, remained in
Jerusalem. We pick up this story in I Kings, chapter 12. Jeroboam reasoned as
follows:

> If this people continues to go up to offer sacrifices in the house of the
> Lord at Jerusalem, the heart of this people will turn again to their mas-
> ter, King Rehoboam of Judah; they will kill me and return to King Re-
> hoboam of Judah.

Jeroboam recognizes that if the house of the Lord is in the south, and if the
people go there to worship, they'll eventually depose him and relieve his
shoulders of the burden of his head into the bargain. His solution is to make
two calves of gold. He set one up in Dan and the other in Bethel and told his
people they are to worship there, not in Jerusalem. TWO calves. Plural. Jeroboam said to the people of the northern ten tribes:

> Here are your gods, O Israel, who brought you up out of the land of
> Egypt[20].

Did you hear that? These are the exact words the people are reported to have
said to Aaron centuries before,

> These are your gods, O Israel, who brought you up out of the land of
> Egypt!

Jeroboam is doing exactly the same thing Aaron did. He's suggesting that the

---

20 1 Kings 12:27-30

people worship the right God, but in the wrong way, and in the wrong place, to boot. Like Aaron, he wants to make God more flexible, more negotiable to the conditions of the time. Why do I bring this up? To point out that we are altogether too good at doing the same thing, bending the word of the Lord to meet our convenience.

You see, the word of the Lord is not contained in the Bible in the same way that the news of the day is contained in the words of the newspaper. The word of the Lord comes to us through the stories in Scripture, but is greater than them. Whether you, personally, want to view these words as having been written by a 6th Century BC editor writing from Babylon under the inspiration of God, or the words of Jeroboam speaking from Shekem in the 10th Century BC, or the words of the people to Aaron in the 14th Century BCE, the word of the Lord is clear: "What part of 'Thou shalt not' did you fail to understand? I said no graven images. Not even images of me, for I cannot be contained in an image. I cannot be contained in any categories of thought open to you. If you make an idol, you will think you have captured me in this image, and you will worship the image. And no, that's not up for discussion."

Some 900 years ago, the great Torah scholar Maimonides described the qualitative chasm between us and God:

> God is not physical and there is absolutely no comparison between Him and any of His creations. His existence is not like their existence; His life is not like that of any living being; His wisdom is not like the wisdom of the wisest of men. The difference between Him and His creations is not merely quantitative, but absolute ...

God demands of us a right view of our relationship with Him, right intentions in our approach to Him and His Creation, right words, right action, and right obedience. We can't shove things around to make it safer or more comfortable for us. It is our role to serve God, not to impose compromises on Him.

That's not something anybody is glad to hear. I'm much happier shouting, "Thank God!" when something goes right, and "Please God" when something goes wrong. I'm much more comfortable taking my troubles to God and expecting Him to fix them than I am thinking God has need of me to serve Him. I had a classmate who told me she held herself back from her church because she was sure that if she gave herself completely, she'd be sent as a missionary to "Darkest Africa." I don't know what part of Africa is the darkest, but I sympathize with her anxiety. Taking God seriously as the master of our lives, the sovereign of our world, is a scary thought, indeed.

If we approach a passage like our Gospel text for today from Matthew without having done the homework we just did, we're likely to be shocked by Jesus' words. This just doesn't sound like the loving, accepting, forgiving, undemanding, comfortable, negotiable Jesus we're accustomed to.

> But when the king came in to see the guests, he noticed a man there who was not wearing a wedding robe, and he said to him, "Friend, how did you get in here without a wedding robe?" And he was speechless. Then the king said to the attendants, "Bind him hand and foot, and throw him into the outer darkness, where there will be weeping and gnashing of teeth." For many are called, but few are chosen.

Really, Jesus? The guy didn't wear the right clothes and for this he gets thrown out, bound hand and foot? No. Not really. This is a parable. Jesus is speaking metaphorically. What is Jesus telling us? In view of what we have learned about Aaron, the calf and Jeroboam, isn't Jesus telling us of God's uncompromising demand for right view, right intention, right speech, right action and right obedience? Isn't He hinting strongly that God is not interested in corner cutters?

I get lectured pretty regularly by visitors to the Chapel of St. Starbuck on the topic of the "wrathful" Old Testament God and the "loving" New Testament God. I point out that there is only one God. The point is absolutely foundational to our understanding of our relationship with God. There is only one. There are lots of distractions, many shiny things that vie for our interest, there are many times when our nerve fails us and we try to make compromises to hide from God's demands on us, but there is only one God. This one God is the foundation, the rock, upon which everything is sustained, and, as such, He is sovereign. That scares us, and in our fear, we have come up with the idea of a "loving" New Testament God, personified by Jesus. We want to think that Jesus is more open to negotiation than the wrathful God of the Old Testament. It does not work this way. Jesus may be all of God we can perceive, but He is not in competition with His Father.

It is precisely this which we have painted over in our pursuit of a negotiable God. If we are to live up to our calling as children of God, we absolutely have to attain a right view of our relationship so as to embrace totally our role as servant and God's existence as the Creator and Source of all being — the un-created One Who must exist, has always existed and will always exist.

Christians see in the life and death of Jesus an example of uncompromising obedience, even unto death on a cross. This is "The Way" which Jesus brought us – the path of uncompromising obedience.

I suppose that the role of a servant to a sovereign God could be discouraging. Will we ever get it right? Are we to be cast into the outer darkness where is weeping and gnashing of teeth for the smallest infraction?

No. That's not the proper view of Jesus' words, either. Better that we turn to Paul's words to his church at Philippi

> Rejoice in the Lord always; again I will say, Rejoice. Let your gentleness be known to everyone. The Lord is near. Do not worry about anything, but in everything by prayer and supplication with thanksgiving let your requests be made known to God. And the peace of God, which surpasses all understanding, will guard your hearts and your minds in Christ Jesus.

Rejoice, church! For your Lord has formed you from the dust of the earth through His great love. Follow the path Jesus laid out with rejoicing, for you are no less than children of the Most Holy God.

The Coin

"Render unto Caesar is not advice from Jesus to pay your taxes. Caesar leaves any dispute with Jesus a beggar."

Exodus 33:12-23

Moses said to the LORD, "See, you have said to me, 'Bring up this people'; but you have not let me know whom you will send with me. Yet you have said, 'I know you by name, and you have also found favor in my sight.' Now if I have found favor in your sight, show me your ways, so that I may know you and find favor in your sight. Consider too that this nation is your people." He said, "My presence will go with you, and I will give you rest." And he said to him, "If your presence will not go, do not carry us up from here. For how shall it be known that I have found favor in your sight, I and your people, unless you go with us? In this way, we shall be distinct, I and your people, from every people on the face of the earth."

The LORD said to Moses, "I will do the very thing that you have asked; for you have found favor in my sight, and I know you by name." Moses said, "Show me your glory, I pray." And he said, "I will make all my goodness pass before you, and will proclaim before you the name, 'The LORD'; and I will be gracious to whom I will be gracious, and will show mercy on whom I will show mercy. But," he said, "you cannot see my face; for no one shall see me and live." And the LORD continued, "See, there is a place by me where you shall stand on the rock; and while my glory passes by I will put you in a cleft of the rock, and I will cover you with my hand until I have passed by; then I will take away my hand, and you shall see my back; but my face shall not be seen."

Matthew 22:15-22

The Pharisees went and plotted to entrap Jesus in what he said. So they sent their disciples to him, along with the Herodians, saying, "Teacher, we know that you are sincere, and teach the way of God in accordance with truth, and show deference to no one; for you do not regard people with partiality. Tell us, then, what you think. Is it lawful to pay taxes to the emperor, or not?" But Jesus, aware of their malice, said, "Why are you putting me to the test, you hypocrites? Show me the coin used for the tax." And they brought him a denarius. Then he said to them, "Whose head is this, and whose title?" They answered, "The emperor's." Then he said to them, "Give therefore to the emperor the things that are the emperor's, and to God the things that are God's." When they heard this, they were amazed; and they left him and went away.

In 1960, young Cassius Clay stepped off the podium at the Rome Olympics with the gold. I can't begin to imagine the pride this young man felt as he received the world's acclaim for what he had accomplished. He later related that was the first night he had ever slept on his back. If he had slept on his stomach, he said, the medal would have hurt his chest.

Back in his home country to which he had brought such honor, he sat down in a segregated diner.

The counter man said, "We don't serve Negroes."

Clay snapped, "I don't eat them either!"

The crowd in the diner shouted, "Boy get out!"

Frankly, it would never occur to me to get smart-mouth with the holder of the Olympic light heavy weight gold medal. What made the guy behind the counter think <u>he</u> could do that? The answer, of course, is that in 1960, the black man was always wrong and the white man was always right. The society in which they lived was unjust, and that injustice favored one group at the expense of the other. An unjust society empowers unjust action by people. An angry and humiliated Clay later tossed his gold medal into the Ohio River say-ing, "This thing ain't worth nothin' – it can't even get me a hamburger!"

It is extraordinarily hard, church, to oppose evil and extraordinarily easy to do nothing. It's extraordinarily hard to police our own hearts and our own ac-tions, so the temptation is to just go along with the injustice that exists in our world while we work on the bad stuff we see in our internal world. I want to shock you with something. God's passion is not the redemption and salvation of individuals *from the world*, but the redemption and salvation *of the world*[21]. The world, and all that is in it, is the Creation of God. When we take the view that we need to be saved <u>from</u> the world, we have made an enemy of God's own handiwork! Our story today speaks about the conflict between God's law, and the statutes of man.

Sometimes, when the Lectionary gives us a well-known parable like this one, I do an informal poll at the Chapel of St. Starbuck to get a sense of what people understand Jesus to be saying. When I asked about the parable in today's text, some told me that "render unto Caesar" meant that Christians should be care-ful to obey the civil law because our leaders are ordained by God to lead us. Given the current situation in Washington, that may be a bit of a stretch, and it's certainly not what I learned from Ruth Huddy Justice in American History class about the American position on the divine right of kings.

Several people told me that Jesus was telling us to pay our taxes on time. Good Americans pay their taxes, but I have some difficulty reading this pas-sage as an endorsement by Jesus of the Internal Revenue Service. I can think of many very good reasons to pay your taxes, but not many of them have to do with the life and teaching of Jesus.

Surprisingly, many people told me that Jesus was demonstrating the impor-tance of separation of church and state – some things belong to Caesar, they explained, and some belong to God, and you should keep them separate. This, it seems to me, is a very strange reading. How can anything in God's cre-ation belong to Caesar and not to God?

One thing I do know – this conversation wasn't an amusing bit of thrust and parry in the drawing room. This was deadly serious. Jesus' life was on the line. The text tells us, right at the beginning, "The Pharisees went and plotted

---

21 Marcus J. Borg, "The Heart of Christianity" (HarperOne, 2004)

to entrap Jesus in what he said." The Jewish authorities were after His life. And, eventually, they got it. Couldn't keep it, to everyone's surprise, but they initially got it.

The plot was a simple one, couched in a simple sort of question. Those opposing Jesus sent their disciples and some Herodians (who would have been enthusiastic collaborators with the Romans during Jesus' life) to ask, "Tell us, then, what you think. Is it lawful to pay taxes to the emperor, or not?"

Well, Roman law certainly imposed a head-tax, beginning in 6 AD, and the Romans could certainly extract severe penalties for NOT paying it, but the questioners aren't talking about Roman law. They are asking if it is lawful under God's Law as set out in Torah, part of our Old Testament, to pay the Roman tax. Torah governs everything an obedient Jew does, and the disciples sent to trap Jesus are from the Pharisaic sect, one noted primarily for its strict adherence to Torah. Indeed, the Pharisee's strict adherence to Torah caused them to bitterly resist this tax because it impoverished Jews while enriching Romans and because it had to be paid in Roman coin. You really can't overestimate the importance of that coin in this discussion. I'll show you why in a minute.

It's a neat trap they've laid for Him. If Jesus answered, "Yes, Torah permits Jews to pay taxes to the Emperor," He would be discredited in the eyes of the people, and perhaps the crowd would turn on him. If He answered, "No, Torah does not permit Jews to pay taxes to the Emperor," Rome could be counted on to kill him. Jesus gave neither answer. Instead, He asked to see the coin used to pay the tax.

> But Jesus, aware of their malice, said, "Why are you putting me to the test, you hypocrites? Show me the coin used for the tax." And they brought him a denarius.

It sounds so distant and strange to our ears, but it isn't. They are asking Jesus, "What law governs you? God's law or Caesar's law?" When you are measuring a position you will advocate, or an action you will take, do you weigh it against how much trouble you might get into with your neighbors and friends or do you weigh it against God's Word? Worse yet, do you perhaps push the whole issue into the back of your mind when you sense some conflict between what your community is doing and your understanding of God's requirements? To put it even more plainly, if you had been in that diner with young Cassius Clay, would you have shouted "Boy get out" with the crowd, would you have remained silent, or would you have spoken up in defense of the young man?

This old world creaks along doing almost everything wrong, and we're carried along with it, whether we like it or not. What are we supposed to do? All that, and more, was wrapped up in that coin Jesus asked to see.

None of us here is familiar with the coin, so the major drama of this encounter goes whistling right by us. Everybody listening, though, would know exactly what was going on. We need to catch up to His first century listeners so that we can understand, too.

This was in the reign of Tiberius Julius Caesar, the Second Emperor of Rome. Like all emperors, he minted coins. The Tiberius silver denarius was minted in its thousands, so many that one can be bought today for as little as $80. It'll be in lousy shape for that price, but you can buy one. A good one will cost you about $300.

On the front is the head of Tiberius, in profile. Around the rim are the words:

TI CAESAR DIVI AVG F AVGVSTVS
(Tiberius Caesar son of the Divine Augustus, Augustus!)

On the back is his mother, Livia, dressed as the goddess Pax. Around the rim are these words:

PONTIF MAXIM
(Roughly, "High Priest")

Remember, this conversation is taking place within the actual Temple itself! Let's imagine how many ways this coin Jesus has caused his accusers to produce from their very own pocket would make a Jew of the time see red.

1. The coin is a Roman coin. It is the coin used to pay the hated head-tax which impoverished Jews and enriched Romans for no better reason than that the Romans could get away with it.
2. It has a graven image on it. Two of them, in fact. Jews were not permitted to carry coins with graven images in the Temple. That's why there were money changers there.
3. The graven images portray Tiberius' mother dressed idolatrously as a goddess.
4. The caption around the obverse identifies Tiberius as "son of the

divine Augustus," simultaneously reminding the holder not only that Augustus had been proclaimed divine by the Roman Senate and that Tiberius is "majestic," but that the Roman Senate fancied that they had the power to create gods of mortals.

5. The caption on the reverse identifies Tiberius as "High Priest."

Jesus calls them hypocrites and hypocrites they are. If they truly had the best interests of the Jewish people at heart, if they were Jewish leaders and not Roman pawns, what were they doing walking around in the Temple jingling a pocketful of unlawful Roman coins depicting Roman politicians as gods? To the people watching, and the first readers of Matthew's Gospel, Jesus had won the argument at this point. He had no such idolatrous coins in his pocket. That coin, so foreign to us, is central to the exchange.

> Then he said to them, "Whose head is this, and whose title?" They answered, "The emperor's."

Jesus then told them, "If it's the emperor's coin, give it back to him." The strong implication is that the coin is worthless.

I disagree most sharply with those at the Chapel who told me that some things belong to Caesar and some belong to God. If we acknowledge that the world and everything in it is the creation of God, and we render unto Him all that there is, doesn't Caesar go home a beggar?

Indeed he does. And those at St. Starbuck who would read this parable as Jesus telling us to go along with anything the civil authorities cook up have misunderstood Jesus as well. Such a reading would have Russian Christians supporting Stalin's murder of 20 million people and German Christians supporting Hitler's horrors.

The people confronting Jesus represented the society of the time – a society in which one group, the Romans, are enriched at the expense of another group, the Jews. This enrichment is unjust because it is enforced at the point of a Roman sword. Might does not make right, but might very often makes the laws of the time, and those laws sometimes operate unjustly.

Which law guides our hands? When we say we are law-abiding people, do we mean that we pay our taxes on time and don't speed through red lights, or do we mean that we are strict followers of the way taught by Jesus? Those opposing Jesus had made their choice. When Jesus forced those questioning him to produce a Roman coin, He was showing that they had counted themselves in with the unjust Roman system which was impoverishing Jews and enriching Romans. The unjust coinage of Rome had become "just money" to them, and the Roman system "the law." Such assent to an unjust system grants it legitimacy. All that is necessary for the triumph of evil is that good men do nothing, or, as Dr. Martin Luther King put it:

> He who passively accepts evil is as much involved in it as he who helps to perpetrate it. He who accepts evil without protesting against it is really cooperating with it.

I said that God's passion is not the redemption and salvation of individuals **from the world**, but the redemption and salvation **of the world**. God so loved the world, we are told, not just me and you. God's elect are called upon to address the unjust societies which empower unjust actions just as much as they are called upon to confess their own sins. As we say each Sunday, "In the words of Scripture we are called upon to confess the reality of sin in personal <u>and common life</u>."

It is extraordinarily hard, church, to oppose evil and extraordinarily easy to close our eyes to the unjust systems of the world which unjustly impoverish some and unjustly enrich others. Dom Hélder Câmara, a Roman Catholic bishop in Brazil, took a clear position for the poor. It was not an easy thing to do. He was reviled by secular leaders and even opposed by forces within his own church. He said,

> When I feed the poor, they call me a saint. When I ask why the poor have no food, they call me a communist.

Everybody feels great if you volunteer to scrounge some food for the poor. If you start asking too many questions about what injustice in the society itself produces so many poor people, they'll sic the Herodians on you, every time.

Numbering ourselves as among the followers of God's only Son cannot mean anything so trivial as a pursuit of our own salvation. To be a practicing Christian means to share God's passion for His Creation and His children. To be a practicing Christian means to seek always justice and compassion, even when we find ourselves in a society which has turned its back on these Godly qualities.

In a just world, Cassius Clay would have gotten his hamburger. In a compassionate world, Bishop Câmara would not have to ask why the poor have no food. We do not live in such a world, and it is not acceptable to silently go along with it. We are to speak up, for there is this about you: you are a child of the Most High.

Folding the Pope's Vestments

"Treat my children with love. You who speak with full mouths, make the suffering of my children your business."

Micah 3:5-12

Thus says the LORD concerning the prophets
who lead my people astray,
who cry "Peace"
when they have something to eat,
but declare war against those
who put nothing into their mouths.
Therefore it shall be night to you, without vision,
and darkness to you, without revelation.
The sun shall go down upon the prophets,
and the day shall be black over them;
the seers shall be disgraced,
and the diviners put to shame;
they shall all cover their lips,
for there is no answer from God.
But as for me, I am filled with power,
with the spirit of the Lord,
and with justice and might,
to declare to Jacob his transgression
and to Israel his sin.
Hear this, you rulers of the house of Jacob
and chiefs of the house of Israel,
who abhor justice
and pervert all equity,
who build Zion with blood
and Jerusalem with wrong!
Its rulers give judgment for a bribe,

its priests teach for a price,
its prophets give oracles for money;
yet they lean upon the LORD and say,
"Surely the LORD is with us!
No harm shall come upon us."
Therefore because of you
Zion shall be plowed as a field;
Jerusalem shall become a heap of ruins,
and the mountain of the house a wooded height.

Matthew 23:1-12

Jesus said to the crowds and to his disciples, "The scribes and the Pharisees sit on Moses' seat; therefore, do whatever they teach you and follow it; but do not do as they do, for they do not practice what they teach. They tie up heavy burdens, hard to bear, and lay them on the shoulders of others; but they themselves are unwilling to lift a finger to move them. They do all their deeds to be seen by others; for they make their phylacteries broad and their fringes long. They love to have the place of honor at banquets and the best seats in the synagogues, and to be greeted with respect in the marketplaces, and to have people call them rabbi. But you are not to be called rabbi, for you have one teacher, and you are all students. And call no one your father on earth, for you have one Father — the one in heaven. Nor are you to be called instructors, for you have one instructor, the Messiah. The greatest among you will be your servant. All who exalt themselves will be humbled, and all who humble themselves will be exalted."

There's a famous Jewish story about Yom Kippur. Yom Kippur is a very solemn day for Jews. It is the Day of Atonement, the day that Jews bring before God their sins for the last year, confess that they have failed God, and ask to be sealed in the book of life for a good year ahead. On one Yom Kippur, the rabbi rose formally before the congregation, tore his garments and shouted, "Lord! I am nothing!".

Next the president of the Synagogue rose, rent his garments and confessed, "Lord! I am nothing!"

To everyone's surprise, the lowly little beadle then went to the front, rent his garments and shouted, "Lord! I am nothing."

The president elbowed the rabbi and pointed at the janitor, "Ha! Look who thinks **he's** nothing!"

Religious pride. We all have a touch of it. It's the feeling that because of our secular position in society, or our accomplishments, or all we do for the church that we are blessed by God for our activities. It's another way of thinking we can win our own salvation.

For the past few Sundays we have been following Matthew's dispute accounts between Jesus and the religious authorities of the time, taking place in the Temple. Jesus can be awfully hard on people in the religious life, and that's hard for them to accept. Jesus, it has to be remembered, is nobody from nowhere. He has no part in the Temple. He has no part in the administration of the government. He has no bone fides, no diploma, no Levite connection. He's not a kohan (that is, a priest) nor a rabbi in a synagogue. Those who are confronting him are all of these. They've dedicated their lives to religious life, and because they have worked so hard, they take ownership of their position. In a very human sort of way, they are proud of their accomplishment, and protective of it. Well, who could blame them? Wouldn't you?

Without earthly credentials Jesus is the natural target for those who see themselves as the guardians of orthodox worship. He has answered all their trick questions, silenced the Sadducees, trapped the Pharisees, disputed with the lawyer. Now it is Jesus' time to address spiritual pride with the crowd and his disciples. His dispute isn't that the teachings of the leaders are false. He agrees they are teaching God's law correctly. His dispute is that they themselves fail to follow the teachings they impose on everyone else. Those he is being critical of are seeking the acclaim of their peers through public displays of piety, but refuse to do the hard work that God has laid before them. It is a scathing attack, and one that resonates with our current time when the church is much more likely to be seen in the papers in the context of someone in the church doing something terribly wrong than it is to be seen in the papers doing something right.

It's a big problem for preachers everywhere. A colleague of mine often said that he was uneasy when people complimented a sermon because if he took credit, then it wasn't the word of God, and if it was the word of God he spoke, he couldn't take credit for it. Yet, he was sure his congregation would think poorly of him if he claimed to speak for God – nobody likes a prophet. Mostly, he just blushed. This is one of the reasons many of us involve ourselves so thoroughly in the business end of running a church. That's easier than undertaking to speak for God by a long shot and if you put together a really good committee structure, or start a really effective youth program, you CAN take credit for that, so there's a very human tendency to focus our attention on that which will bring us acclaim.

I know this because my one and only gift is to spin tales to you in the hope that by doing so I am throwing light upon the Gospel. I confess to you that, since that seems to be my only gift, sometimes I'm tormented by the thought that if I do that well, that's all that God requires of me. Of course, that is entirely wrong and I know it. Still, it is very human. We all want to feel we are doing what we do well, and that others appreciate it.

I was watching something on TV about the Catholic Church the other night. There was an appearance by the Pope in St. Paul's Basilica. After the Pope entered, two Cardinals assisted him to his throne and folded and arranged his vestments after he was seated. The Cardinals performed their duties with great care, folding the vestments just so. What would have happened, I wonder, if the beadle from our story had tried to help with the vestments? Would one Cardinal have elbowed the other and said, "Look who thinks HE can fold a vestment"?

I've looked the Scriptures over carefully. Nowhere do I find the word of God directing us to fold the Pope's vestments, yet that job and the countless others that are involved in keeping a church going have to be done. Since they HAVE to be done, the temptation is to focus on these, more manageable, tasks at the expense of the more difficult spiritual tasks that we are really supposed to be tending to. In other words, if you are up to your waist in alligators, it's sometimes hard to remember that your objective was to drain the swamp. We allow ourselves to be overwhelmed by the secular aspects of the job, and neglect the spiritual tasks which are really our only important jobs.

We do what we do, not as an end unto itself, but in obedience to God's command to love God with all our heart and all our might and all our strength, and to love our neighbor as ourself. Those in the dispute texts we have been reading who fancied that they are holier than Jesus had lost sight of that underlying objective. They thought their teaching and their grasp of Jewish law was all God required of them. Jesus reminded them that opening their hearts to let God empower them to love His creation as He does is our only real task. God works through the church to change hearts, one by one.

Unfortunately, we're a stiff-necked people. If we're faced with an alternative between doing what we know God would have us do at great expense to ourselves, or refusing to do so to our great remorse, we're very likely to search about for a third course which we can undertake and which will restore our feelings of self-worth. We go and find a Pope and fold his vestments, in other words. We invent easier paths to follow.

Seven hundred and fifty years before Jesus, the prophet Micah looked about him and brought the word of God to the prophets who were wrongly advising the leaders of the people of the southern kingdom.

> Thus says the LORD concerning the prophets
> who lead my people astray,
> who cry "Peace"
> when they have something to eat,
> but declare war against those
> who put nothing into their mouths.

I said nobody likes a prophet, and it is true. Prophets always speak in opposition to the status quo. How often can you find an Old Testament prophet declaring, "Great job! Just what I wanted. Take a couple weeks off and treat yourself to a trip to Disneyland on me"? It is a prophet's job to speak the word of God to the imperfect structures we create, to say to the establishment, "I don't care what the Pope's robe looks like. My children are starving." Regrettably, if you're dependent on your position as a prophet, you're likely to ignore the voice of God and tell those paying the freight what they want to hear. When you do that, you stop being a prophet, and that is the consequence of their action which Micah reports.

> Therefore it shall be night to you, without vision,
> and darkness to you, without revelation.

Those prophets who have lost sight of the objective and substituted for it public displays of piety, who have not trusted God to make to them the gift of love we spoke about last Sunday, will be cut off from the word of God. That's not good news if you're heavily invested in the prophet business, but really it's terrible news for anyone. If we can't do it by ourselves, and if, by our lack of trust in God, we fail to take the opportunities to refocus our lives that God gives us, then we have cut ourselves off from the Gospel path the life and death of Jesus showed us.

What would a Gospel-centered path look like in 21st Century America? This is where I speak as a prophet, and make you mad. Nobody likes a prophet. ABC News recently reported that over the last 30 years, the income of the richest 1 percent of the population nearly tripled while the poorest people got poorer[22]. The poverty rate in 2010 was the highest poverty rate since 1993[23]. A rising tide lifts all boats, but over the last three decades, we haven't been creating wealth — we've been consolidating it.

Set aside the arguments about socialism and wealth redistribution and the rest of the political noise we hear. Disregard everything you know about the proper way to fold the Pope's vestments and ask yourself: is this an acceptable situation in the richest country the world has ever known? Is it the Gospel path Jesus trod to have the rich get richer and the poor get poorer? I'm not speaking of how we might address this. That's a political question. I'm asking you to evaluate the direction this country has gone in the last three decades and to measure it against the Great Commandments that Jesus gave. What do you think?

Kathy's favorite book is "A Christmas Carol" by Charles Dickens. As the story opens, Scrooge has been visited by two men who wish him to make a charitable gift. Scrooge asks after the poor houses and the treadmill, then in his spiritual pride, his certainty in his own righteousness, he refuses to donate, telling them:

> "I don't make merry myself at Christmas and I can't afford to make idle people merry. I help to support the establishments I have mentioned — they cost enough; and those who are badly off must go there."

---

22 The National Poverty Center reports, that in 2010, 15.1 percent of all persons lived in poverty.

23 See also http://www.census.gov/prod/2011pubs/p60-239.pdf

"Many can't go there; and many would rather die."

"If they would rather die," said Scrooge, "they had better do it, and decrease the surplus population. Besides — excuse me — I don't know that."

"But you might know it," observed the gentleman.

"It's not my business," Scrooge returned. "It's enough for a man to understand his own business, and not to interfere with other people's. Mine occupies me constantly. Good afternoon, gentlemen!"

Contrast these heartless words with the anguished words of Marley's ghost:

Business! Mankind was my business. The common welfare was my business; charity, mercy, forbearance, and benevolence, were all my business. The dealings of my trade were but a drop of water in the comprehensive ocean of my business!

Over and over again, from Micah and Amos to Jesus himself God's words ring loudly, "Treat my children with love. You who speak with full mouths, make the suffering of my children your business." God's church has inherited the prophetic role, to speak the word of God truthfully, and courageously. If the church involves itself in folding the Pope's vestments and does not speak the prophetic word, who will? God's church cannot be the spokesman for the status quo but must be the advocate for the kingdom.

In 15th century Romania, the ruler of Wallachia ended sickness and poverty in his province. He invited the poor and sick to a dinner, locked the doors and set fire to the place. The ruler's name was Vlad Tepes, but you may know him by his patronymic, Dracula. When our spiritual pride tell us that the sick and the poor are that way because they are lazy or druggies or drunks and we declare war on them, we are locking them in a room where we can no longer see their suffering, then setting the place on fire.

Mankind is our business. The common welfare is our business; charity, mercy, forbearance, and benevolence, are all our business. Reading the Bible is good. Attending church is good. Memorizing the Bible is good, but if your reading and singing and attendance and praying does not open your heart to the gift of love your Father is offering so that you may see His children through the eyes of His Love, you might as well memorize the crossword puzzle. No matter how the Pope's vestments lay, the original intent is to change your heart so that you see the suffering of others through the eyes of God's compassion and act upon it.

Active Voice

"A commitment to follow the Christ
is an active statement of life in the world in which we
find ourselves. It cannot be accomplished behind stained
glass."

Judges 4:1-7

*The Israelites again did what was evil in the sight of the LORD, after Ehud
died. So the LORD sold them into the hand of King Jabin of Canaan, who
reigned in Hazor; the commander of his army was Sisera, who lived in
Harosheth-ha-goiim. Then the Israelites cried out to the LORD for help; for he
had nine hundred chariots of iron, and had oppressed the Israelites cruelly
twenty years.*

*At that time Deborah, a prophetess, wife of Lappidoth, was judging Israel. She
used to sit under the palm of Deborah between Ramah and Bethel in the hill
country of Ephraim; and the Israelites came up to her for judgment. She sent
and summoned Barak son of Abinoam from Kedesh in Naphtali, and said to
him, "The LORD, the God of Israel, commands you, 'Go, take position at
Mount Tabor, bringing ten thousand from the tribe of Naphtali and the tribe
of Zebulun. I will draw out Sisera, the general of Jabin's army, to meet you by
the Wadi Kishon with his chariots and his troops; and I will give him into your
hand.'"*

Matthew 25:14-30

*Jesus said, "For it is as if a man, going on a journey, summoned his slaves and
entrusted his property to them; to one he gave five talents, to another two, to
another one, to each according to his ability. Then he went away. The one
who had received the five talents went off at once and traded with them, and
made five more talents. In the same way, the one who had the two talents
made two more talents. But the one who had received the one talent went off
and dug a hole in the ground and hid his master's money. After a long time
the master of those slaves came and settled accounts with them. Then the one
who had received the five talents came forward, bringing five more talents,*

saying, 'Master, you handed over to me five talents; see, I have made five more talents.' His master said to him, 'Well done, good and trustworthy slave; you have been trustworthy in a few things, I will put you in charge of many things; enter into the joy of your master.' And the one with the two talents also came forward, saying, 'Master, you handed over to me two talents; see, I have made two more talents.' His master said to him, 'Well done, good and trustworthy slave; you have been trustworthy in a few things, I will put you in charge of many things; enter into the joy of your master.' Then the one who had received the one talent also came forward, saying, 'Master, I knew that you were a harsh man, reaping where you did not sow, and gathering where you did not scatter seed; so I was afraid, and I went and hid your talent in the ground. Here you have what is yours.' But his master replied, 'You wicked and lazy slave! You knew, did you, that I reap where I did not sow, and gather where I did not scatter? Then you ought to have invested my money with the bankers, and on my return I would have received what was my own with interest. So take the talent from him, and give it to the one with the ten talents. For to all those who have, more will be given, and they will have an abundance; but from those who have nothing, even what they have will be taken away. As for this worthless slave, throw him into the outer darkness, where there will be weeping and gnashing of teeth.'"

To steal an old joke, Sundays in my childhood were all about drugs. I was drug to church, then I was drug to my grandparents' house for an exciting afternoon of over-cooked vegetables and Lawrence Welk in a house perpetually heated to the low 90s Fahrenheit. It's probably why I am suspicious to this day of people who tell me that being a Christian is fun.

What Jesus has been involved in for the past few Sundays was no fun at all. It is the preparation for the crucifixion, for next Sunday we celebrate Christ the King Sunday and the end of the liturgical year. For a full year, we've followed Matthew's telling of the story of Jesus. Things are now coming to a head. The cross looms before Jesus.

The following Sunday will begin Advent, and we will turn our minds again to the coming of our Lord. Today, however, Jesus shares with us and his disciples a lesson in parable about discipleship. To understand, we need to recap.

Jesus entered Jerusalem on Palm Sunday. On Monday, Matthew tells us:

> Then Jesus entered the Temple and drove out all who were selling and buying in the Temple, and he overturned the tables of the money-changers and the seats of those who sold doves. He said to them, "It is written, 'My house shall be called a house of prayer'; but you are making it a den of robbers."

Jesus acted with authority toward people in the Temple, even though he had no official standing, then he did deeds of power, performing healings in the very Temple itself, demonstrating his authority. The crowds, as you might imagine, raised a great cry of approval, and that got the attention of the Temple authorities. Believe me! I've been on the police end of a riot stick. Riots do not make those in temporal power happy campers. The last thing you want, if your job is to protect the status quo, is a bunch of people excited about someone outside your organization.

When they confronted him about it, he gave them an answer certain to inflame them further.

> Jesus said to them, "Yes; have you never read, 'Out of the mouths of infants and nursing babies you have prepared praise for yourself'?"

Jesus' words "have you never heard" are not a question — they are a rebuke, and the passage he is quoting is from a Psalm by David in praise of God himself. For Jesus, this is the crossing of the Rubicon. I don't think there is any place for him to retreat from this exchange.

Jesus left the Temple, but he returned the next day, Tuesday, and at that point, the battle was really joined. Jesus fenced with the Temple authorities, besting them on every occasion, and posing questions they could not answer. In the end, Matthew tells us, "nor from that day did anyone dare to ask him any more questions." The time for fencing has passed. Jesus has thrown down the gauntlet before the authorities of the time. The Passion is inevitable.

If that were the end of it, we would be aware that this Jesus of Nazareth was one very clever man. He came from an area so removed from the center of Jewish religious studies that it was called "Galilee of the Gentiles," yet he best-

255

ed in debate the best that the very Temple administration itself could offer.

Of course, that's NOT the end of it at all because Jesus also healed the blind and lame, and reinterpreted passages from the Hebrew Scriptures in a way to claim his authority for himself. He didn't have to do that. He could have had as large a following as he wished as a rabbi and spread his teachings widely. It was really the most foolish course imaginable if you wish your teachings to be spread. We might even say, "Poor Jesus! Think what he could have accomplished if he had been a little more tactful with the Temple authorities." You got to go along to get along, you know.

Jesus did not go along. He directly attacked the Temple authorities, calling them hypocrites in a section of Matthew called "Woes of the Pharisees" because they start out with "Woe to you, scribes and Pharisees, hypocrites!" Now he has not only bested them, he is rebuking them.

When I try to mentally place myself in 1st Century Palestine, I see a man and his followers in a loud confrontation with the Session of the Church (assuming they were Presbyterian Jews, of course). By his voice, I can tell he's not from around here. Someplace up north, I'd guess. Galilee, perhaps. My first impression of the group would be something along the lines of "outside agitators," I think. My second thought would be that this whole loud discussion is unseemly in the church. If they want to talk politics, they should do it somewhere else.

To my shame, I think the whole thing would be one of those "Huh!" incidents that cross our paths from time to time. I think I might have slowed my step to hear what was going on, but I think my attention wouldn't be riveted to it. I think I would have said, "Huh!" and gone about my business. What the odd man from up north was speaking about was change, and, honestly, I've got a full plate. I don't want to think about change. I'm booked three months in advance. I want stability, not upset; tradition, not novelty. And, by the way, have you forgotten about the Romans? We do NOT want to upset the Romans. I don't have time for that kind of trouble.

I'm most often instructed by folks who want to tell me where I went wrong that Jesus was abolishing the old forms of Temple worship and Torah study in favor of something else. I don't think you can go very far down that path before you run up against Jesus' own words:

Then Jesus said to the crowds and to his disciples, "The scribes and the Pharisees sit on Moses' seat; therefore, do whatever they teach you and follow it; but do not do as they do, for they do not practice what they teach."

Jesus is picking a fight that will result in his death, certainly, but the fight he is picking isn't with the Jewish form of worship or even with Jews generally. It is with those who understand the law but fail or refuse to put it into operation in their own lives. Jesus is rebuking passive Jews who give lip service to the teachings, but do not actively incorporate Torah into their lives.

As he leaves the Temple, Jesus discusses with with his disciples what is to come. He predicts the destruction of the Temple, the end of the age, persecutions and the coming of the Son of Man, an image from the book of Daniel. Jesus then tells a series of parables about what must be done to be ready for the end of the age. Our passage today is one of those parables.

I think there is a very real tendency for us to see Jesus as offering the modern, familiar understanding of our relationship with God to the Temple authorities who stubbornly cling to the old, foreign understanding. If we do that, we have nothing much to learn from this parable, since we've already decided that in this encounter, Jesus is on our side.

That would be a shame, because this parable speaks very clearly to us about the business of being faithful disciples. The active slaves who presented the master with increase are referred to as "good and faithful." The passive slave, who has acted with laudable caution to preserve what was given him, is condemned. Clearly, when Jesus calls the first two slaves "good and faithful" he means more than passive waiting, more even than strict obedience to clear instructions for the master did not give any instructions as to what each slave is to do with the talents entrusted to him. "Good and faithful" means active responsibility that takes initiative and risk.

Active responsibility means being prepared and willing to undertake new ways of relating to God and His children as the present age ends and a new age, ushered in by the Resurrection of our Lord, begins. Change of any sort always requires sacrifice. Diverting the river at Pikeville benefited many, but required sacrifice from those whose property was in the proposed new course of the river. You cannot make change without mashing toes.

I told a group I spoke to this week that the deadliest poison God's children can be fed is comfort. I called comfort poison because comfort leads to complacency. Complacency leads to a sense of entitlement. Entitlement leads to demand and demand ends our relationship with God for we can no longer serve God from such a position.

When do you look to God most fervently, pray most actively, seek Him most intently — when you just finished Thanksgiving dinner, or when you have gotten bad news from the doctor, or lost a friend, or sat beside a loved one in their last moments? We draw near to God in fright and sorrow. We recede from God in comfort and satisfaction. Comfort draws our attention away from God at precisely the time when we should roll up our sleeves, draw from our plenty, and do the work of God. We're passive Christians, more often than we should be. We really need to acknowledge that, for we are the most comfortable people the planet has ever known.

To maintain their comfort during Roman occupation, the religious leaders of the time had blessed economic systems imposed by Rome which impoverished God's people. Jesus' actions in confronting the Temple authorities are also a confrontation with the societal injustices being protected by the Temple. Inevitably, Jesus' actions will afflict the comfortable to comfort the afflicted. It cannot be done without terrible cost, and that cost, Jesus will take on himself.

I'm not telling you that to make you mad, or even just because I want you to stay awake. I'm saying that because I want you to focus on what brings us here — what being a Christian means.

In the parable told by Jesus, the master entrusted his three servants with five talents, two talents and one talent. A talent was a unit of weight. When applied to money, it amounted to about fifteen YEARS wages for a working man. We're talking big bucks here. Primarily because of this parable, the word talent came into English to mean God-given gifts. Those slaves who won the master's approval presented him with increase in the value of the investment the master had made with them. The slave who was condemned, in fear of the risk of failure, did nothing with the talents entrusted to him.

God has gifted each of us far in excess of our own abilities to gift ourselves. If you doubt that, come to my house at bill paying time, and try to imagine how I might set aside 150 years of salary all by myself. This enormous investment by God is made with the expectation that we will treat it with active responsibility.

So ... are we doing that? When I engage folks on the topic of why the church does such and such a thing, the most common answer I get is, "We've always done it that way." The second most common answer is, "That's the way I always heard it."

Those are the voices of comfort and satisfaction, the lullaby of complacency whispering to us, "Don't you know that God is fearsome and His ways complicated? Don't get above yourself. Do it as we have always done it. That's safest." It leads to the old joke, "How many Presbyterians does it take to change a light bulb?" the answer to which is, "You can't change that light bulb. It's always been there."

God spoke to the injustices of the 1st Century in the person of Jesus of Nazareth. Jesus did not go along with the way we always did it, and He paid a terrible price for His obedience. The Risen Christ speaks to us today and says, "You shall love the Lord your God with all your heart, and with all your soul, and with all your mind, and your neighbor as yourself. Touch my Creation ONLY with the hands of love. Hate no one. Tend to my sick, my poverty stricken, my blind and lame. Live with compassion."

It cannot be done without paying the price for rocking the boat. Jesus tells us this when he said, "If anyone would come after me, he must deny himself and take up his cross and follow me." Opposing the inertia of complacency, overcoming our willingness to overlook the suffering of others in the name of personal comfort, will always extract a price. That is the price Christians take upon themselves. The voices of comfort and satisfaction, the lullaby of complacency will exact a price for your disobedience, but Jesus has shown us the way. Follow Him.

J. STEWART SCHNEIDER

Dust and Water and Seed

"God's seed cannot spring up in us without the living water that can be obtained only from a deep well, a well dug deep with the hard work of prayer, of study, of worship, of a relentless pursuit of justice and healing for God's children. "

1 Corinthians 4:1-5

Think of us in this way, as servants of Christ and stewards of God's mysteries. Moreover, it is required of stewards that they should be found trustworthy. But with me it is a very small thing that I should be judged by you or by any human court. I do not even judge myself. I am not aware of anything against myself, but I am not thereby acquitted. It is the Lord who judges me. Therefore do not pronounce judgement before the time, before the Lord comes, who will bring to light the things now hidden in darkness and will disclose the purposes of the heart. Then each one will receive commendation from God.

Matthew 6:24-34

'No one can serve two masters; for a slave will either hate the one and love the other, or be devoted to the one and despise the other. You cannot serve God and wealth.

'Therefore I tell you, do not worry about your life, what you will eat or what you will drink, or about your body, what you will wear. Is not life more than food, and the body more than clothing? Look at the birds of the air; they neither sow nor reap nor gather into barns, and yet your heavenly Father feeds them. Are you not of more value than they? And can any of you by worrying add a single hour to your span of life? And why do you worry about clothing? Consider the lilies of the field, how they grow; they neither toil nor spin, yet I tell you, even Solomon in all his glory was not clothed like one of these. But if God so clothes the grass of the field, which is alive today and tomorrow is thrown into the oven, will he not much more clothe you—you of little faith?

Therefore do not worry, saying, "What will we eat?" or "What will we drink?" or "What will we wear?" For it is the Gentiles who strive for all these things; and indeed your heavenly Father knows that you need all these things. But strive first for the kingdom of God and his righteousness, and all these things will be given to you as well.

'So do not worry about tomorrow, for tomorrow will bring worries of its own. Today's trouble is enough for today.

Huston Smith said once, "If what you're looking for is water, better to dig one well sixty feet deep than to dig six wells ten feet deep." There is a lot to that very simple sentence. We live in a time of "cafeteria Christians", people with a sort of general idea about the Gospel of Jesus Christ gained from childhood, or their parents or just...wherever, who then take a bit from here and a bit from there and try to form a relationship with God from that. Surprisingly enough, that doesn't work very well. If you just want to convince your brothers and sisters that you're gainfully occupied, you might as well dig six wells ten feet deep. The logistics are simpler. But, if you wish to find something productive, you're going to have to commit yourself to the enterprise and dig a deeper well.

Rev. Garrett Bugg and I met at the Chapel of St. Starbuck Tuesday morning, as we often do, to celebrate vigils, lauds and coffee beans. We were talking about the decline in church membership, particularly among young professionals, and what might be at the root of that. In particular, we wondered why it might be that the Presbyterian church is shedding members faster than other mainline Protestant churches. I thought it might be a matter of perception — that the Presbyterian church is perceived by younger people as being filled mostly with elderly people. Waddie Mitchell and Don Edwards, in a live performance of cowboy songs, tried to get the audience to sing along to "Home, Home on the Range". They didn't get much response, and Waddie said to the audience, "Come on! You sound like a bunch of Presbyterians." I told Garret that I thought we might seem to the younger people to be a "dusty" faith, a church filled with grandmothers.

Rev. Bugg didn't agree with that assessment, but then he asked, "What grows in dust? Nothing. Without water and seed, nothing grows in dust. It just blows away with the wind and is gone."

Garrett is right; we need to talk about water, dust and seed. We want to bring some water to bear on the dustiness of the Presbyterian worship experience. And the best way to do that is to dig a deep well, and tap into the reserves laid up there by the church.

I mentioned last Sunday that the voice of God always speaks in protest to culture. What I meant by that is that any society, whether we are speaking of ours or a village on the Orinoco, lives by certain agreed behaviors. That's the voice of the village, you might say. Those behaviors are not always in accord with the teachings of Jesus of Nazareth. I'll go out on a limb here and hazard that those behaviors are NEVER in accord with the teachings of Jesus of Nazareth. This is because the voice of the village is there to insure the survival of the village, culture or corporation. The Gospel of Jesus Christ is never about the survival of a culture or a village or even a country. It is about a relationship with the light of the world which enables us to bring that light into the world, and comfort it, responding to the suffering of God's children. Since much of that suffering is the inevitable result of the flawed agreements that we, sinners that we are, have devised to preserve our cultures, the Word of God always speaks in protest to culture.

Attempts to integrate the teachings of Jesus into a culture inevitably lead to a clash between the two. I'm going to get emails about that, but I believe it is true. If your loyalty is to the United States of America, and what is good for her, and the demands of Jesus lead you into something that is not good for the United States of America, what do you do?

You could find no better example of how this works than in the conversation between the counsel of Jerusalem and Caiaphas, the chief priest, during Jesus' entry into Jerusalem. Jesus had brought a voice of protest to a system that has served to enrich the rich at the expense of the poor, That kind of talk is dangerous. The Temple authorities have a working arrangement with the Romans and no one wants that upset. The counsel met to discuss Jesus, and what to do about him.

"If we let him go on like this, everyone will believe in him", said one of the counsel. "And the Romans will come and destroy both our holy place and our nation." This is the voice of the village speaking.

John goes on, "But one of them, Caiaphas, who was high priest that year, said to them, 'You know nothing at all! You do not understand that it is better for you to have one man die for the people than to have the whole nation destroyed.'"

That's how it works when you try to serve two masters — the voice of the village and the voice of God.

> "No one can serve two masters; for a slave will either hate the one and love the other, or be devoted to the one and despise the other."

We usually blow past that part of Jesus' words and focus on the remainder, "You cannot serve God and wealth", then comfort ourselves by assuring ourselves that we are not servants of our purse. That is much easier to say when you are living in the richest country that history has ever recorded. We look to the historical kings and queens of Europe for our ideas of what conspicuous wealth looks like, but wine sometimes froze in the decanters at the Palace of Versailles, and Louis XIV did not have access to indoor plumbing, but was made to resort to a chamber pot. You live grander than did Louis XIV, and if you think you are not wedded to your wealth, imagine for a moment giving up indoor plumbing in favor of a chamber pot at night and a walk to the garden during the day.

It is this observation of Jesus about divided loyalties which makes me uncomfortable with flags on the chancel. It's not something I would pick a fight over, but it does make me uncomfortable. Our culture has many things that we honor. We honor veterans. We honor the flag. We honor motherhood, and parenthood, and caring for the elderly. We could have displays of all these things on the chancel — a sort of museum of the things spoken of with honor by the voice of the village. These are all, worthy though they be, shallow wells. Pretty much everyone, Christian or not, honors mother and country, and apple pie, too, if you like. Including God in that display, though, would mean that God is just one more of the things we honor. Not to nag, but...

> No one can serve two masters; for a slave will either hate the one and love the other, or be devoted to the one and despise the other.

It is the same reason that I'm not altogether comfortable with public prayer before public events. It looks to me as if we were lumping prayer and the pledge together in a sort of display of the things which are important to us, something to give a non-serious event an air of solemnity. That's not really how I understand prayer.

Nevertheless, my sense is that this is the place where religion finds its home in our culture — in weddings, funerals and public events requiring solemnity. And this is the place where I will say something that will REALLY get me letters. These are dust. These are the places where the water of the Spirit is rarely experienced. At weddings, we're all excited for the new couple. That's where our minds are. At funerals, we grieve, and that's where our minds are. The water of the Spirit is seldom seen in such events, however important they are to us. To reach the spiritual water that will bring fertility to our dusty faith, we have to dig deeper wells.

Last week, we observed, with Professor N.T. Wright, that the 18th Century movement we call "The Enlightenment" or the "Age of Reason" offered a way of peace, but at a cost. In Prof. Wright's words:

> Following the post-Reformation European wars in which religious allegiance played a major role, the Enlightenment offered a way of peace, though at a cost: make religion a matter of private opinion, and we will sort out the world without reference to God.

Our Evangelical brethren who press with such energy for greater inclusion of God in our classrooms and public life miss the point, I think. The living water Jesus speaks of doesn't flow to man-made structures or cultures. It bathes us, individually. No matter what the Supreme Court thinks about the "personhood" of corporations, we don't Baptize corporations or countries. We Baptize people, and for very good reason. To use Paul's words, "Think of us in this way, as servants of Christ and stewards of God's mysteries." That is you and I, church. Servants of Christ and stewards of God's mysteries. Quality may or may not be "Job One" at Ford, but this is "Job One" for Christians. If you are about Job One, then the dust of your efforts, watered by the living water of God and the seed of Jesus Christ will sprout wonderful things. Not necessarily things you'll enjoy, or like, as we saw in the tragic death of four American missionaries at the hands of Somali pirates, but you have to believe that God can bring forth wonders, or you'll never dig that deep well.

All of us here are old enough to remember when our sanctuaries were full, every Sunday. When I look at the empty pews today, I'm not as discouraged as you might think I would be. In our youth, religion informed culture, and to do well within the culture, it was important to be connected with organized religion. That's cart before the horse, church. When religion stopped informing culture, these are the people who melted away. I'm reminded of Jesus' teaching in the parable of the sower:

> "A farmer went out to sow his seed. As he was scattering the seed, some ... fell on rocky places, where it did not have much soil. It sprang up quickly, because the soil was shallow. But when the sun came up, the plants were scorched, and they withered because they had no root."

God's seed cannot spring up in us without the living water that can be obtained only from a deep well, a well dug deep with the hard work of prayer, of study, of worship, of a relentless pursuit of justice and healing for God's children. Many, who filled our pews in our youth, did not do the hard work of digging a deep well, and when their shallow wells produced only dust, they withered because they had no root.

Digging a deep well is hard. It requires commitment and effort, and that is not easy in this sort of a culture where distractions come at us from every side. Digging that deep well means refusing to be satisfied with a shallow relationship with God, but insisting on a committed relationship. Tony Campolo was asked to pray before some event, and responded, "What? Just like that? I need time to prepare to go to God." That kind of insistence is what we need. Prayer without commitment is just showing yourself to be gainfully employed. Such prayer is a shallow well. It will produce only dust.

Some of the noisiest expressions of Christianity we hear today are from groups who pursue some agenda important to themselves and hang the name Christian on it. I recall news footage from some years ago showing a group out west calling themselves a church, who believed that the right to bear arms was given by God. The news footage of a worship service showed each worshiper carrying a sidearm. In this same connection we would have to remember the hate-filled group that marches at funerals protesting gays. Certainly, they are noisy. Where do they get their enthusiasm? Ah, for an explanation of that we go to Charles Darwin, of all people, for the observation that "Ignorance more frequently begets confidence than does knowledge." Digging shallow, unproductive, dusty wells for the sake of appearance yields — dust.

I'd like to ask you to think back to your courting days. Specifically, to the time when you just knew you were making the right decision about your future mate. Did you just pick the first one that came along, or did you spend time with him or her to deepen the relationship? Did you think about whether or not the person could aid you in becoming wealthy? Did you think about whether or not the person would advance your business opportunities, or make you universally happy? Or did you come to know, down to your socks, that this person was the yin to your yang, the answer to your question, the prop for your leaning side?

That's the deep well I wish for you in your walk with God. I don't want you to worry about what you will eat, or wear because you know that God walks with you and will sustain you as you are about His business.

J. STEWART SCHNEIDER

Christt the King

"The unavoidable consequences of recognition of a king are vulnerability and powerlessness. Of all the things Americans don't relate to, vulnerability and powerlessness are most certainly on the short list. "

Colossians 1:11-20

May you be made strong with all the strength that comes from his glorious power, and may you be prepared to endure everything with patience, while joyfully giving thanks to the Father, who has enabled you to share in the inheritance of the saints in the light. He has rescued us from the power of darkness and transferred us into the kingdom of his beloved Son, in whom we have redemption, the forgiveness of sins.

He is the image of the invisible God, the firstborn of all creation; for in him all things in heaven and on earth were created, things visible and invisible, whether thrones or dominions or rulers or powers – all things have been created through him and for him. He himself is before all things, and in him all things hold together. He is the head of the body, the church; he is the beginning, the firstborn from the dead, so that he might come to have first place in everything. For in him all the fullness of God was pleased to dwell, and through him God was pleased to reconcile to himself all things, whether on earth or in heaven, by making peace through the blood of his cross.

Luke 23:33-43

When they came to the place that is called The Skull, they crucified Jesus there with the criminals, one on his right and one on his left. Then Jesus said, "Father, forgive them; for they do not know what they are doing." And they

269

cast lots to divide his clothing. The people stood by, watching Jesus on the cross; but the leaders scoffed at him, saying, "He saved others; let him save himself if he is the Messiah of God, his chosen one!" The soldiers also mocked him, coming up and offering him sour wine, and saying, "If you are the King of the Jews, save yourself!" There was also an inscription over him, "This is the King of the Jews."

One of the criminals who were hanged there kept deriding him and saying, "Are you not the Messiah? Save yourself and us!" But the other rebuked him, saying, "Do you not fear God, since you are under the same sentence of condemnation? And we indeed have been condemned justly, for we are getting what we deserve for our deeds, but this man has done nothing wrong." Then he said, "Jesus, remember me when you come into your kingdom." He replied, "Truly I tell you, today you will be with me in Paradise."

Christ the King Sunday – the last Sunday of the liturgical year. We began our walk with Jesus, through the anticipation of Advent, the miracle of Christmas, the revelation of Epiphany, the introspection of Lent, the horror of the Crucifixion, the joy of the Resurrection. Then, we entered a time called "Common Time" when we followed Jesus through His ministry.

Does that strike you as odd? It's as if we were to read a book by first reading the beginning then skipping to the end, and only after we know how the story is going to end do we read the middle and watch the plot develop. The liturgical year has been this way for a very long time. Why do you suppose we approach this story in this odd way?

Years and years ago I thought, if I bothered to think about it at all, that the pastor of a mainline church prepared his sermons by picking something out of the Bible that interested him, or supported something he wanted to say, then writing a sermon around that. So, I was surprised to learn of something called the Revised Common Lectionary, and even more surprised to learn that the Revised Common Lectionary offers passages for each Sunday that direct us through the Gospel story in this fashion. That means that this odd way of experiencing the Gospel story is done on purpose. Why would we need to know how the story ends in order to read the story?

I think the answer to that question is in the Feast of Christ the King, this Sunday. The only way to really experience the ministry of Jesus is in this odd fashion because the story of the ministry of Jesus isn't just another story from long ago. The story of the life of Jesus of Nazareth, known as the Christ, is utterly, stupefyingly unique and its uniqueness is contained in the phrase "Christ the King."

And … there's the rub. We're Americans. We don't DO kings. **We** do politicians, and we don't think much of them as a general rule. Occasionally, we see photographs of people interacting with the Queen of England. There is a great deal of bowing and curtsying that looks odd and, well … foolish to American eyes. We just don't have the mental toolbox to DO kings.

When Christ the King Sunday comes around, then, it's perfectly understandable that we don't have a way to relate to it other than in the way in which we relate to other special days of the year. Christ the King Sunday must be something like Valentine's Day or the Fourth of July. Or, maybe, because it sounds a little Anglican, it's something a little foreign, a little exotic, like Guy Fawkes Day. Maybe it's just the signal for the change of seasons. How nice — it's Christ the King Sunday. Time to start getting ready for Christmas. We just don't DO kings in this country.

The unavoidable consequences of recognition of a king are vulnerability and powerlessness. Of all the things we **don't** do in this country, vulnerability and powerlessness are most certainly on the short list. If our government does something we don't like, we whoop and holler and take to the polls. If the policeman who has pulled us over for speeding doesn't treat us with respect, we want his badge number and we make a big stink with the department.

Christ the King is different, so it is fitting that this sad Sunday, when we meet to celebrate and remember our beloved Sexton, John Bell Judd, should also be Christ the King Sunday. From John Bell's passing we can come to understand better the consequences of a king because the finality of death is one of those consequences.

John Bell is gone from us. His quiet performance of his duties will become someone else's responsibility now. His seat on the pew is empty. The small bottle of water he placed on the pulpit each Sunday to ease my throat won't be there. As much as I miss John Bell, it is the finality of his passing that actually helps me most to see around my American hostility to authority in order to perceive the reality of Christ the King.

It is not an easy thing to do. Since we, as Americans, lack the emotional mechanisms to deal with the finality of a world in which Christ is King, we try to deal with it as we do with the other things in our lives that we don't like — often we get angry. We get angry at God for taking John Bell from us earlier than any of us would have chosen. We want to make a complaint to the citizen ombudsman that it is unfair to take John Bell from us this early. We didn't have a chance to say goodbye. We didn't have the time we needed to prepare. The whole thing was done badly, and we want to register a complaint!

The writer of Colossians writes of Jesus:

> He is the image of the invisible God, the firstborn of all creation; for in him all things in heaven and on earth were created, things visible and invisible, whether thrones or dominions or rulers or powers — all things have been created through him and for him. He himself is before all things, and in him all things hold together. He is the head of the body, the church; he is the beginning, the firstborn from the dead, so that he might come to have first place in everything. For in him all the fullness of God was pleased to dwell, and through him God was pleased to reconcile to himself all things, whether on earth or in heaven, by making peace through the blood of his cross.

And now, maybe we can see why the Revised Common Lectionary forces us to read the Gospel story in so odd a fashion — knowing how it will turn out before we have a chance to read the story. If the story of Jesus' time on earth were told in the customary way, we would see Him as a good man among other good men of history; a prophet among other prophets; a teacher among other teachers; a role model among other role models. We would not see Him as Christ the King. Only by viewing His life through the lens of the Resurrection can we hope to understand the unparalleled uniqueness of Jesus of Nazareth, known as Christ the King. In this way we can come to know that God is to us as water is to a fish — Jesus, the image of the invisible God, the firstborn of all creation upholds us, supports us and grants us life just as water supports and gives life to fish. It is God, whose image we are privileged to see in Jesus of Nazareth, who holds everything together.

What a blessing that is! Because, with John Bell's passing, we can see that each of us fit into the lives of the others, that none of us would be whole if the holes in our lives weren't filled with the people we love.

My very Baptist cousin sent me an email on this topic. It read:

> Their marriage was good, their dreams focused. Their best friends lived barely a wave away. I can see them now, Dad in trousers, tee shirt and a hat and Mom in a house dress; lawn mower in his hand, and dish-towel in hers. It was the time for fixing things. A curtain rod, the kitchen radio, screen door, the oven door, the hem in a dress. Things we keep.
>
> It was a way of life, and sometimes it made me crazy. All that re-fixing, reheating, renewing, I wanted just once to be wasteful. Waste meant af-fluence. Throwing things away meant you knew there'd always be more.
>
> But then my mother died, and on that clear summer's night, in the warmth of the hospital room, I was struck with the pain of learning that sometimes there isn't any more. Sometimes, what we care about most gets all used up and goes away ... never to return. So ... While we have it ... its best we love it ... And care for it ... And fix it when it's broken ... And heal it when it's sick.
>
> This is true ... For marriage ... And old cars ... And children with bad report cards ... Dogs and cats with bad hips ... And aging par-ents ... And grandparents, aunts and uncles and friends. We keep them because they are worth it, because we are worth it.

We've suffered a terrible loss, you and I. But we've also gained an opportunity to see beyond ourselves. We have an opportunity to see Jesus, not as our fish-ing buddy, as one of my colleagues put it, but as Christ the King, "the image of the invisible God, the firstborn of all creation, He who holds all things to-gether."

And we have gained the opportunity to see each of us as the completion of our brothers and sisters, the fillers of the holes in each other's souls. From such perspective, we can pray:

> O God, what are we, that You have regard for us? What are we, that You are mindful of us? We are like a breath; our days are as a passing shadow; we come and go like grass which in the morning shoots up, renewed, and in the evening fades and withers. You cause us to revert to dust, saying: Return, O mortal creatures! Would that we were wise, that we understood wither we are going! For when we die we carry nothing away; our glory does not accompany us. Mark the whole-hearted and behold the upright; they shall have peace. You redeem the soul of Your servants, O God, and none who trust in you shall be desolate.

We have cause for rejoicing for the time John Bell was with us. We have cause for continued rejoicing as we remember the many times he touched each of us. And we have greatest joy in the knowledge that we live in a universe which is the domain of a loving God, who pursued us even unto taking on flesh.

Benediction

Take courage. Go in the knowledge that the loving God is your eternal friend and companion. And may the God of peace, which is beyond our understanding guard your hearts and your thoughts in Christ Jesus, AMEN

Appendix

Thirty-six Sentences on Lamed Vovniks

Mikhail Horowitz
(Used by permission)

It snows on one of them; rains on another.

Both are without shoes.

Another is schlepping a heavy box and not complaining; another is stroking the sodden fur of a blind cat.

Another of their calling, more recondite still, is employed as a lighthouse keeper at the edge of a lunar sea.

We are speaking figuratively, here.

That we are speaking at all is a miracle, and the miracle is thanks to them.

In their own sight they are small as mesons; to most of us they are smudges on the sills of the world, shmutz on the discarded shmattas of the quotidian.

But when one of them has gooseflesh, the universe trembles; when one of them sneezes, there is a momentary brownout throughout the Milky Way.

I thought I sussed one out, once, at a soup kitchen in Minneapolis.

He was doling out stew to a bunch of losers, not the beautiful kind but the other kind, whose dreams have been flattened by steamrollers of neglect, that bastard offspring of capitalism.

But he was beaming, beaming at each of the stubby shadows as they shuffled in front of him, rekindling the dead light in their eyes with the light in his, if only for a moment.

If only for a moment the world would stop.

If only for a moment that greatest of angels, the one who frees us from suffering but at such cost, would weep for shame.

Suppose for a moment that they could know themselves, and not immediately combust, or crumble to dust.

How then would it be?

Would it mean that Moshiach had finally arrived, redeeming the bleached coupon in each soul?

That the mountains would skip like lambs in spring, the sky roll up like a scroll, the seas dissolve like snowflakes? It would mean, of course, there was no longer any need for them, that all of us were now the thirty-six, the pillars of the universe.

But that day, by definition, is eternally postponed. "Moshiach" is Hebrew for "mañana," and tomorrow and tomorrow and tomorrow creep in this petty pace from Shabbos to Shabbos, from naked seder to naked seder, to the last syllable of recorded tsuris.

And so they linger, continuing to abide in the world, which hides them in plain sight, unassuming as dust.

They are gelt not meant to be given; afikomens not meant to be found.

Their number remains constant in every age; should one die, another is born in that same instant, somewhere else.

Even their mothers do not know who they are.

They have manifested on every continent, but always in the villages and cities, always among the throngs.

They are not necessarily Jewish.

They have been cobblers, carpenters, ostlers, masons, blacksmiths, but these days are just as likely to be nurses, garage attendants, pizza flippers, computer technicians.

They have not, will never be, brokers, bankers, politicians, attorneys, or journalists.

They are flies on the wall that have melded with the wall; they are undetected by any radar, even and especially their own.

At this moment, the sun scorches one of them; the wind is making it difficult for another.

Neither of them complains.

Another is rummaging through a dumpster; still another, sitting on a park bench, is humming as he tosses crumbs to pigeons.

They will go on doing these things, being this thing, until the world ends, or finally begins.

Did I just hear one of them sneeze?

There is no way to know, and for that I say hosanna.

Perhaps one of them is even reading this.